MW00608619

Trading and Price Discovery for Crude Oils

Adi Imsirovic

Trading and Price Discovery for Crude Oils

Growth and Development of International Oil Markets

Adi Imsirovic
The Oxford Institute for Energy Studies (OIES)
Oxford, UK

ISBN 978-3-030-71717-9   ISBN 978-3-030-71718-6   (eBook)
https://doi.org/10.1007/978-3-030-71718-6

© The Editor(s) (if applicable) and The Author(s), under exclusive license to Springer Nature Switzerland AG 2021, corrected publication 2021
This work is subject to copyright. All rights are solely and exclusively licensed by the Publisher, whether the whole or part of the material is concerned, specifically the rights of translation, reprinting, reuse of illustrations, recitation, broadcasting, reproduction on microfilms or in any other physical way, and transmission or information storage and retrieval, electronic adaptation, computer software, or by similar or dissimilar methodology now known or hereafter developed.
The use of general descriptive names, registered names, trademarks, service marks, etc. in this publication does not imply, even in the absence of a specific statement, that such names are exempt from the relevant protective laws and regulations and therefore free for general use.
The publisher, the authors and the editors are safe to assume that the advice and information in this book are believed to be true and accurate at the date of publication. Neither the publisher nor the authors or the editors give a warranty, expressed or implied, with respect to the material contained herein or for any errors or omissions that may have been made. The publisher remains neutral with regard to jurisdictional claims in published maps and institutional affiliations.

This Palgrave Macmillan imprint is published by the registered company Springer Nature Switzerland AG
The registered company address is: Gewerbestrasse 11, 6330 Cham, Switzerland

To those whom I love most: Edin, Haris, Jasmine, Manik, Nana & Meda.

The original version of the book was revised: Affiliation in the copyright page has now been updated. The correction to the book is available at https://doi.org/10.1007/978-3-030-71718-6_16

Acknowledgements

I am grateful to my family for their patience and understanding of my frequent antisocial behaviour during this project. Especially, I am grateful to my wife, Dr. Manik Imsirovic, who found the time and patience to read every single chapter.

This book would not have been possible without a number of colleagues and friends who helped with their advice, comments, recollections, and opinions.

I would particularly like to thank (roughly in chronological order).

Prof. Antonio Fatas, Prof. Dimitra Petropoulou, Ken Leask, Michael Lynch, Owain Johnston, Jorge Montepeque, Kurt Chapman, Liz Bossley, Colin Bryce, Simon Andrews, Daniel Brusstar, Javier Blas, Adrian Binks, Paul Horsnell, Dave Ernsberger, Robin Mills, Jonty Rushforth, Nick James, Ben Pryor, Ronny Davidson, and Florian Thaler. Needless to say, any omissions and errors are entirely mine.

I would like to thank the Oxford Institute for Energy Studies for the use of the excellent Institute library. My personal thanks go to the Institute director, Prof. Bassam Fattouh and Ms. Kate Teasdale for making it available.

Lastly, I am grateful to my editor, Ms. Tula Weis for her understanding, support, and encouragement.

This list is certainly not exhaustive and should be extended to a number of my friends and colleagues who I worked with and learned from throughout my trading, teaching and research careers.

Ascot
February 2021

Contents

List of Figures

1

Introduction

Why This Book?

In the early 2019, I was asked to write a chapter on the topic of trading and price discovery in oil markets for the Palgrave Macmillan 'Handbook of International Energy Economics'.[1] Writing this chapter, I realised that it was impossible to do justice to the topic without taking a broader historical perspective with regard to the growth and development of the oil markets. Later, I decided to expand this chapter into a short book on the same topic.

There is a vast amount of literature on the subject of oil industry and prices. What should make this book different is a focus on the oil markets (rather than the oil industry as a whole) and a synthesis of three of my key experiences: I spent over thirty years trading in the international oil markets, almost half of which in Asia (Singapore), trading physical oil, all the key benchmarks and associated derivatives; I spent a number of years of teaching undergraduate courses in Energy Economic and Resource and Environmental Economic at Surrey University; and my work on the contemporary issues in the oil markets at the Oxford Institute for Energy Studies (OIES).

It is well known that the international oil markets have hardly ever been competitive. It is often assumed that this is inevitable. It is said that natural monopolies are common in energy markets, generally resulting in either private or government monopolies. There is some substance in this, and it is discussed in Chapter 2 of the book. Like other commodity markets, oil markets are assumed to be 'unstable' and 'volatile' and in need of some market power as a stabilising force.

© The Author(s), under exclusive license to Springer Nature
Switzerland AG 2021
A. Imsirovic, *Trading and Price Discovery for Crude Oils*,
https://doi.org/10.1007/978-3-030-71718-6_1

I hope that this book will dispel that thinking. Markets have been destroyed by unregulated monopolies with government regulation of such monopolies often coming only when it was too late. For example, Rockefeller's oil monopoly was already under pressure at home, but especially abroad, when the US government intervened and broke up the Standard Oil Trust.[2] Soon, however, governments stepped in and supported the old colonial and crony capitalist relationships, all in the interest of a supposed 'energy security'. In the process, both producers and consumers suffered.[3]

Legislators have often been keen to intervene in markets where they are not needed, but reluctant to regulate market failure. Presumably, the former is a source of political power, whereas the latter is hard work. Failed government intervention when it was not needed and a lack of it when it was needed is one of the key themes of this book. The urgent need for them to do just the opposite, regulate market failure[4] and keep out of the well-functioning markets is one of the book's conclusions. Only the policies designed to keep new, independent firms from monopolised incumbents, ensuring that the markets are transparent and competitive and rules of the game clear, can be the basis for flexible, responsive, yet stable and reliable energy system. Such policies will not only ensure a speedy and smooth energy transition but also prevent the new technologies from turning into new monopolies.

Plan of the Book

The book is roughly divided into two parts. A historical overview is covered in Chapters 3–10 and contemporary markets are covered in Chapters 11–15.

The book begins with a discussion about some theoretical concepts in economics that underpin the whole book. As a result, it may be a bit dense for a general reader who may prefer to move straight to Chapter 3. It starts with a simple concept of market power. Market power manifests itself by firms that do not take market prices as given. In trader speak, if all the participants are price takers, the market is competitive. When firms influence the market price, they have some form of market power. Oil industry has some characteristics which make it prone to concentration of market power. Oil projects tend to be big, risky, capital intensive with long gestation periods, with project-specific assets, lasting very long-time periods. There are large economies of scale and often one refinery or pipeline is more efficient than two or more. Economists refer to this as 'natural monopolies'.

Large, vertically integrated firms may even be beneficial to both firms and society as a whole. Modern antitrust policy has its roots in the Chicago school of economics, combining economics, organization theory, and contract law to study how vertical integration of related activities within a firm can resolve some market failures. Rather than focusing just on the size of the firm in relation to the size of the market, this approach is based on the economic theory, considering the economics of scale, transaction costs, and uncertainty.

Instead of simply breaking up a dominant firm in the market, such as in the case of the Standard Oil Trust in 1911, this approach would consider each case individually, on its economic merits. For example, a large electric utility may have both elements of natural and 'pure' monopoly. While transmission and distribution of power have all the characteristics of natural monopolies, there is no reason for generation and retail parts not to compete in the marketplace. In a similar fashion, parts of national oil, gas, and pipeline companies that can be competitive could be privatised, creating efficient markets. Monopolies are often disrupted by new technology. A good example is gas markets being shaken up by the rapid expansion of the liquified natural gas (LNG) trade. However, it is always the job of governments to regulate market power. It was the government policies in the United Kingdom and the United States that successfully privatised most of the energy sector in these countries after 1980. Markets flourished and the privatised companies reduced costs, increased output, and improved their profitability.[5]

Early Days of Competition

Chapter 3 discusses the early days of the oil industry. The first 'killer app' for oil was illumination. Coal oil, manufactured by distilling cheap and widely available coal, was just beginning to take off. It did not go unnoticed that using crude oil would remove the need for the first part of the production process. The key concern was whether there was enough crude oil available at the right price to substitute coal. This concern was soon dispelled by applying the existing technology for salt water drilling.

As the drilling technology improved,[6] costs fell dramatically. Not only was oil a widely available source of illuminating oil, but it was becoming cheap as well. By 1860, all aspects of the oil industry as we know them today were in place: exploration and production technology was originally borrowed from the drilling for salt water and refining and the transportation and distribution infrastructure were already in place for the coal-oil production. The coal-oil refineries had established technology, easily adaptable to the refining of oil. They already had markets for wax, lubricants, naphtha, and solvents for cleaning and kerosene for gas making and anaesthetics. This explains the lightning speed by which the oil industry expanded in the 1860s.

The first 'gusher' wells appeared in 1861 overwhelming the markets, and transportation and storage became a problem. Between 1860 and 1862, oil prices fell from almost $20 to $0.10 per barrel. This was the first 'oil shock'. Then, as now, producers made attempts to reduce output, but cheating and free riding were common, and the results were disastrous.

The first oil traders were known as 'dump men'[7] on Oil Creek. They would make markets for small producers who had to sell oil relatively quickly due to limited tankage. They provided liquidity in illiquid markets and took price risk. They provided the earliest price discovery mechanism.

The real breakthrough came with the introduction of gathering pipelines, taking oil from the wells to the nearest railway hubs. The gathering lines started issuing 'tickets' as proof of oil delivery. They were made in duplicates and denominated in volume and not value. They were tangible assets that could be traded for cash and an excellent vehicle for speculation. Each barrel of oil could be traded many times, providing price liquidity, and creating the first 'paper' markets for oil.

Soon, the first exchanges were established at Oil City, Titusville, Parker, Bradford, Pittsburgh, New York, Philadelphia and elsewhere. The spread of telegraphy greatly facilitated the transmission of information and trading. They attracted not just producers and refiners, but also investors and speculators, providing ample liquidity. The oil markets were born.

Building a Monopoly

It was the Rockefeller's refining monopoly that destroyed them. The rise of the Standard Oil monopoly is discussed in Chapter 4. Both Rockefeller and his right-hand, Henry Flagler started as traders.[8] They made their money in their early thirties, trading grain and other commodities, but saw a better opportunity in the new and thriving market for kerosene. The early 1867 partnership of 'Rockefeller, Andrews & Flagler' was a means of attracting additional capital for a massive refinery expansion and addition of new oil depots, rail tank cars and general efficiency improvements.

In the early 1870s, half of the delivered cost of oil was rail transportation. This is where Flagler came to the fore: He had an in-depth knowledge of the transportation aspect of trade and a personal relationship with many officials on the railways.

Unlike roads and canals, railways were generally being built by private capital, utilising state legislation granting them a 'charter' or a concession, to be exercised in a way to provide public utility. The growing business of railroads as well as the oil industry was well ahead of the development of legislation. There was little federal legislation to facilitate and regulate business across several states. In such an environment, 'combinations' and abuses were common and in a hunt for revenues, 'anything went'. Railroads usually gave rebates for a guaranteed volume of agreed business. But it was the drawbacks that were rewarding large shippers with additional compensation from the fares paid by their competition. Flagler made sure they got a better deal from the railways than anyone, making the partnership eventually a monopoly.

Eventually, the Standard Oil Company controlled all the plants in Cleveland and key refineries in Pittsburgh, New York and the Oil Regions as well as the best refiners, officers, and agents throughout the country. By mid-1880s, it also controlled the key pipelines which gradually replaced railroads as the primary carriers of oil and refined products. In January 1895, in the final act of stamping its monopoly power in the marketplace, the main Standard Oil buyer of oil,[9] posted a notice to the oil producers informing them of the end of the oil purchases based on the exchange prices. The Trust would only buy oil at prices which they 'posted' themselves. They became the sole price maker.

Oil Markets Go Global

While the Standard Oil monopolised the domestic refining market, they did not have their own way overseas. The emergence of the international oil markets is the subject of the fifth chapter. Foreign sales were becoming important for the growing American oil industry and there they faced stiff competition from Russia which was soon to become the largest oil producer in the world. Standard Oil might have been a price maker at home, but it had to accept the going market price for kerosene overseas. The key competition came from the Noble brothers who brought drillers from the United States and produced Russian oil in 'Pennsylvania fashion'. They run an efficient operation, bringing cheap and plentiful oil supply by pipeline to a well-organized refining plant. Just like Rockefeller, the Nobel brothers realized that the key missing link to the operation was a cheap and efficient transportation system. Not unlike Rockefeller's New York headquarters, Nobels' central office in St. Petersburg ran a sleek logistical operation.

At the same time, the Rothschilds established their own export monopoly via the Southern route, formed the Caspian and Black Sea Company in 1884 and quickly became the biggest kerosene exporter from Russia. That very same year, there was some dissatisfaction with the quality of the American product in the UK, then the biggest European market. The Nobel brothers skilfully exploited it to enter this new market. Both Nobels and Rothschilds strengthened their positions by forming companies and exclusive distributors in the country.

1890s Asia, not unlike a century later, was a large and growing market and Russian kerosine had a competitive advantage—it was much closer than the American product. This is where another trader had an established operation: 'Marcus Samuel & Co'. Having seen the first kerosine tankers on the Caspian, his audacious plan was to copy it for bulk transportation to the Orient. Eventually, his branded kerosine in 'Shell oil' tins was a huge success in Asia.

But the real prize was to find a steady supply of oil within the region. One well-capitalized company producing oil in Asia was the Royal Dutch. The company had a well-established production in Sumatra, including a refinery, railroad, pipeline, and a harbour. In charge of the operation was an ex-trader, Henri Detering. Intense competition in the region was ripe for consolidation and in 1906 Marcus Samuel's Shell Trading had to accept difficult terms[10] to create a new company, the Royal Dutch Shell.

Tectonic Shifts and Governments

The first decade of the century saw the widespread application of internal combustion engines both for power and mobility and the adoption of electricity for lighting. The result was a fall in the use of kerosine and exponential growth in the use of gasoline, fuel oil and lubricants. The intensity of the fighting in the First World War could never have been possible without mechanization and the oil that powered it. The importance of oil in the mobility of the armies would make the commodity one of the ultimate goals (or 'The Prize'[11]) in the World War Two. Chapters 6 and 7 deal with the subject of the post-colonial era, government intervention and growth of oil majors.

After the war, government involvement and the post-imperial nature of the international relations resulted in oil markets being largely controlled by the national champions of the US, Britain and France, an oligopoly of the oil 'majors'. Aside from being vertically integrated, these companies were also integrated 'horizontally' to ensure maximum control of the market and profits. Oil was carefully supplied from various geographic areas at the lowest possible cost and to ensure that supply and demand were balanced, and prices were kept stable. Such integration enabled the supply of oil to be fine-tuned to the prevailing demand for end products, thus ensuring political as well as market stability. The ascent of the majors came primarily through the post-colonial government intervention in the Middle East with the Foreign Office orchestrating various agreements in the former Turkish empire. This angered the American allies who saw it as imperial and discriminatory. After the war, Americans saw the world through a non-exclusive, competitive, 'open door' lens. At least until they got in and then slammed the door shut.

Also, the British government was the first to intervene in the private sector, by the acquisition of a controlling share in the Anglo-Persian (later BP). The role of American majors was particularly prominent in the 'Marshall Plan', which was partly designed to affirm the dominant position of the American companies in the Middle East. With the US majors in a dominant position, it was only natural that oil price was US-centric. Oil prices were based on the 'US Gulf Plus'[12] pricing. With increasing volume of oil and petroleum products coming from the Middle East, 'phantom freight' was generating oil majors large, unjustified profits. The British Auditor General learned it the hard way, being charged bunker prices for the Royal Navy, based on very high USG prices plus some non-existent freight to the Middle East, for the product refined from cheap Iranian oil in the Abadan refinery.

The majors were making lots of money from selling Middle Eastern oil to their own governments, from the concessions they obtained with their very help. The arbitrary pricing continued with shifts to the UK and then New York as delivery points, the latter effectively becoming 'Gulf Minus' formula, discriminating against the oil produced in the Middle East. To avoid embarrassment, the majors tweaked freight rates in a totally arbitrary manner. They were price makers with such market power that allowed them to do as they pleased.[13] In 1949, the majors controlled 82 per cent of reserves outside the United States, produced 95 per cent of oil in the Easter Hemisphere and 99 per cent of the oil from the Middle East. They owned 77 per cent of the global refining capacity outside the US and Russia, two-thirds of the privately owned tanker fleet and pretty much every single, important pipeline outside the United States.

Consuming country governments, and the US government in particular, used the majors not only to keep the supply of oil stable and affordable but also as an instrument of their foreign policy. Under the threat of Communism, the policy started to develop after the war, with the goal of supporting pro-Western governments. The companies would take care of appeasing some rulers (often the Shah of Iran) by increasing output, while the Shah would buy American weapons 'to keep his country safe from Communism', supporting the US military industry and balancing the books. To facilitate this oil balancing function, the American Majors were explicitly exempt from the antitrust sanctions by the US Justice Department.[14] This cosy relationship between companies and producing governments contained the seeds of its own destruction. The US government abandoned free markets. At home, the Texas Railroad Commission (TRC) supported the small domestic producers and prices and abroad, the US government abdicated the supply and balancing function to the majors.

Competition

Profits of the major oil companies did not go unnoticed. New companies without integrated systems and national refiners entered the market. More than half of the Libyan production ended up in the hands of companies with no integrated systems in Europe and hence no outlets for the oil. They left the 'balancing of the market' posted prices to the majors and sold their oil at the best price they could get, driving the spot prices down. With the US import quota system protecting the domestic oil producers in place, many independents were 'stranded' with oil which had to find markets elsewhere.

These 'newcomers', not unlike the shale producers in the 2010s, were keen to get the oil out of the ground and sell it as soon as possible, securing a quick return to their investment, thus putting pressure on prices. Lower spot market prices meant higher discounts relative to the posted prices and higher effective tax rate. The majors were losing money, market share, and the ability to balance the market and keep prices stable. The integrated structure of the industry was crumbling. At the heart of the problem was the oil pricing structure that ceased to make any sense. The Majors could no longer balance the market by rationing supplies. Therefore, they could not keep prices fixed. Increasingly, the spot market dictated them.

Producers' Cartel

This was a revolutionary period, a decade marked by the Suez crisis, anti-colonial movements, Sputnik and the Cuban revolution. On the 14th of September 1960, Venezuela, S. Arabia, Iran, Iraq, and Kuwait met in Baghdad and set up the Organisation of the Petroleum Exporting Countries

(OPEC). Chapter 8 discusses the impact of the orgnisation on the market and prices.

OPEC was an expression of oil producers' sovereign right to manage their own resources and align them to the needs of their economic and social development, rather than the needs of consuming nations. Algeria nationalised the oil industry in 1971. By the end of 1972, Libya nationalized BP assets in the country. In June of the following year, Iraq nationalised the Iraq Petroleum Company. In October 1973, the Arab–Israeli War started.

Consuming government policies did not help. In August 1971, President Nixon froze prices and wages. The freeze removed the incentive for refiners to produce the petroleum product, causing shortages. In December 1975, President Ford signed the Energy Policy and Conservation Act.[15] The key provision of the act was a separation of the US production into 'new' and 'old' oil. As a result, the production of all oil significantly declined. European and Japanese governments were trying to dampen the social impact of this transition through the imposition of subsidies and import taxes and supporting the national champions of the oil industry. In the process, price signals were distorted, giving wrong incentives to both domestic producers and consumers, and exacerbating the perception of a shortage of oil.

While OPEC effectively took control of the posted prices for oil, it had no mechanism for balancing the market without the help of the major oil companies. But as long as the oil demand grew and the market remained tight, everything was fine. OPEC could simply continue increasing prices to the levels markets would bear.

OPEC Fails

The end of the vertically integrated structure of the oil majors was brought about by the 1979 Iranian revolution. The new regime in Iran was quick to cancel all contracts with the US and European oil companies, but it was soon followed by other producers. Having lost the oil, the companies were forced to cancel their contractual deliveries to third parties, driving buyers to the spot market. Even though OPEC members agreed to limit spot sales, high spot prices often proved to be too tempting. Iraq, Libya, and Nigeria used the spot market frequently and Iran even used it exclusively for a period of time. As a result, Markets took the lead, and OPEC was following.

Oil production from other sources was creeping up. Britain, Norway, Mexico, USSR, and others would sell their oil at prices at which the markets would clear, effectively setting the 'free market' price. In a weak and falling market environment, OPEC official prices were lagging behind the market. In an effort to support prices, the organisation was losing market share. The fixed system of oil prices was broken and OPEC abdicated their price-making power to the market by linking their official prices to the benchmarks in the three key markets: United States, Europe, and Asia.

Liberalisation and the 'Age of Benchmarks'

Chapter 10 discusses liberalisation of the energy industries in the UK and the US. This was the most significant event in the rebirth of the oil market as an alternative to the OPEC power. In March 1983, the New York Mercantile exchange successfully launched its first crude oil futures contract. In 1988, a successful Brent contract took off the ground. From the mid-1980s, the benchmarks became a pillar of the international oil pricing system. How they work and how they are traded is the subject of the rest of the book.

Chapter 11 discusses the main global benchmark, Brent. It is a pricing reference for as much as 70 per cent of the world exported oil.[16] History and details of the workings of the benchmark are explained.

The most peculiar feature of the physical Brent benchmark is that the deliverable basket of cude oils are generally traded as a differential to Dated Brent assessment. Therefore, the price reporting agencies (PRSs) are challenged to assess the Dated Brent price based on physical trades which are themselves differentials to Dated Brent. We discuss this and the whole ecosystem of Brent derivatives ('paper markets') that facilitate better assessments. The Brent market is highly concentrated and the top five traders make up almost 60 per cent of all the cash trades. However, it does not necessarily mean they have a major influence on the outright prices. Brent is traded on the two exchanges as well, and any major deviation from the exchange prices could be easily arbitraged by any other trader.

For historical reasons, most grades of oil trading 'East of Suez' base their prices on the basis of the Dubai benchmark. This benchmark is discussed in Chapter 12. This has resulted in monthly Dubai swaps being the primary hedging instrument. These swaps are regularly traded as a differential to Brent futures[17] or a spread to Brent swaps. This spread is the heart of the international trade flows. We discuss the history and evolution of the benchmark. Market power in Dubai is even more concentrated than Brent. The top three players account for about sixty per cent of the market and just half a dozen players accounted for almost all the deals in Dubai cash partials.

Oman benchmark is also mentioned in this chapter. In spite of a large exposure to this benchmark, the liquidity of the Oman contracts is relatively poor. The chapter discusses the reasons and possible remedies.

Chapter 13 is about the grand old benchmark, West Texas Intermediate (WTI). Throughout modern history, the United States have been the world's single largest regional oil market. The benchmark WTI assessment is based on one of the world's most liquid contracts, physically delivered in Cushing, Oklahoma. The interaction between the oil gathering centres, pipelines, storage, refining and import/export facilities are the key to understanding the history, development, and dynamics of the benchmark. The pipeline links to the US Gulf Coast are essential in keeping the benchmark linked to the international oil markets. The launch of the NYMEX WTI futures contract in March 1983 heralded a return of the oil futures trading in the United States and the world. The timing of the launch was perfect, as OPEC was struggling to control the market and price volatility was growing.

Being land-locked, WTI has had a fair share of problems over the years. The greatest challenge came from rising Canadian and domestic shale production while the oil export ban was still in place. Eventually, common sense prevailed among the US legislators, and the US oil export ban, imposed in 1977 was lifted in 2015. This relieved the glut at Cushing and lifted domestic oil prices. WTI price reconnected with the international oil markets, increasing, and eventually achieving record volumes of open interest.

The Chapter 13 also addresses the shale phenomenon and its impact on the domestic and internationally oil markets. The benchmark was severely tested in April 2020 when it traded in deeply negative territory. Possible reasons and remedies are discussed at the end of this chapter.

Market Lives On

Chapter 14 follows the benchmarks in action, under the stress of the 2020 demand shock. After the April debacle and the increasing importance of oil exports, the focus of the WTI benchmark may be shifting towards the US Gulf Coast exporting facilities. While the Brent complex performed relatively well, the falling volume of the physical crude underpinning the benchmark was becoming a concern. Brent assessments are increasingly including delivered barrels and the addition of WTI in the Brent basket is the next obvious step. Asian benchmarks experienced some disconnects and issues with Dubai, Shanghai INE, and DME Oman contracts are discussed. Abu Dhabi, in conjunction with ICE have launched a Murban futures contract. The consequences for the country and OPEC may be profound and are discussed. The Demand shock of 2020 also had an impact on the way artificial intelligence is used in the oil markets and this is addressed at the end of the chapter.

Chapter 15 is a short epilogue, pointing to possible future developments in the international oil markets. Depending on government policies, the structure of the market will probably be very different, partly due to the limitations imposed by the remaining carbon budget. The chapter draws on the lessons from the history of the oil markets and how they may be applied to other markets, especially at this age of energy transition.

Notes

1. Hafner M. and Luciani G. (Eds), Handbook of International Energy Economics, Palgrave Macmillan, 2021.
2. Standard Oil started posting monopsony prices in 1895 and it was finally broken up in 1911. See Chapters 4 and 5.
3. See Chapter 6.
4. As in the case of climate change and general environmental degradation.
5. See Chapter 10, endnote #60.
6. Mainly by reducing the number of dry holes (from four in five to five in eight) and increasing life expectancy of the well (from 18 months to over three years) in the period 1865–1871. See Chapter 3, endnote #21.
7. After 'dumps' where oil was stored.
8. At the time, they were called merchants.
9. J. Seep.
10. 60:40 split in favour of the Dutch entity and with Detering in charge.
11. Hence the name of the book 'The Prize' by D. Yergin (1991).
12. US Gulf Coast was the price basis with the 'plus' freight cost added to any other delivery location.
13. See Chapter 6, 'Discriminatory Pricing'.
14. See Chapter 7.
15. It was so dense that it was termed '99-page filibuster'.
16. Assuming Dubai is a part of the same complex.
17. Exchange of Futures for Swaps or EFS.

2

Oil, Policy, and Market Power

Market Power

The history of oil markets is a story of rags to riches. In this story, individuals and firms seek to make a fortune exploiting the most important commodity in the world. Some make it, but more often than not, they fail or get swallowed by larger competitors. Cycles of intense competition and volatile prices are followed by consolidation, the emergence of dominant players and stable prices.

In general, market power manifests itself by firms that do not take market prices as given. They have the power to influence those prices. In the market jargon, they are 'price makers' rather than 'price takers'. Market power can be derived from several sources: The ability to differentiate their product, capacity constraints in the market that prevent prices from collapsing if competitive forces are unleashed, barriers to entry, and through strategic vertical integration. High initial capital costs involving risk are usually mentioned as a barrier to entry in the oil industry. Mitigating these risks through vertical integration was a source of market power of the oil majors for very many years.

Dominant players can and regularly do emerge from perfectly competitive markets in which many firms are simply 'price takers'.[1] At the very beginning of the US oil industry, the Oil Region of Pennsylvania in the 1860s had a perfectly competitive, emerging oil industry, consisting of hundreds of small producers and refiners who simply bought and sold the commodity at the going market price. First drillers were rewarded with high prices and made

© The Author(s), under exclusive license to Springer Nature
Switzerland AG 2021
A. Imsirovic, *Trading and Price Discovery for Crude Oils*,
https://doi.org/10.1007/978-3-030-71718-6_2

it rich quickly. Contemporary journalist Ida Tarbell pointed out the 'extravagant' expectations of the early drillers: '*No oil producer thought in the sixties that he was succeeding if his wells did not pay for themselves in six months*'.[2] This caused the 'oil rush' attracting thousands of fortune-seekers, resulting in overproduction, and a collapse in prices. As Figure 2.1 shows, oil price in late 1859 were around $20 per barrel, only to fall below £3 by the end of 1860. Instability and volatility were the norms. The region had an informal but functioning oil exchange, where most of the oil changed hands. Yet, by the mid-1880s, it ended up being dominated by a single entity, Standard Oil Trust, controlled by Rockefeller.

While most of the major actors in this story abused their power at some stage or another, there also may have been genuine attempts to reduce costs, improve efficiency to achieve economies of scale, stable prices and predictable profits. Rockefeller's 'Standard Oil' was vilified for the abuse of market power, but it was also synonymous with planning, standardisation, efficiency, and attention to detail.[3]

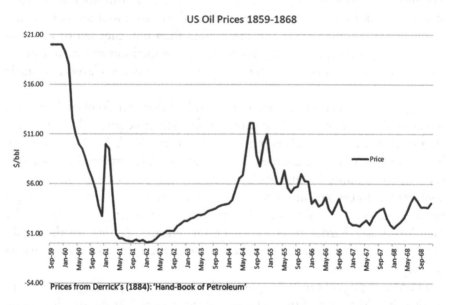

Fig. 2.1 Average crude oil prices at oil wells, oil region, Pennsylvania (Data from 1884 Derrick's Hand-Book of Petroleum)

Oil Projects, Risk and Economies of Scale

One form of market power is a 'natural monopoly'.[4] Economists define it by the presence of both economies of scale and 'sub-additivity'. The former implies cost savings over the whole range of output,[5] while the latter simply means that it is cheaper to have one firm in the market, rather than two or more. To achieve economies of scale, energy investments usually come in discrete, indivisible 'chunks'. Refineries, ships, pipelines, and other assets are often designed and built to an optimal size so that it is difficult to increase output quickly. One larger project is cheaper than several small ones for the same purpose. When scale economics are large relative to the market size, few firms exist. This is especially true in the early stages of the development of the industry.

The oil industry involves not only the exploration and production of oil, but also transportation, refining, distribution, and marketing of finished products. Crude oil demand is derived from the demand for petroleum products. These products are fairly homogenous: kerosene from one manufacturer can easily be substituted for the same product from another one, making competition between firms mainly based on price. In such circumstances, low cost of production and transportation and economies of scale are crucial.

Oil projects tend to be big, capital intensive with long gestation periods, with inflexible, project-specific assets lasting very long-time periods. Large capital spending upfront is the norm, with returns on investments enjoyed many years later. After the capital has been sunk, the operating costs are relatively small, making it harder to reduce or stop the use of assets even in very low price environments. If two or more investments are made, competition can be fierce and prices can, at least for a while, be just enough to cover only operating costs, eventually driving the investors to ruin. As the economics of scale increase the efficient size of the operation, fewer firms remain in the industry.

Large, connected oil projects[6] are also risky: They are sensitive to shifts in demand, prices, interest rates, politics, and conflicts, causing serious financial losses. For this reason, it often makes sense to keep all the interlinked aspects of the projects integrated within a single firm and not to rely on third-party suppliers or customers.

These characteristics explain why oil price wars can be fierce and why it is hard for drillers, refiners, and shippers to agree on cuts to stabilise prices. When markets are oversupplied, there is a strong incentive to 'free ride',[7] benefiting from higher prices, due to cuts by those producers making the effort. Eventually, price wars cause all producers to face ruin. Like stars and planets emerging from the 'Big Bang', players eventually close ranks, cluster and some market leadership appear from the dusty chaos.

Vertical and Horizontal Integration

One of the first economists to look into integration of various activities within a firm was Ronald Coase, probably the most famous British economists most people have never heard of.[8] In his seminal work on the 'Nature of the Firm',[9] he pointed out that all firms existed in order to minimise transaction costs. Each firm was engaged in a myriad of transactions, such as legal, accounting, manufacturing, marketing, transportation, and so on. Left to the market, each of these transactions would need to be contractually specified and agreed in detail. Any change in the circumstances would involve renegotiating such contracts. The time, trouble, and risk involved in doing so would be immense (economists usually account for all of these under the term 'cost'). It was often simpler and cheaper to arrange all of these interactions 'under one roof', namely within one firm.

As the industry activity clustered around few large firms, analysing their behaviour became harder. In 1944, a mathematician John von Neumann and economist Oskar Morgenstern published a ground-breaking book, '*Theory of Games and Economic Behaviour*', which opened new avenues for studying outcomes of the interactive behaviour of firms under a given a set of rules.[10]

Firms are normally integrated through vertical[11] and horizontal structures. Horizontal integration is between companies that are competitors in the same industry. Seen as collusion and detrimental to the general welfare, it is usually considered illegal. However, even horizontal integration can be seen as efficient: Using a game-theoretic model, a Chicago economist L. G. Telser[12] showed that, assuming indivisibility of investments (he used auto industry as an example) and steeply rising costs, large producers may not create a market equilibrium in a competitive environment.[13] In such a case, a quota-based production restraint, not unlike the one used by OPEC, can avoid a 'free-rider problem, reduce costs and still achieve a market equilibrium'.[14]

However, collusion among such firms has generally been seen as detrimental to economic welfare and large conglomerates were broken up, regulated or even nationalised,[15] under the banner of maximising 'social welfare'. The beginning of the oil industry in the United States (US) at the end of the nineteenth century was rife with complaints against the power of individual firms. Railroads were especially being accused of price discrimination for obvious reasons: they were prone to natural monopoly. It was common for them to collude and share the market, as well as price, discriminate (charge different customers, different prices). Facing 'ruinous' price competition in the early 1870s, a number of refineries 'merged' around Rockefeller's Standard Oil in order to reduce oversupply, increase efficiency and obtain lower transportation rates. Since transportation of crude oil and products is an important part of both oil and the railroad business, it is no coincidence the first monopoly in the oil industry, Rockefeller's Standard Oil, utilised railways to protect its dominant position.

Challenges in the New Age

This was a period of major economic change, challenging legal, political, and economic structures of the economy. As Telser puts it: '*Until the coming of the railroad in the 1820s, most large-scale enterprise was the creature of government... Large private enterprises are a recent phenomenon. ... Railroads marked the beginning of the new era. Building and running a railroad created new problems vastly more difficult than any ever seen before. Other industries, and some new, also posed new problems of coordination and competition like those presented by the railroads. By the late nineteenth century there were companies larger than some of the smallest nations in Europe and Latin America. Some private firms borrowed larger sums than did some of these governments. The legal forms of business enterprise changed in response to the new technology. The corporation, with its limited liability, became the leading form of private business enterprise... These changes in the economy create puzzles to challenge economic science, and among the puzzles the nature of competition in a modern economy*'.[16]

By 1872, twenty-one out of twenty-six refineries in Cleveland, Ohio, ended up in Rockefeller's control.[17] Initially, his objective was to achieve economies of scale: having so many small refineries, each with their own supply and distribution chains did not make much sense. A larger conglomerate (they called it a 'combination') could not only achieve better economies of scale in production but obtain cheaper transportation—which was a very big part of the overall cost at the time—transport of oil by rail could cost as much as the oil transported.[18] Caught in the intense competition themselves, railways commonly offered rebates and even 'drawbacks' for a guarantee of large shipments. Through such arrangements, Rockefeller and his associates could not only ship oil up to a dollar cheaper than the competition but could also 'draw' back another dollar from every barrel which its competition paid the railway for shipping. While clearly illegal, it was a common practice at the time. A refining company with a large volume of business was the lifeblood of railroads and could command such concessions.

The market power yielded by these new, large and complex entities attracted the attention of the economists. If a firm can command market power in one activity, such as transportation, could they not extend that market power to other areas such as production or marketing? An American economist, Lester Telser noticed that monopoly manufacturer could potentially project that power to the retail sector as well.[19]

The US political scene of the early twentieth century was tough on 'Standard Oil'. In 1906, Using Sherman Act[20] of 1890, the administration of President Roosevelt broke up the conglomerate into thirty-six separate oil companies in order to promote competition. Many of them continued to carry on business as usual for a while, maintaining the old market structure, stability and prices.

Others saw integrated companies in a different light. Schumpeter was one of the first economists who saw large corporations as necessary vehicles for modern capitalist innovation and temporary monopolies as sometimes unavoidable to develop new products and technologies. For him, large, integrated corporation did not preclude competition, and 'perfect' competition never really existed: '... *an entirely imaginary golden age of perfect competition that at some time somehow metamorphosed itself into the monopolistic age ... it is quite clear that perfect competition has at no time been more of a reality than it is at present*'.[21]

New Antitrust Views

The main criticism of the prevailing antitrust views of the time came from the 'Chicago School'[22] economists such as Director, Bowman, McGee, Stigler, and Telser.[23] Aaron Director, a friend of Milton Friedman, saw 'industrial organisation', as too vague and descriptive field of economics, distanced from the prevailing economic theory.[24] The 'Chicago School' attitude was that the markets were competitive and operated reasonably well, while cartels were unstable structures, unlikely to last. It is not a coincidence that many followers of this line of thought have predicted the collapse of OPEC for decades.[25] Equally, vertically integrated companies would find it hard to maintain barriers to entry and discriminate. The only exceptions that should be dealt with were the horizontal collusion of firms and blatant price-fixing. Suspects should be examined using economic theory, especially the price theory.

Some economists saw vertical integration as perfectly normal and present in everyday life: as we drive to work, buy, and wash our cars, we engage in it. There are markets for these and many other services, but it can be inconvenient and costly to engage in them. It is simply easier to 'own' them. What is more, such ownership does not say anything about competition in such markets.[26]

The sage of petroleum economics, Morris Adelman, was particularly harsh in his assessment of the Sherman Act, calling it an *'accidental result of railroad-building after 1860'*, and observing that: *'The economists were of little help precisely because they were more interested in doing good than with understanding facts'*. He added that: *'Neither professional economists nor public opinion of any shade could then distinguish among business, monopoly, and efficiency'*.[27]

The 'Chicago School' approach to antitrust issues was vindicated, at least as far as the Nobel Committee was concerned: Oliver Williamson, a follower of Ronald Coase's approach to economic organisation, was awarded the Nobel Prize in 2009 for combining economics, organisation theory, and contract law to study how vertical integration of related activities within a firm can resolve some market failures, by reducing transaction costs and uncertainty.[28] When transactions involve a simple or generic commodity or service, markets usually provide the cheapest solution for trade. According to Williamson, when trade involves specific products or services where two firms depend on each other for a long-term relationship which can change over time, vertical integration may be a better solution. For example, it is hard for an investor to sink a large amount of capital into a plant producing lubricants without having a regular supply of quality, petroleum feedstock from a refinery. Therefore, the two would normally be integrated into one firm. If they were to be independent firms, the contracts between them would have to account for virtually every eventuality over the lifetime of the project and that usually means decades. As a result, a successful lubricant business is usually a part of an integrated oil company.

In a rapidly growing and changing oil industry, long-term planning of the upstream and downstream facilities is often required, and this is generally done within integrated firms better than with new entrants, due to available information from the vertically integrated system.[29] Economists refer to this problem as 'asymmetry of information'. For example, a planned refinery expansion may take several years to accomplish, but the expanded plant will also need better transport facilities such as pipelines, barges, jetties, and so on. Making such planning within a larger, integrated oil company is a lot easier.

A study carried out by the American Enterprise Institute for Public Policy Research in 1976 claims that: *'There is no evidence the large vertically integrated oil companies are now exercising monopoly power in any of the four major stages of the oil business: the production of crude oil, the transportation of crude oil and refined products, the refining of crude oil, and the marketing of refined oil products*[30] ...Vertical integration helps companies reduce risk as well as capital costs,[31] making it particularly attractive for the oil industry. The study goes as far as to say that vertical integration may well be a necessity, saving consumers money: '... *oil company profits in a non-integrated petroleum industry would have to be at least 20 percent higher than they are now in order to offset the greater riskiness of non-integrated companies*'.[32]

In 1978, an influential legal scholar and judge, Robert Bork published a particularly important book, '*The Antitrust Paradox: A Policy at War with Itself*', in which he argued that the promotion of consumer welfare was the original principle behind the adoption of the Sherman Act in 1890. Since vertical integration is in many cases efficient and therefore beneficial to the general welfare, prosecuting integrated monopolies is against the spirit of the Act. Therefore, the practice of punishing vertically integrated firms as monopolists, in order to preserve smaller, less efficient firms was contradictory and 'at war with itself' and therefore contrary to the spirit of the Sherman Act. Gradually, the 'Chicago school' approach extended to the US Supreme Court[33] and became part of the mainstream legal practice in the United States.

Antitrust and Policy

Today, judging by the prevalence of behemoths such as Amazon, Alphabet, Microsoft, and Facebook, this view is still alive and well.[34] But regulating possible abuses of market power is not always about 'science'. The antitrust law and it's enforcement in the United States remain heavily politicised and subject to the political whim of the president and the Congress.[35] This is well reflected in the US attitude towards the international oil cartel, OPEC: A number of times, some version of NOPEC[36] bill has been proposed in the last twenty-plus years in order to extend the arm of US law to such international cartels such as OPEC. However, as soon as the 2020 COVID-19 pandemic caused a collapse in demand and threatened the US oil industry, the president of the United States reacted by turning the pressure on OPEC to cut oil production and effectively brokered[37] an agreement to forge an alliance between OPEC and producers outside the organisation, including by Russia creating 'OPEC+'.

The gradually accepted application of economic 'science' to market structure points out that normally, not all the parts of the energy supply chain are necessarily subject to natural monopolies. The best examples are electricity utilities: While transmission and distribution of power have all the characteristics of natural monopolies, there is no reason for generation and retail sales not to compete in the marketplace. Along the same lines of argument, parts of national oil, gas, and pipeline companies that can be competitive could be privatised, creating efficient markets.[38]

This approach was first applied to energy industries in the US and UK during the era of Thatcher and Regan. Lifting of US price controls by the administration of President Reagan in 1981, spurred the creation of the West Texas Intermediate (WTI) crude oil futures contract on the New York Mercantile Exchange (NYMEX) in March 1983.[39] Development of the Brent market started in a parallel and similar fashion: The Prime Minister Thatcher government's opening of the energy markets to competition in the UK in 1981 and 1982 was instrumental in the emergence of the market for the North Sea Brent crude oil.[40] Following the policies of liberalisation (or deregulation),[41] spot markets quickly grew, and the price reporting agencies (PRAs) started assessing and publishing prices for the key oil benchmarks, creating transparency and helping the establishment of the Brent futures contract in 1983.

While political and government intervention are keys to resolving monopolies, new technologies, firms, and sources of supply can equally well shake and break the foundations of a monopolised market. Breaking nationalised monopolies in the UK has generally led to the emergence of competitive markets, lower prices, and further technological improvements.

Historically, both have occurred in the oil industry.[42] What that history can teach us about this process is a subject of the next chapters.

Notes

1. In economic-theory, there is a free entry in such markets (as indeed was the case in the early oil industry which required little known technology and capital outlay other than hard labour), which erodes profits in the long run and price equals marginal cost of production. However, in the short run, there is a scope for large profits as it was indeed the case with the early producers. Prices in 'perfect markets are volatile' and as some firms enter the industry, some also exit it.
2. Tarbel (1904, p. 184).
3. Ibid., p. 196. Even a fierce critic such as Ida Tarbell, admits it in her book, in the chapter 17 titled: 'The legitimate greatness of the Standard Oil company'.

4. For an overview of the early economic thought on the subject, see Sharkey W.W. (1982, pp. 12–28).
5. A shorter but more technical definition is a falling long-term average cost curve over the whole range of output where long-run marginal cost curve is always below it. See Begg D. et. al. (2014, p. 191).
6. For example, oil exploration, pipelines, storage tanks and loading facilities.
7. If only one firm reduces output, the other one benefits, 'free riding' on the effort of the first one.
8. When I taught economics at the undergraduate level, most final-year economics students had never heard of him.Coase received a Nobel Memorial Prize in Economics in 1991. He had a major influence on the 'Chicago' school of economic thinking (where he taught at the faculty of Law) and pretty much started the field of 'Law and Economics'.
9. Coase R. (1937).
10. Like a game of cards, firms react to decisions of their competitors to achieve best outcomes (maximise utility). Hence the name.
11. Grossman and Hart (1986) define it as: 'Vertical integration is the purchase of the assets of a supplier (or of a purchaser) for the purpose of acquiring the residual rights of control,' p. 716.
12. Telser (1985).
13. One of the key assumptions is that the output increases over and above the optimal level.
14. In game theory, equilibrium is where neither player has an incentive to deviate from their initial strategy.
15. Oil nationalisations first started in 1914, with the Winston Churchill government acquiring 51% of The Anglo-Persian Oil Company (today BP); Mexico in 1938, Iran in 1951 (BP and British assets) and then from 1960s onwards, the rest of OPEC.
16. Telser (1985, p. 272).
17. Tarbell (1904, pp .33, 82).
18. Ibid., p. 31.
19. Telser (1960, p. 87). 'Some British data are consistent with the hypothesis that only manufacturers enjoying some degree of monopoly power use resale price maintenance'.
20. The Sherman Antitrust Act of 1890 is a federal statute, prohibiting restrictive interstate commerce and competition.
21. Schumpeter (1943, p. 81).
22. Wright J.D. (2012) defines the Chicago School as: ' … a set of methodological commitments embedded into the research agenda of the set of scholars associated with the law and economics movement at the University of Chicago. Three commitments stand out as the defining characteristics of the Chicago School: (1) a rigorous application of price theory; (2) the centrality of empiricism; and (3) an emphasis on the social cost of legal errors in the design of antitrust rules, p. 245.

23. For an excellent summary of the 'school', history and views, see Posner A. (1979).
24. Ibid., '… kinked demand curve," "workable competition," "cut- throat competition," "leverage," "administered prices," and the other characteristic concepts of the industrial organization of this period had this in common: they were not derived from and were often inconsistent with economic theory, and in particular with the premises of rational profit maximization. They were derived from observation, unsystematic and often superficial, of business behaviour. Director's approach was the opposite,' p. 931.
25. This point is discussed in detail in the chapter on OPEC.
26. See Liebeler J. (1976).
27. Adelman M.A. (1965, pp. 32–33).
28. Williamson O. (1971).
29. Adelman M. A. (1955).
30. Mitchell (1976, p. 70).
31. Ibid., p. 73.
32. Ibid., p. 3.
33. See Priest G.L. (2014, p. 14).
34. *Perhaps the best way to describe the current state of the antitrust thinking is a general consensus towards a 'scientific approach' to economics: '… (1) any theory ought be judged by distinct phenomena; (2) iterative testing can refine predictive power over time; and (3) that a theory other theory demonstrates predictive power'*, Wright J.D. (2012) p. 256.
35. Salop (2014, p. 637).
36. The No Oil Producing and Exporting Cartels Act (NOPEC) is an U.S. Congressional bill, never enacted, proposing a removal of the state immunity OPEC, and its national oil companies to be sued under U.S. antitrust law.
37. *The Financial Times*: 'OPEC secures record global oil cuts deal under US pressure', April 13, 2020.
38. For a summary of arguments and empirical evidence for and against privatisation, see Megginson (2005, p. 42).
39. Following a success of heating oil and gasoline futures contracts. See Chapter 13.
40. See Chapter 10.
41. The two are often used interchangeably and refer to the freeing of markets from state intervention.
42. Mitchell (1976, p. 108).

References

Adelman M.A. (1965): 'An Economist Looks at The Sherman Act', *Section of Antitrust Law*, Vol. 27, Proceedings at the Spring Meeting, Washington, DC., April 8–9, pp. 32–46.

Begg D, Gianluigi V., Stanley F. and Rudiger D. (2014): *Economics*, 11th Edition.

Coase R. (1937): 'The Nature of the Firm', *Economica*, pp. 386–405.

Grossman, S.J. and Hart O.D. (1986): 'The Costs and Benefits of Ownership: A Theory of Vertical and Lateral Integration', *Journal of Political Economy*, Vol. 94, No. 4, pp. 691–719.

Liebeler J. (1976): *Integration and Competition*, in: Mitchell E.J. (Ed), 'Vertical Integration in the Oil Industry'.

Megginson W.L. (2005): *The Financial Economics of Privatisation*, Oxford University Press.

Mitchell E.J. (1976): 'Vertical Integration in the Oil Industry', *National Energy Study*, No. 11 (June).

Posner A. (1979): 'The Chicago School of Antitrust Analysis', *University of Pennsylvania Law Review*, Vol. 127, No. 4 (April), pp. 925–948.

Priest G.L. (2014): 'Bork's Strategy and the Influence of the Chicago School on Modern Antitrust Law', *The Journal of Law & Economics*, Vol. 57, No. S3, The Contributions of Robert Bork to Antitrust Economics (August), pp. S1–S17.

Sharkey W.W. (1982): *The Theory of Natural Monopoly*, Cambridge University Press, Reprinted version 2008.

Telser (1985): 'Cooperation, Competition, and Efficiency', *The Journal of Law & Economics*, Vol. 28, No. 2 (May), pp. 271–295, Antitrust and Economic Efficiency: A Conference Sponsored by the Hoover Institution.

Telser (1960): 'Why Should Manufacturers Want Fair Trade?', *The Journal of Law & Economics*, Vol. 3 (October), pp. 86–105.

Tarbell I.M. (1904): *The History of Standard Oil Company*, Brief Version, Chalmers D.M. (Ed), Dover Publications. Reprint 2015.

Williamson H.F. and Daum A.R. (1959): *The American Petroleum Industry, 1859–1899 The Age of Illumination* (Vol. 1), Northwestern University Press.

Wright J.D. (2012): 'Abandoning Antitrust's Chicago Obsession: The Case for Evidence-Based Antitrust', *Antitrust Law Journal*, Vol. 78, No. 1 (2012), pp. 241–272, an Economic Association, pp. 112–123.

3

Looking at the Mirror: Early Days of the Oil Markets in the United States

Markets in History

History does not necessarily repeat itself. But markets do. The common denominator to all the historical epochs is the human who continues to react to events in similar fashion. The Early history of oil in the late nineteenth century in the United States offers us a glimpse of most events in the industry in subsequent periods: the riches of new discoveries, competition and oversupply, transport bottlenecks, collapsing prices and price wars, the emergence of markets and speculation, changing technology, large new oil finds, emerging domestic and foreign competition, and struggle for market power.

The First Killer App: Lighting

In some places, the oil naturally seeps from the ground where it has been gathered in small quantities since ancient times.[1] The first attempts to use oil in Britain date back to the late seventeenth century along the banks of the River Severn in Shropshire. Eventually, the manufacture of 'British Oil' was taken over by the Darby family, the descendants of Abraham Darby who first introduced coke smelting and was one of the pioneers of the Industrial Revolution.[2] The market for oil was rather limited and was promoted as a medicine for 'the Cure of Rheumatic and Scorbutic Affections'.

© The Author(s), under exclusive license to Springer Nature Switzerland AG 2021
A. Imsirovic, *Trading and Price Discovery for Crude Oils*, https://doi.org/10.1007/978-3-030-71718-6_3

The 'British Oil' was imported and sold in the United States in 'apothecaries' of New York, Philadelphia, and Pittsburgh as medicine for as high as $16 a bottle. It was soon substituted by domestically produced oil. It was collected in small quantities, only in the dry season by soaking blankets in oil seeps[3] and sold in the 1830s for as little as $0.75–$1.00. By 1840s, medicinal demand was steady and firmly established.

One of the pioneers who introduced drilling for oil was Samuel Kier, He used his extensive experience of salt-boring and applied it to gathering oil. He opened a shop in Pittsburgh in 1849 and sold half-pint bottles of 'Rock Oil' at $1. This first, established price for oil was rather high—it is equivalent to $559 per barrel in todays money,[4] a price justified by high advertising and distribution costs, generating modest profit. Before the 'Age of Oil' was to happen, a new 'killer application' had to be found, and that turned out to be illumination.

In the 1850s, most illumination was done by lard oil, sperm oil, and camphene (produced by distillation of turpentine and alcohol). The latter was by far the cheapest option, roughly at half the price of highly prized oil produced from whales.[5] Another source of illumination, manufactured by distilling cheap and widely available coal into coal oil, was just beginning to take off. First experiments in low-temperature distillation of coal, were done in Europe. In the late 1840s. James Young of Scotland refined coal into naphtha and lubricating oil.[6] The process involved several stages of distillation as well as treating with chemicals to remove impurities. As whale oil was getting expensive, James Young in Britain built his oil illuminating business based on several patents.

In 1854, Abraham Gesner patented a distillation process from coal which produced a few different kinds of oil, one of which was soluble in alcohol and could be used for burning in camphene lamps. It was claimed to be cheaper to produce, burned brighter, with less smoke, was less explosive, and therefore less dangerous than camphene. Two years later, Gesner established a New York Kerosene Company (NYKC), which was the first commercial venture to produce coal oil for illumination.[7] Together with James Young in Scotland and Samuel Downer in Boston, Gesner continued experimenting with refining the coal oil. Young managed to obtain a patent and the trademark for 'kerosene', while the NYKC developed a 'cracking' process, a foundation of modern petroleum refining. For a royalty of 2 cents per gallon, NYKC bought a licence from Young for rights to market their illuminating oil under the brand 'kerosene' and to distribute Young's specially designed lamps for burning it. Burners were as cheap as $3.50 a dozen, making illumination by coal oil attractive, especially in rural areas where city gas was not available.[8]

By 1859, retail distribution of lamps and oil was well developed, helped by a growing network of railroads. Illuminating with coal oil was cheap and efficient: for the same price, safer coal oil had almost 5 times the luminosity of camphene. It was selling in shops for roughly $1per gallon and in the 1860s, fierce competition brought the price down to $0.75 a gallon and, on occasion, even lower.[9] It even started competing with city gas in smaller towns.

From the producers' point of view, the economics of 'coal oil' distillation was compelling: A ton of coal would yield 110 gallons of 'crude coal oil' which, when distilled, yielded 65 gallons of illuminating oil and 5 gallons of lubricants.[10] With coal at $3 per ton,[11] and illuminating oil at $1 per gallon, $3 worth of coal turned into at least $70 worth of various products.[12] What made coal such a successful resource of oil was its widespread availability, originally imported from Britain, but later from Canadian and domestic mines and at low prices. However, it was not unnoticed that crude petroleum could also be refined using the essentially same process as coal-oil refining, simplified by the absence of the first step of coal-distillation. The problem was that petroleum was not widely available in sufficient quantities and it was not obvious that it ever would.

Drilling for Oil

Commercial salt production was well established before the end of the eighteenth century, especially in Virginia. While drilling for salt water, petroleum and gas were frequently found and considered a major nuisance. Salt is impermeable and does not dissolve in oil, so it often sets boundaries of the oil deposits in the ground. It was only natural that drilling of the first commercial oil well was carried out with the help of salt drillers. By the 1820s, they could drill as deep as several hundred feet and with the introduction of copper tubing, they could drill as deep as 2000 feet.[13] To increase their chances of finding oil, the drillers employed the 'science' of hydrology, a branch of geology that started in France in the 1850s, where divining rods were used to locate water, and later oil. Such 'scientists' were sought after and paid good money even by today's standards—up to $100 per well, depending on their performance.[14]

In 1853 George H. Bisell and J.G. Eveleth, partners in a stock marketing venture, had an oil sample from Titusville, Pennsylvania where it was naturally seeping from the ground and had it tested by a Yale University chemist, Benjamin Silliman, who produced a now-famous report[15] a couple of years later. It was a very encouraging report, estimating that about 50% of crude oil could be distilled into illuminating oil. After distillation, the leftover material could be used in producing illuminating gas and wax for the manufacture of candles. Eveleth and Bisell jumped on the opportunity, incorporated the 'Pennsylvania Rock Oil Company of Connecticut' and leased acreage in search for oil. They hired Edwin L. Drake, a retired railway conductor to coordinate the operations. Using well-established techniques of drilling for salt water and after many setbacks, Drake struck oil at a depth of only about 70 feet. Using a hand pump, he was able to extract up to 10 gallons a day, a volume large enough to cause first oil storage problems.[16] Drake's well proved that oil could be produced in sufficient quantities for further processing. His drilling techniques soon expanded and improved all around the Oil Creek which became known as the 'Oil Region', A number of oil rush towns mushroomed south of Titusville with telling names such as Oil City, and Petrolea City.

Prospecting for oil was hard, but with luck, the returns were attractive. In the early years, leasing costs, paid in cash were anywhere between $200-$600, plus a royalty payment of between a quarter and a third of the oil produced, to be delivered to the landlord in barrels.[17] So, assuming a 1/5 probability of finding a well producing 20 barrel per day (bd), royalty of 25%, daily operating costs of $5 and oil price at the well of $5, a driller could pay off the initial investment in a couple of months.[18] Barriers to entry were low. However, this assumed a well-skilled, organised, and capitalised effort which was usually not the case. After a few unsuccessful attempts, most drillers would simply be wiped out.

In order to spread the risk, many prospectors sold shares in their leases and bought shares in several others. Together with the 'rule of capture'[19] embedded in the US law, this created chaos and waste with wells drilled near each other, substantially reducing the pressure and life of the well. The sage of oil economics, Morris Adelman wrote: '*Given the rule of capture, ... the discovery of every new field will mean a sudden and wasteful rush to overproduce. But this results from a legal system peculiar to the United States... the waste is not only a burden on society, but even on the producers themselves...*'[20]

By 1860, all aspects of the oil industry as we know them today were in place: exploration and production technology was originally borrowed from the drilling for salt-water and refining and the transportation and distribution infrastructure were already in place for the coal-oil production. In particular, the coal-oil refineries had established technology, easily adaptable to refining of oil. They already had markets for wax, lubricants, naphtha and solvents for cleaning and kerosene for gas making and anaesthetics. This explains the lightning speed by which the oil industry expanded in the 1860s.

Beginning of the 'Age of Oil'

New production gradually spread to the 'Lower Oil Region' and supply kept outrunning demand. With learning, drilling produced deeper wells, safer and more efficient operations, increased output, while the economies of scale reduced operating costs. In 1865, the estimated daily cost of a producing well was $6.37.[21] In 1871, it fell to $2.20, mainly by reducing the number of dry holes (from four in five to five in eight) and increasing the life expectancy of the well (from 18 months to over three years). This meant that oil was getting close to being able to compete with coal, head to head. This success, as it is usual in extractive industries, eventually lead to falling prices. While a calamity for the producers, it was a boon for the competitive position of oil versus coal. Not only was oil a widely available source of illuminating oil, but it was becoming cheap as well. A simple 'netback' calculation shows that oil, at $1 per barrel, despite very high transportation costs (assumed at $9/ bbl to New York or Philadelphia)[22] could start to compete with quality Albert coal delivered to refinery at $10 per ton.[23]

As the oil refining process improved, the yield of illuminating fuel increased. But it was the other products of the refining process which were also becoming attractive. A small yield of gasoline found use in the air-gas machines, naphtha was used in the manufacture of illuminating gas, which at 5 cents per gallon could compete with coal gas. The light products, pentene and butene found use as anaesthetics and sold well at $1 per gallon.[24] Later, they became important in ice-making machines. After kerosene, lubricants were most important, but the problem of colour and odour required additional treatments and high refining skill. Eventually, removing these through slow distillation opened markets and helped to accelerate the industrial revolution. The extra effort to produce lubricants was very profitable as these 'deodorised' or 'mineral sperm oils' were often selling at twice the price of kerosene. By 1865, the paraffin uses also exploded with the advent of 'paraffin chewing gum', and application in pharmaceuticals, electricals, and medicine. Oil products such as petroleum jelly or 'Vaseline', a well-known brand even today, appeared. What is more, these new products improved the quality of kerosene by reducing adulteration—before, these products were dumped into kerosene, compromising its quality.

At the end of the refining process, at the very 'bottom of the barrel' remains a residue or fuel oil. Its only use was for burning and refineries were very keen to promote it as a substitute for coal in steam engines. Their efforts worked, and the Congress sponsored an investigation into fuel oil use for naval vessels substituting coal, resulting in practical trials for the US navy as early as 1867. The results of the trials were presented in the 'Isherwood Report'[25] in the same year. The report found that less than 4 barrels of oil did the equivalent work of 6–8 tons of coal with 50% gain in the speed of a vessel, without any machinery alterations, saving the fuel storage space and labour by up to 75%. However, it found serious drawbacks that the technology of the day could not mitigate: Evaporation of oil produced highly volatile and explosive gases which, if it hit, could disintegrate the ship. Gas odour was also hard to bear by the crew. Most importantly, coal remained about eight times cheaper fuel: *'From these considerations, it appears that the use of petroleum as a fuel for steamers is hopeless; convenience is against it, comfort is against it, health is against it, economy is against it, and safety is against it. Opposed to these, the advantages of the probably, not very important reduction in bulk and weight, with their attending economies, cannot prevail'*.[26]

With coal prices around $4.60 in 1867, fuel oil only became attractive at or below $1.00 per barrel.[27] It would take new, large oil fields in Ohio with high fuel oil and sulphur content and very low prices to break the monopoly of coal in fuelling steam engines.

Transportation Bottlenecks

A major problem for the oil industry was transport. It was expensive and irregular. In the early days of the Oil Region, the cheapest form of transportation was by boats with very shallow draft or 'flatboats', moving 25–50 barrels down the shallow creek to Oil City at $0.25–$1.00 each.[28] In winter months, the Allegheny river was closed for navigation. Wagons, usually in two-horse teams (hence name for them 'teamsters') loaded with only half a dozen barrels, would struggle to the nearest railway without getting stuck in snow and mud. The 'teamsters would charge at least $3 per barrel and often, as much as $5 per barrel, incurring massive losses along the way.[29] Barrels were a prized commodity, costing at least $2 each and had to be transported back to the wells empty. Once used for oil transport, could not be used for anything else. This was expensive and wasteful.

Railroads played a key role in transportation, connecting the pipelines with refineries in consuming centres. Improvements in bulk storage and transportation and their lower per barrel cost made the location of refineries in major consuming centres such as New York, Philadelphia, and Cleveland more attractive. However, reaching railroads was not the end of the problems. While their network was reasonably extensive in the 1860s United States, roads often had different ownership and gauge so that oil had to be re-loaded, further increasing costs and losses. Rocking and shaking would produce dangerous, flammable gasses and large water deposits at the bottom. Accidents were frequent.

Attracted by large transportation charges, new ideas were tried. In the spring of 1862, fifteen steamers and barges started transporting oil from Oil City to Pittsburgh. Bulk transportation by railway was introduced in 1867, within tank cars (wagons with oil tanks), improving safety and losses. On top of that, handling cost alone was reduced by at least $0.05 per gallon,[30] equivalent to $2.10 per barrel! It made delivered oil to the refinery more regular, safer, and much cheaper.

Gathering Lines, Storage, and the First Price Shock

The real breakthrough came with the introduction of gathering pipelines, taking oil from the wells to the nearest railway hubs. Attempts to build pipelines were made as early as 1860.[31] The first successful pipeline[32] was built by Samuel Van Syckle, who completed a two-inch line from Pithole to Miller Farm in 1865 and charged only $1 per barrel for the transport (compared to teamsters charging $3–$5 a barrel). Samuel was also heavily speculating in oil and despite his brilliant ideas, he lost all his money and assets. In the early days, these pipelines were built to substitute the most difficult and expensive leg of transportation and were complementary to the railroads.

Soon, the gathering and 'accommodation' lines (which connect wells with pipeline storage or 'dump' tanks) fees fell further, to $0.75 and even $0.25.[33] From 1862, more, better, and safer iron tanks became common and gradually, the cost of storing started to fall as well, from $2.50 in 1862 to $1.00 in 1865.[34] One reason for the falling costs was saving in the capital by not building expensive wooden barrels. The other reason was a large increase in production, resulting in low unit prices (see Fig. 3.1).

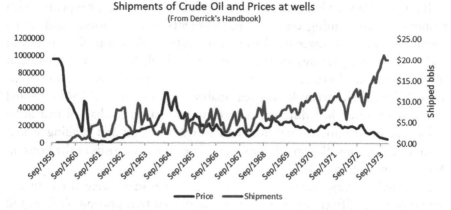

Fig. 3.1 Oil prices at wells and volumes of shipments in barrels (Data: Derrick's Handbook of Petroleum, 1884)

As the spring of 1861 brought about the first 'gusher' wells,[35] market was overwhelmed with supply, so that transporting and storing such volumes of oil became a problem.[36] Between 1860 and 1862, oil prices fell from almost $20 to $0.10 per barrel.[37] Even pits were being dug to 'store' oil. This was the first 'oil shock'. Then, as now, producers made attempts to reduce output,[38] but cheating and free riding were common, with disastrous results.

Storing any commodity is costly and risky. It ties up precious capital. But storing oil serves a key function and creates a buffer in the market, soaking up excess supply which is then released when demand picks up. Given sufficiently low prompt or 'spot' prices, storing makes sense when the price of oil for future delivery, is high enough to pay for the costs of storage, the price of capital and insurance.[39] Essentially, it is an arbitrage[40] in time. For storage to work without prohibitive risk (by hedging the price risk), the industry needed not only the market prices for prompt delivery, but also a liquid market for future delivery of oil.

The First Physical and 'Paper' Oil Markets

The first oil traders were known as 'dump men' on Oil Creek.[41] 'Dump' referred to a storage tank for oil, pretty much of any size, but usually not large. The 'Dump men' would make markets (they would bid for oil at a firm price) for small producers who had limited tankage and had to sell oil relatively quickly, but not in quantities large enough to be of interest to bigger refiners. They provided liquidity in illiquid markets and took price risk, relying on better market information than these small producers. Also, they provided the earliest price discovery mechanism. Refinery representatives or agents would scout the Oil Region, meet with producers, discuss business, and make deals, usually in the late hours of the day. Once their hours were regulated, they would be the foundations of an organised exchange. The first example of a 'forward' market (market for future delivery) was Captain Jacob Jan Vandergrift (who later ended up working for Rockefeller) buying July 1862 delivery of 5,000 barrels of oil agreed six months earlier, in November 1861.[42]

The gathering lines started issuing 'tickets' as proof that a producer delivered oil. Made in duplicates and denominated in volume and not value, these tickets were proof of ownership of a quantity of oil in the line, tangible assets which could be traded for cash and an excellent vehicle for speculation. In such a way, each barrel of oil could be traded many times (changing hands through multiple trades), establishing the going price and creating the first 'paper' markets for oil. Trades were made in offices, at oil wells, on streets, trains and pretty much everywhere. Normally, the deals concluded were for certificates of 1,000 barrels[43] and delivery within 10 days ('regular' delivery) but could also be for 'spot' (immediate) or 'future' delivery at any time and any volume.[44] The forerunner of oil exchanges was "the Curbstone Exchange" at Oil City in 1870 where the bulk of the buying and selling was done on Centre street, near the railroad track. Producers, dealers, and spectators would gather on the pavement, discuss the market and trade.

From the earliest days, oil trading was conducted with a very strong sense of honour: *The men of the oil-region have ever been noted for their commercial honor. It passed into a proverb—"honor of oil. "The spirit of the saying, "his word is as good as his bond," has always been lived up to more closely in Oildom than in any other section of the country. The force of business-obligation ran high in the exchanges and among the early dealers in crude. Transactions involving hundreds-of-thousands of dollars occurred every day, without a written bond or a scrap of paper save a pencil-entry in a memorandum-book. Certificates were borrowed and loaned in this way and the idea of shirking a verbal contract was never thought of. The celerity with which property thus passed from man to man was one of the striking features of business in the bustling world of petroleum. And the record is something to be proud of in these days of embezzlements, defalcations, breaches of trust and commercial deviltry generally.*[45] Many prominent citizens were regularly involved in speculation.[46]

As trading took off, there was a clear need for permanent premises. The exchanges were established at Oil City,[47] Titusville, Parker, Bradford, Pittsburgh, New York, Philadelphia and elsewhere. The spread of telegraphy greatly facilitated the transmission of information and trading. First broker-ages were started earlier, in 1868 by refinery buyers in Pittsburgh, Baltimore and Philadelphia, taking orders by telegraph and charging a commission of ten cents per barrel from buyers and five from sellers. These institutions took off strongly. On 30 March 1876, Derrick's reported: '*Great excitement in Oil City Exchange; bulls and bears have a warm contest; aggregate sales nearly 250,000 barrels*'. Over time, volumes grew significantly, and the same source recorded monster trading days (even by today's standards) in 1882: 4,727,000 barrels on 27 August; 8,462,000 barrels on 12 September; 12,731,000 barrels on September 26th and, having established a clearinghouse in October that year, the exchange hit a record number of transactions at 17,765,000 barrels trading on November 7th.[48]

Outside the oil city, the New York 'Consolidated Stock and Petroleum Exchange' grew particularly large with 2,400 members and a 'lordly building' at Broadway and Exchange Place. It had one of the largest memberships in the country with seats sold as high as three-thousand dollars and volumes of traded oil often exceeding the transactions on the New York's Stock Exchange.[49]

For a period of some 20 years, from 1875 to 1895, virtually all the oil trading was done on one of the exchanges.[50] But one day, it all suddenly ended. In January 1895, 'Seep Agency', the sole oil buying agency of Standard Oil company, in a fine display of market power, announced that it was to stop the use of exchange prices for oil purchases and would simply 'post' prices at which it would buy oil:

'*NOTICE TO oil PRODUCERS*'.[51]
The small amount of dealing in certificate oil on the exchanges renders the transactions there no longer a reliable indication of the value of the product. This necessitates a change in my custom of buying credit balances. Hereafter in all such purchases the price paid will be as high as the markets of the world will justify, but will not necessarily be the price bid on the exchange for certificate oil. Daily quotations will be furnished for you from this office.
Joseph Seep. "January 1895.'

The free market died and from then on, the key arbiter of what price the oil should trade at, the price maker was a refiner with the greatest market power in the land—Standard Oil. How and why one of the most competitive industries in the country became dominated by a refining 'combination' led by Rockefeller to set its own prices is the subject of the next chapter.

Notes

1. See McLaurin (1896, p. 4).
2. See Craig J. et al. (2018, p. 5).
3. Williamson and Daum (1959, p. 13).
4. Ibid., p. 22. There are 42 gallons in a barrel.
5. In 1852, end year prices for illuminating oils were: sperm oil $1.34, lard oil $0.95 and turpentine $0.635 per gallon. Ibid., p. 36.
6. Henry (1873, p. 32).
7. Williamson and Daum (1959, p. 47).
8. Ibid., p. 55.
9. Ibid., p. 59.
10. Ibid., p. 53.
11. White J.H. (1979, p. 87).
12. On per gallon basis, lubricants consistently had higher market value than illuminating oil.
13. Williamson and Daum (1959, p. 17).
14. Ibid., p. 91.
15. '*Professor Silliman's report, published in the fall of 1855, attracted attention in New Haven, and led to the reorganization of the Pennsylvania Rock Oil Company, with that gentleman as President*'. Henry (1873, p. 348).
16. Williamson and Daum (1959, p. 80).
17. Ibid., p. 100.
18. 20 bd at 1/5 risk and 25% royalty is 3 b/d; at $5/ bbl, revenue is $15/ day minus daily cost is $10/ day. Over 60 days, a $600 leasing cost could be paid off.
19. This peculiar feature of the US law of the time, gave property rights of the subsoil resources to those who find them first.
20. Adelman (1972, p. 44).
21. See J.T. Henry (1873, p. 221).
22. At least 2/3 of the delivered price was handling and transportation cost. Williamson and Daum (1959, p. 136).
23. A ton of Albert coal is assumed to yield 60 gallons, while a barrel of oil is assumed to yield 70% kerosene. Processing coal is assumed to be $0.19 and oil at $0.06 per gallon. For assumptions, see Williamson and Daum (1959, pp. 105–107).
24. Williamson and Daum (1959), p. 237.
25. Annual Report to the Secretary of the Navy (1867).
26. Ibid., p. 175.
27. Using energy contents of coal of 28 m Btu per ton and fuel oil at 6.3 m Btu per barrel, with coal prices at $4.6, fuel oil would need to be roughly at $1/ bbl or below to be competitive: $28/6.3 = 4.44$ and $4.6/4.44 = 1.03$
28. Williamson and Daum (1959, p. 166).

29. 'Even after a plank-road had been built from Titusville to Pithole, cutting down the teaming one-half or more, the cost of laying down a barrel of crude in New York was excessive. In January of 1866 it figured as follows:

Government tax	$1 00
Barrel	$3 25
Teaming from Pithole to Titusville	$1 25
Freight from Titusville to New York	$3 65
Cooperage and platform expenses	$1 00
Leakage	$0.25
Total	$10.40

McLaurin (1896, p. 316).

30. Williamson and Daum (1959, p. 183).
31. 'The first suggestion of improvement in transportation was made in 1860, at Parkersburg, W. Va., by General Karns to C. L. Wheeler, now of Bradford. An old salt-well Karns had resurrected at Burning Springs pumped oil freely and he conceived the plan of a six-inch line of pipe to Parkersburg to run the product by gravity. The war interfered and the project was not carried out. At a meeting at Tarr Farm, in November of 1861, Heman Janes broached the idea of laying a line of four-inch wooden-pipes to Oil City, to obviate the risk, expense and uncertainty of transporting oil by boats or wagons. He proposed to bury the pipe in a trench along the bank of the creek and let the oil gravitate to its destination... The opposition of four-thousand teamsters engaged in hauling oil defeated the bill and the first effort to organize a pipe-line company. The Legislature granted a pipe-line charter in 1864 to the Western Transportation Company, which laid a line from the Noble & Delamater well to Shaffer. The cast-iron pipe, five inches in diameter, was laid on a regular grade in the mode of a water-pipe. The lead points leaked like a fifty-cent umbrella, just as the Hutchings line had done, and the attempt to improve transportation was abandoned'. McLaurin (1896, p. 318).
32. Pipelines were a game changer on many levels: 'The producer can leave his oil in the line, subject to a slight charge for storage after thirty days or sell it immediately. He can take certificates or acceptances of one thousand barrels each, payable on demand in crude-oil at any shipping-point in the oil-region. These certificates, good as gold and negotiable as certified checks, the holder can use as collateral to borrow money, sell at sight or stow away if he looks for an advance in prices... In an hour from the time of notifying the office his oil may be run, the amount figured up, the sale made and the currency in the owner's pocket. He has not tugged and perspired loading it in wagons or on cars, worn out his patience and his team and his profanity driving it through an ocean of mud, or risked the chances of a jam and a wreck ferrying it on the bosom of a pond-freshet. Nor has he put up one penny for the service of the pipe-line, which collects twenty cents a barrel when the oil is delivered to the purchaser. The company is not a holder of oil on its own account,

except what it necessarily keeps to offset evaporation and sediment, acting merely as a common-carrier between the producer and the refiner. The system is the perfection of simplicity, accuracy and cheapness'. As McLaurin (1896, p. 432).

33. Williamson and Daum (1959, pp. 187–178).
34. Ibid., p. 192.
35. Fountain well was discovered, followed by Empire and Phillips no. 2, all very large finds at the time.
36. When storage and transportation become overwhelmed with available commodity, prices in certain location can go to zero or even negative. This has happened on several occasions, including very relatively recent history and will be discussed in later chapters.
37. Derrick's (1884), p. 51. In January 1860 it was $19.25 and in January 1862 $0.10 per barrel.
38. The first ever association of producers, the Oil Creek Association formed in Pennsylvania on 14th of November 1861. See Miller (1968): '*In an attempt to bolster the market and limit production, producers met at Rouseville, Pa., formed the Oil Creek Association, and accomplished practically nothing!*' p. 54.
39. The price structure where prompt delivery is cheaper than future delivery is called 'contango'.
40. Arbitrage involves buying in a cheaper market and selling in a more expensive one. For arbitrage to work profitably, the cost of moving the commodity between the markets must be less than their price difference. The same applies to the arbitrage in time—future price of commodity must be high enough to cover all the costs involved in storing the commodity, and that involves storage fees, insurance, and the cost of capital.
41. Hearings of the Industrial Commission, p. 450.
42. Vandergrift, in partnership with Forman 'piped and railroaded oil from Pithole, extended their lines through the different fields, devised many improvements, perfected the methods of handling the product and developed the system that has eliminated jaded horses, wooden-barrels, mud-scows, slow freights and the thousand inconveniences of early transportation'. Apparently quite an ingenious character, he was a president of the United Pipe-Lines (and of the United Division of the National-Transit after the consolidation in 1884), founder of the Oil-City Trust-Company, several banks, manufactured steel pipes and was 'a pioneer, a guide and a leader in natural-gas'. He was prominent in organizing the Oil Exchange in Pittsburgh in 1881 by providing the premises. See McLaurin, p. 326.
43. 1,000 barrels (or one 'lot') remains a minimum volume traded on the major exchanges to this day.
44. 'The Farmers' Railroad, completed to Oil City in 1867, brought so many operators to town that a car had assigned them, in which they bought and sold 'spot', 'regular' and 'future oil'. There were no certificates, no written obligations, no margins to bind a bargain, but everything was done on honour and no man's word was broken. 'Spot oil' was to be moved and paid for at once,

'regular' allowed the buyer ten days to put the oil on the cars and 'future' was taken as agreed upon mutually. Large lots frequently changed hands in this passenger-car, really the first oil-exchange. Ibid., p. 335.

45. McLaurin (1896, p. 342).
46. Ibid., p. 333.
47. Derrick's Handbook (1884, p. 30). The first regular exchange was established in 1874, while the original exchange dates back to 1871.
48. Ibid., p. 33, 45, 46.
49. Smith (1887, p. 141).
50. Preliminary report (1900, p. 451).
51. Ibid., p. 436.
52. Ibid., p. 436.

References

Adelman M.A. (1972): *The World Petroleum Market*, The Johns Hopkins University Press.

Craig J., Gerali F., Macaulay F. and Sorkhabi R. Eds. (2018): *The History of the European Oil and Gas Industry (1600s–2000s)*, Geological Society, London, Special Publications, 465, pp. 1–24.

Derrick's (1884): *Hand-Book of Petroleum*, Derrick Publishing Company.

Henry J.T. (1873): *The Early and Later History of Petroleum*, Jas. B. Rodgers Co. Printers, Philadelphia.

McLaurin J.J. (1896): *Sketches in Crude Oil*, Harrisburg, PA.

Miller, E.C. Ed. (1968): *This Was Early Oil, Contemporary Accounts of the Growing Petroleum Industry, 1848–1885*, Commonwealth of Pennsylvania, The Pennsylvania Historical and Museum Commission, Harrisburg, 1968.

Smith E.V. (1887): *Plain Truths About Stock Speculation, How to Avoid Losses in Wall St.*, Brooklyn, NY.

White J.H. (1979): *A History of the American Locomotive: Its Development, 1830–1880*, Dover Publications New York.

Williamson H.F. and Daum A.R. (1959): *The American Petroleum Industry, 1859-1899 The Age of Illumination* (Vol. 1), Northwestern University Press.

4

From Competition to Monopoly

'The Butcher, Baker, and the Candle Maker'

Markets are born in competition. What economist call 'perfect competition' is often focused on the 'long run equilibrium' or a steady state of affairs, where free entry into the market erodes firm profits to zero and the price eventually equals the marginal cost of production. What is often missed is tremendous scope for profit-making in the short run.

The early days of oil production demonstrate this point well: Pennsylvania discoveries turned to a rush for drilling and a speculative boom in oil-producing, not unlike the shale boom in the United States of 2010s: *'Well owners could pay all expenses and make profits of $3 to $7 a barrel. Many of them rolled in wealth. Men were feverishly boring fresh wells in old areas and prospecting and "wildcatting" new fields. Investors rushed to pour more money into speculative enterprises… the Federal Revenue Commission estimated in 1866 that more than $100,000,000 had been applied to the purchase and development of oil lands'.*[1]

As new producers entered the market and others left, money was made and money was lost. *'During these boom years Oildom seemed half a region of gilded romance, half violent melodrama. Almost everybody you meet… has been suddenly enriched or suddenly ruined (perhaps both within a short space of time)'.*[2]

The oil industry operated no differently to any other American business of the time—it was based on partnerships and required relatively little capital, making it highly competitive. With changes in demand and supply,

© The Author(s), under exclusive license to Springer Nature
Switzerland AG 2021
A. Imsirovic, *Trading and Price Discovery for Crude Oils*,
https://doi.org/10.1007/978-3-030-71718-6_4

the industry seemed constantly out of kilt with production, transportation, and refining. This was reflected in the volatility of both crude oil and refined product prices.

The production 'boom' led to overproduction, waste, and the eventual collapse in prices. It was only a matter of time before the oil 'rush' in production reached the refining. Cheaper oil and improvements in refining increased profits and led to a rush of investment. In 1866, Cleveland alone had fifty refineries.[3] They appeared everywhere and, in all sizes and anyone could enter the business. In the words of Rockefeller: '*The cleansing of crude petroleum was a simple and easy process, and at first the profits were very large. Naturally, all sorts of people went into it: the butcher, the baker, and the candlestick-maker began to refine oil, and it was only a short time before more of the finished product was put on the market than could possibly be consumed*'.[4] ... *Any man with $10,000 could establish a small refinery, any one with $50,000 a large one*'.[5]

Competition became fierce. Despite growing demand, by the early 1870s, the refining segment of the oil industry became bloated and unprofitable. Figure 4.1 shows crude oil prices at the well, compared to the prices of the 'refined' product in New York harbour. If one had exact transportation cost to add to the crude prices, refinery margins (refinery profits) would probably be negative for most refiners in 1871 and 1872. They were losing money.

Even the most efficient ones such as John D. Rockefeller were worried.

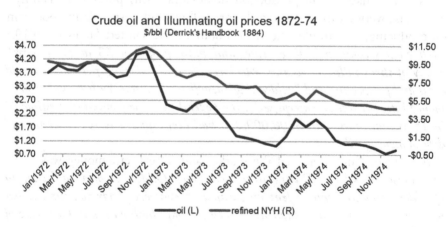

Fig. 4.1 Crude and 'refined' prices (Data from Derrick's Handbook, 1884)

More kerosene than Bibles

Both Rockefeller and his right-hand, Henry Flagler started as merchants or as we call it now, traders.[6] They made their money as young men, in the early thirties, trading grain and other commodities, but saw better opportunity in the new and thriving market for kerosene'.[7] 'We use more kerosene lamps than Bibles', wrote one observer.

From the outset, it was very clear to them that this new oil industry had a huge potential, and the biggest, most efficient refiners would gradually end up consolidating and dominating the industry. Such consolidation could only be done by an efficient dominant entity and the partners got to work to create one. They were not afraid to leverage their investments and borrow heavily from banks when needed.[8] But that was not enough as: '... all the money that Rockefeller could get from Cleveland banks, or from profits, was not enough to develop his enterprises at a rate which satisfied him.[9]

The early 1867 partnership of 'Rockefeller, Andrews & Flagler' was a means of attracting additional[10] capital for a massive plant expansion. The expansion did not just include the Cleveland refinery but also new oil depots, rail tank cars and anything to improve the efficiency of the operation. The Cleveland plant itself trebled in size from 500 barrels in 1867 to 1,500 barrels only two years later.[11] Eventually, most of these investments paid off handsomely.[12]

The 'Railway problem'

The industry constantly suffered from high transportation charges, so this was the area the partners turned next. In the early 1870s, the price of oil at the wells fell below $4 a barrel and rail transportation alone was easily half as much. The growth in the size of the business not only increased the efficiency of production by creating economies of scale, but it also gave the partnership sufficient market power to demand better transportation rates, thus lowering their overall cost. This is where Flagler's key competencies came to the fore: He had an in-depth knowledge of the transportation aspect of trade and a personal relationship with many officials on the railways.[13]

Eventually, it will be the railroads which helped Rockefeller and Flagler tame and ultimately control the oil industry. They were a tool used to integrate the business horizontally and then to strengthen and protect the monopoly and prices from the competition by creating barriers to entry.[14]

Unlike roads and canals,[15] railways were being built primarily by private capital, using state legislation granting them a 'charter' or a concession, to be exercised in a way to provide public utility.[16]

The railway boom of 1830s in the United States was followed by their consolidation a couple of decades later, through mergers or 'combinations'.[17] In 1850s, three main companies consolidated a number of smaller railroads on the Midwest to the East coast route: The Erie, running from the Dunkirk on the Lake Erie to New York, The New York Central from Buffalo on the Lake Erie to Albany and 'New York, and the Pennsylvania, linking Philadelphia to Pittsburgh and Chicago.[18] The alternative to these railroads was the Great lakes-Erie Canal linking Lake Erie to Albany.[19]

The growing business of railroads as well as the oil industry was well ahead of the development of legislation. States focused on their laws and business, bridging several states that were operating in limbo. There was little if any federal regulation to either facilitate or regulate business spanning several states. In such an environment, 'combinations' and abuses were common and in a hunt for revenues, 'anything went'.[20]

Following the consolidation, railways grew in economic and political power and very much begun to exist outside the government control.[21] In the opening of the proceedings of the Chamber of Commerce of the state of New York in 1879, Simon Sterne appeared on behalf of the Chamber and the Board of Trade and Transportation arguing that: '*This vast power has been permitted to grow up and overshadow almost every other interest in society, without any responsibility for its management to anyone, except, as I shall hereafter show, an illusory one to its stockholding interest. The State has ceased to control it; the stockholders have practically ceased to control it*'.[22] For example, in 1850, the state of New York passed a General Railway Act to maintain state supervision and control of the passenger, but not freight traffic which was becoming the main money earner for the railways. This allowed the railways to charge for freight pretty much what they wanted. Different consolidated lines started to offer similar services, especially on the East-West route, creating heated competition amongst them.

At the same time, entirely distinct organizations were established for the purpose of handling the freight involving several railroads and different states, vastly improving the speed and cost of transportation. These 'fast freight' trunk lines usually owned the cars used for through traffic and handled the entire trip. They collected the charges from the shippers and paid the railroads, agreed on tolls for the use of locomotives and railroads, avoiding difficult and costly trans-shipments. This further intensified competition among the consolidated railroads. Having sunk large amounts of capital with a very low running cost for each additional trip on the railway, different railroads, offering pretty much the same service, would get involved in fierce price wars to secure large, regular customers.

To avoid price wars, the railways held several 'conventions', from the late 1850s for a good quarter of a century. The purpose of these conventions was to fix rates and 'pool' the customers, thus avoiding painful competition. They failed each time, primarily because they were amalgamations of local lines, where the rate wars usually started. They took the form of discounts or rebates and drawbacks and were a widespread practice among the railroads. While the main competition was in agricultural products, oil became a significant commodity in mid-1860s. This coincided with the major expansion of the Rockefeller, Andrews & Flagler's Cleveland plant and the increased size of their operations including tank cars and terminals gave them an important bargaining chip in negotiations with the railroads. This together with Flagler's knowledge and the ability to enforce[23] a hard bargain with the railroads made the company a likely beneficiary of such practices.

Such price wars between trunk lines were particularly vicious between 1869 and 1878, exactly at the time when Rockefeller and Flagler were consolidating their position as premier Cleveland refiners. Rebates or discounts were usually given for a guaranteed volume of agreed business. But it was the drawbacks that were a particularly vicious form of rewarding large shippers who not only receive rebates but also additional compensation from the fares paid by their competition. Such arrangements would not only give a dominant player lower rates but would also cripple its competition. While both rebates and drawbacks were practised by railroads well before Flagler started negotiating them, they became '*indispensable*' to the partnership to become the eventual monopoly.[24]

The Years of Depression

The promise of large returns led to overinvestment in railroads, but also in the oil industry, both in production in refining. As a result, the period of 1868 to 1873 were the 'years of depression' in the Oil Region.[25] In December 1767, oil price at the wells fell below $2 a barrel and in January it was only $1.55. Oil producers scrambled to organise and understand the causes of low prices. Just like the first oil price shock in May 1861 set producers to establish the local Oil Creek Association the early 'years of depression' led the producers to establish the Petroleum Producers' Association of Pennsylvania in February 1869. However, this later association mainly focused on gathering production statistics, patent litigation and other administrative tasks, ignoring the causes of the price weakness—massive overproduction.

The excess capacity was even more obvious among the refiners with the capacity growing to as much as three times the prevailing demand.[26] In such circumstances, only one thing could happen—refined product prices fell and with them collapsed the refinery profits. Simple, unsophisticated, and poorly run refineries went out of business. Rockefeller and Flagler, with good facilities in Cleveland, warehouses and tanks in the Oil Region and New York harbour, barrel-making plant, railroad tank cars, lakeside shipping facilities, were in a good place, ready to take advantage of the situation and consolidate the rest of the industry.

'Our Plan'

They called it 'our plan'.[27] It involved mergers with the largest refiners in the region and acquisition of others, closing of the small and inefficient plants and leaving a dominant, large, and stable monolithic entity under their control. To that end, as the rate war between the railroads was raging in 1869 and 1870, the partnership resolved to seek additional investment and set up a joint-stock corporation, while retaining the control of the company. On 10 January 1870, the Standard Oil Company was incorporated in Ohio with $1 million in capital.[28] When other refiners were reeling under pressure, Standard Oil was growing. It had enough market power not to accept the 'official' transportation tariffs, but to negotiate their own, far better ones. When Flagler went to the railroads with a promise of large shipments every day of the year, they were only too eager to listen and oblige with large rebates. In the railroad freight market, Standard became a price maker, not a price taker.

The first serious idea about integrating both refiners and railroads came from Tom Scott, a very prominent well connected local businessman and the vice president of the Pennsylvania Railroad. His idea was to use a special company charter of the Pennsylvania legislature[29] to pool the key refiners as mediators or 'eveners' in order to allocate mutually agreeable shares of freight between the railroads and thus end the price war. The vehicle for this pool was the 'South Improvement Company' (SIC) and at its first official meeting in January 1872 the rules were agreed: Participation would be opened to all the refiners accepting the basic principles of the 'pool' who would hold shares in the SIC which, in turn, would act as the 'evener'[30] of oil traffic on the railroads, agreed to be 45 per cent for Pennsylvania, and 27.5 per cent each to Erie and the New York Central. The 'official' tariffs would be substantially raised for all the shippers, but the shareholders of the SIC would receive rebates in proportion to their shareholding, thus reducing the overall cost. At the time, Standard Oil was shipping about sixty carloads of oil per day and was, almost certainly, already the biggest refining operation in the world[31] and therefore the most influential 'pool' member and the one to benefit most from the arrangement.

Of course, all the refiners outside the 'pool' would face considerably higher shipping costs. On top of the rebates were drawbacks to be paid to the SIC by all the shippers outside the pool, and equal to the amount paid in rebates. For example, the new official rate for shipping crude oil from the Oil Regions to New York was $2.56 a barrel, a massive increase from the earlier rate of $1.65. However, a shareholder of the SIC would receive a rebate of $1.05 a barrel, thus paying about $1.50.[32] Any refiner outside the SIC would pay the full rate of $2.56, out of which a drawback of $1.05 a barrel would also go to the 'pool'.

Thus, the participants in the combination would not only get money back from their own shipments, but also profit from the shipments of their competitors. In his biography of Rockefeller, a historian Allan Nevins commented: '*Of all devices for the extinction of competition, this was the cruellest and most deadly yet conceived by any group of American industrialists*'.[33] Finally, the SIC shareholders were to receive full market intelligence from the railroads regarding shipments of all of their competitors and have full access to the railroad books for inspection.

In the form it was conceived, 'the plan' was clearly designed to eliminate all the refining competition outside the SIC, and Standard Oil was very clearly a major part of it.[34] Nevins concluded: '*The rebate provisions of the contract were brutal, unjust and outside the pale of business ethics even in that loose period. They run counter to the essential spirit of fair play and democracy in American enterprise*'.

The general public in the United States and overseas learned about it through a fascinating and hugely popular, while not entirely accurate piece by H.D. Lloyd published in the Atlantic in 1881: '*The Story of a Great Monopoly*'.[35] While Rockefeller and Flagler eventually achieved 'their plan', negative public opinion created would follow them for the rest of their lives'.[36]

Monopolies at War

As details of the deal leaked into the public, they caused indignation and anger throughout the Oil Region. The producers quickly resurrected the Petroleum Producers' Association, now named the Petroleum Producers Union, cut production and imposed an embargo on all oil shipments to the SIC, starting the 'Oil War of 1872'. This time it was a war between two monopolies, producers versus refiners.

It was not a long war. Under public and political pressure, the railroads were quick to fold the 'pool'. On 2 April 1972, the Pennsylvania Legislature passed two very popular bills: one revoking the SIC charter and another passing the 'free pipeline bill', giving the pipeline companies the right of eminent domain[37] thus increasing competitive pressure on the railroads. Rockefeller offered producers an olive branch by proposing to buy oil at a guaranteed, high price, provided they cut their production. Also, less than a week following the Pennsylvania Legislature decisions, Standard Oil announced it had no more contracts with the railway companies or the SIC.

Producers were equally restive. Shipments were low, oil stocks were growing, and the war seemed to have been won. Standard Oil managed to buy oil from Oil City firms once again and the ice seemed to have been broken. But behind the scenes, Rockefeller and Flagler used the threat of the SIC to proceed with their original plan—to consolidate the oil refining industry.

Roughly at the time of formation of the Petroleum Producers' Association, refiners were openly in discussions about a comprehensive, yet loose association which would ration production, procure crude oil, fix product prices, and negotiate freight rates with the railroads. The Petroleum Refiners' Association (often referred to as the National Refiners' Association) was formally established in August 1872 with Rockefeller as president and with officers from two other key refining regions: J. Vandergrift from the Oil Region and Charles Pratt, from New York. While this association also failed in less than a year,[38] Rockefeller and Flagler learned some valuable lessons: Firstly, they realised that a loose association would not work, and any consolidation would have to be under the umbrella of Standard Oil and their direct control. Secondly, it put them in touch with key individuals in charge of refining such as Archbold and Vandergrift from the Oil Region and Pratt and Rogers of New York, whose companies and personnel will eventually be absorbed and become an important part of the Standard Oil empire.

The Giant

In this, final version of 'the plan', Rockefeller and Flagler were to approach the large, key refiners first, use the stick of the falling profits and the threat of the SIC combination[39] and merge or simply buy outright the assets of these refiners, directly under the umbrella of the Standard Oil Company. The smaller, less efficient plants with no market power would simply fold.

Rockefeller and Flagler threw money at the problem. Standard's biggest competitor in Cleveland, Clark, Payne & Co. agreed relatively quickly, in return for a very generous offer for their assets, goodwill and the expertise of James Clark, one of the proprietors, who was offered employment in the enlarged company.[40] Outside Cleveland, a big addition was the plant of Bostwick & Company of Long Island, New York, a prominent exporter of refined products with excellent terminal facilities. Within only three months,[41] twenty-two out of twenty-six Cleveland refineries sold out, increasing the refining capacity of Standard Oil from about 1,500 to more than 10,000 barrels, which was almost half of all the oil then produced in the country at the time.[42]

While the whole nation was fixated by the 'oil war', a giant was born, with the capacity to refine more oil than any of the entire regions in the United States.[43] However, this was not the end of 'the plan'. The next four years were to see a snowball effect and expansion of the company both horizontally, by acquiring the remaining refineries and vertically, by integrating within the firm oil purchases, pipelines, marketing and exports.

In the area of oil purchases, Standard Oil was generally conservative.[44] In the mid-1880s, all its oil supplies were bought through one of the two agencies: a wholly owned brokerage of Henry Lewis & Company (originally focusing on the Cleveland plants) and Seep Purchasing Agency (a sole agent in the Appalachian region). Both were later consolidated within the National Transit Company where a highly centralised operation of the 'Crude Stock Department' would closely monitor global supply and demand fundamentals, advising the Executive Committee who, in turn, would issue purchase orders to be executed through one of the two agencies. All the Standard refineries would then procure the oil from the crude stock department directly. This was a very sophisticated operation, not unlike the 'supply and trading' departments of the international oil companies today.

Buying was done in pipeline certificates on one of the exchanges, or directly in negotiations with the producers. Standard avoided speculation and most of the direct purchases were done on the bases of the average of the 'high' and 'low' prices on the exchange for the day. This was a neutral, price-taking approach familiar to many refining companies today. Most of the volume on the exchanges was speculative and daily volumes traded were large for even today's standards, at some 300–400 times the total regional production.[45] However big, the Standard Oil monopoly could not significantly influence prices set on such liquid exchanges. It might have achieved a monopoly in refining and transportation, but in terms of oil purchases, it was still a price taker. This was to change very soon.

Just like during the 'Great Depression', the trigger for further consolidation was another crisis, only this time the financial crisis or 'the Panic of 1873'. Desperate railroads continued to cut sweet deals for the Rockefeller and Flagler. In the atmosphere of fierce competition and mistrust among themselves, railroads appointed the Standard Oil Company as an 'evener', collecting rebates in the process and continuing to undermine the remaining independent refiners. In 1874, this 'pool' included pipelines as well, further tightening the control of the Standard monopoly. None of the transportation prices were fixed as normal common carriers would do—they were all arranged in a complex web of 'pools' and rebates with Standard Oil, like a spider, in their heart.[46]

Most of the mergers, acquisitions, and 'pools' were done in secret, undermining the trust among the remaining independent companies. To tie up these remaining independents, Rockefeller and Flagler resurrected the National Refiners' Association – this time called the Central Refiners' Association. It was a 'pool' of refining interests open to all, linked through an ingenious system of asset leases[47] and under the absolute control of an Executive Committee of the association, headed by Rockefeller.

By 1877, the Standard Oil Company controlled all the plants in Cleveland and key refineries in Pittsburgh, New York and the Oil Regions as well as the best refiners, officers, and agents throughout the country. By mid-1880s, it also controlled the key pipelines which gradually replaced railroads as the primary carriers of oil and refined products. This highly integrated operation across most of the States of America was way ahead of the legal corporate framework of the times. The only options available to such large and complex business were partnerships, holding companies or trusts. Rockefeller and his associates chose the last one, probably not as best, but least bad option.[48]

In January 1882, Standard Oil was incorporated in Ohio as a trust, with nine trustees controlling all the properties owned and controlled by Standard Oil, thus legitimising the initial 'combination'. Trusts were a novelty in the industrial organisation of the country and soon, many other companies with market power extending across the continent followed the suit.

While trusts might have been a welcome innovation for growing corporate giants, among the general public, they remained synonymous with monopoly and abuse of power. This backlash will haunt Rockefeller and his associates for the rest of their lives.

The Death of Oil Exchanges

In the early days, Rockefeller never saw a need to get involved in the production of oil. For him, it was a highly speculative, chaotic, and unruly enterprise, best left to adventurers and gamblers. After all, producers were many and their attempts to 'pool' had been sporadic, with very limited success. As the Oil Region production diminished, Standard Oil did get involved in production in places like Ohio and later overseas, but these were always calculated, strategic decisions. For example, when heavy but prolific Lima oil, rich with sulphur came on stream in Ohio in 1885, it was important to secure supply for Standard plants. Given the loss of other regular sources, its cheap yet difficult to process oil was a challenge as well as an opportunity for the Standard Oil engineers to reap large profits.[49]

Once the consolidation of the refining, transportation and marketing was taken care of, the company was finally ready to do something about the price of purchased oil as well. Rockefeller was never happy with leaving the price of his raw material to the vagaries of the market, especially speculation, which was rampant at the time. Standard Oil now had a refining monopoly in the industry and a virtual monopsony[50] in buying oil. But the company could not influence the oil prices on the exchanges. There are several reasons why a dominant company may want to kill a well-functioning futures markets[51]: It can reduce volatility, make it harder for the producers to organise and increase prices and it can stamp its existing virtual monopsony power.

After 1895, the independent or 'fringe' refiners represented only about 15% of the products market. They benefited from the exchanges providing the information and liquidity.[52] When the oil exchanges died, companies such as Sun Oil, Pure Oil Company and others were forced to vertically integrate. That left the independent oil producers, the 'happy victims of monopoly' with Standard Oil Trust as the only buyer.

This was an important victory for Rockefeller, as there was evidence that producer cartels such as Petroleum Producers' Union did have a direct effect on oil prices. A study[53] shows that, during the periods when the producers were organised, prices were, on average, 14% higher. The same study shows Standard's monopoly over transportation had an even greater effect on oil prices, making them 26% lower. Further, killing the exchanges and competitive oil markets, might have reduced the average oil prices by up to 40%.[54] So, Standard Oil had every reason to get rid of the oil exchanges and become a price maker.

In January 1895, J. Seep, the main Standard Oil buyer of oil, posted a notice to the oil producers informing them of the end of the oil purchases based on the exchange prices.[55] From that day, the sole agents of the Standard Oil Trust would only buy oil at prices which they 'posted' themselves. They were the sole price maker. The oil was paid in cash[56] and the agents would stop trading pipeline certificates, the lifeblood of the oil exchanges. Slowly, the exchanges and with them, free, independent oil markets waned and died.

Notes

1. See Nevins (1859, p. 19).
2. Ibid., p. 21.
3. Ibid., p. 21.
4. Rockefeller (1933, pp. 81–82).
5. Ibid., p. 22.
6. Ibid., p. 25.
7. Lloyd (1881, p. 5).
8. 'It required many hundreds of thousands of dollars — and in cash —securities would not answer. I received the message at about noon and had to get off on the three-o'clock train. I drove from bank to bank, asking each president or cashier, whomever I could find first, to get ready for me all the funds he could possibly lay hands on. I told them I would be back to get the money later. I rounded up all of our banks in the city, and made a second journey to get the money, and kept going until I secured the necessary amount'. Rockefeller J. D. (1933, p. 49).
9. It seems that Flagler was able to attract a fair bit of investment capital, including his wife's wealthy uncle, Stephen V. Harkness. Nevins (1859, p. 25).
10. Flagler married into a wealthy Harkness family and made a small fortune himself from this association. Stephen Harkness was a silent partner in the company. Andrews was an expert in refining and the original partner of Rockefeller in the venture. Akin E.N. (1988, preface).
11. Ibid, p. 26.
12. 'I remember a case where we paid only $1,000 or so an acre for some rough land to be used for such purposes, and, through the improvements we created, the value has gone up 40 or 50 times as much in 35 or 40 years.' Rockefeller (1933, p. 91).

13. See the Preliminary Report (1900): '... the Standard Oil Company, for these men even at that early date seemed to have an advantage in freight rates that enabled them to market oil at a profit when no one else could', p. 384.

14. Producers without transportation would face higher costs, refiners without petrol stations would be forced to sell cheaper and so on; soon they would be driven out of business.

15. "The navigable waters leading into the Mississippi and St. Lawrence, and the carrying places between the same, shall be common highways and forever free, as well to the inhabitants of the said territory as to the citizens of the United States, and those of any other States that may be admitted into the confederacy, without any tax, impost, or duty therefor." Northwest Ordinance, Congress of the Confederation of the United States, Art. 4. 1787.

16. Proceedings of the Special Committee on Railroads (1879, p. 111).

17. A combination was simply joining or merging of different companies through horizontal integration with the aim of reducing competition and increasing the monopoly power. 'The earliest combinations of railroads in the United States were those made by several lines jointly engaged in the carriage of through traffic. This form of combination was merely a consolidation of different links into one connecting line, in order to secure the benefits of unified management.' Langstroth C. and Stilz W. (1899, p. 29).

18. The fourth great trunk line was Baltimore & Ohio, but less important for the oil transportation.

19. Williamson and Daum (1959, p. 195).

20. Rockefeller himself admitted that: ' *Our Federal form of government making every corporation created by a state foreign to every other state, renders it necessary for persons doing business through corporate agency to organize corporations in some or many of the different states in which their business is located. Instead of doing business through the agency of one corporation they must do business through the agencies of several corporations... These different corporations thus become cooperating agencies in the same business and are held together by common ownership of their stocks. It is too late to argue about advantages of industrial combinations. They are a necessity.*' Rockefeller (1933, p. 67).

21. Tom Scott, the Vice president of the Pennsylvania Railroad virtually controlled the Pennsylvania legislature. Williamson and Daum (1959, p. 347).

22. Ibid, p. 99.

23. Akin E.N. (1988, p. xii, Preface).

24. In the probably the best single biography of Rockefeller (which was rather kind to him), Nevins (1859, p. 31), admits the key role of the railways in development of the monopoly.

25. Nevins (1859, p. 31).

26. Ibid., p. 32. Also, demand in Europe fell sharply due to the 1870–1871 Franco-Prussian War.

27. Ibid., p. 89.

28. Other large shareholders were John's brother William Rockefeller, Andrews and Harkness. Ibid., p. 33.
29. '*By an act of the Pennsylvania legislature on May 1, 1871, the South Improvement Company had been created and vested with all the powers conferred by the act of April 7, 1870, upon the Pennsylvania Company. The powers of the company included authority " to construct and operate any work or works, public or private, designed to include, increase, facilitate, or develop trade, travel, or the transportation of freight, livestock, passengers, or any traffic by land or water, from or to any part of the United States.*' The Report of the Industrial Commission, 1900, p. 607.
30. An 'evener' is a guarantor of the agreement. The competing railroads did not trust each other and needed a third party, in this case the SIC, to guarantee the agreed partition of freight traffic.
31. Nevins (1859, p. 39).
32. Williamson and Daum (1959, p. 349). The numbers were taken from the reference. There is some disagreement as to the actual 'new' rates and rebates as they were never really exercised. Nevins (1859, p. 43) is using somewhat different numbers. In any case, they prove the point.
33. Nevins (1859, p. 43). Interestingly, Nevins was commissioned by the Rockefeller family to write the biography, making him, if anything, likely to be somewhat biased in favor of the billionaire.
34. While Rockefeller later insisted that the SIC was his 'second best plan', as the biggest refiner in the country and possibly the world, he 'threw himself into the enterprise with tremendous zeal'. Ibid., p. 45.
35. Lloyd (1881). It was so popular that it was translated into many languages.
36. In his own writing, Rockefeller tried to justify these unequal shipping arrangements: "*The Standard Oil Company of Ohio, being situated at Cleveland, had the advantage of different carrying lines, as well as of water transportation in the summer; taking advantage of those facilities, it made the best bargains possible for its freights. Other companies sought to do the same. The Standard gave advantages to the railroads for the purpose of reducing the cost of transportation of freight. It offered freights in large quantity, car-loads and train-loads. It furnished loading facilities and discharging facilities at great cost. It provided regular traffic, so that a railroad could conduct its transportation to the best advantage and use its' equipment to the full extent of its hauling capacity without waiting for the refiner's convenience. It exempted railroads from liability for fire and carried its own insurance. It provided at its own expense terminal facilities which permitted economies in handling. For these services it obtained contracts for special allowances on freights*". Rockefeller (1933, p. 109).
37. The right to acquire necessary land and property in return for a fair compensation.
38. It was disbanded on 23 June 1873. Derrick's (1884, p. 28).
39. This point comes from Tarbell (1904) but seems controversial. Tarbell argued that any refiners not accepting the SIC combination would simply give up and sell their assets. See Williamson and Daum (1959, Vol. 1, p. 353).

40. Nevins (1859, p. 58).
41. Tarbell (1904, p. 33).
42. Using Derrick's Handbook data, average daily production in 1872 was 16,389 barrels.
43. '*The new Standard Oil Company with its 10,000 barrels a day capacity was ready to refine more oil than all the (Oil) Regions plants (with an estimated 9,231 barrels capacity), or all those in the New York area (9,790 barrels capacity), or those in Pittsburgh, Philadelphia, and Baltimore combined (9,249 barrels)*'. Nevins (1859, p. 59).
44. Most of this discussion is based on Hidy R & Hidy M. (1957, pp. 87–89).
45. Ibid., p. 88.
46. 'By now, the Standard was so powerful that when it called the tune, refiners and railroads both had to dance.' Nevins (1859, p. 83).
47. Ibid., p. 88.
48. Ibid., p. 152.
49. At first, Lima oil was virtually impossible to refine. It was primarily used as fuel for burning and traded for as little as 15 cents a barrel. Finding a process to remove sulphur and refine this crude was a great and very profitable success for Standard Oil. Standard got involved in the production of this crude and by 1891 accounted for about a half of its production. See Williamson and Daum (1959, Vol. 1, pp. 601–607).
50. Market with only one buyer.
51. Most literature on the subject hinges on the ground-breaking work of Newbery (1982).
52. Indeed, one of the leading pioneers in the oil region, Captain Vandergrift helped establish the oil exchange in Pittsburg.
53. Brown and Partridge (1998, p. 573).
54. Ibid., p. 582.
55. See the end of the previous chapter and endnote #50.
56. '*Since the elimination of exchanges producers generally sell their oil in the shape of credit-balances. For their convenience, the Standard Oil-Company has established purchasing-agencies throughout the region. The quantity of crude to the credit of the seller on the pipe-line books is ascertained from the National-Transit office, a check is given and all the trouble the producer has is to draw his money from the bank. It is handier than a pocket in a shirt, easier than rolling off a log in a mill-pond, and the happy "victim of monopoly" goes on his way rejoicing after the manner of Philip's converted eunuch*' McLaurin (1896, p. 336).

References

Akin E.N. (1988): *Flagler: Rockefeller Partner and Florida Baron*, University Press of Florida.

Brown JH and Partridge M (1998): 'The Death of a Market: Standard Oil and the Demise of 19th Century Crude Oil Exchanges', *Review of Industrial Organization*, Springer, Vol. 13, No. 5 (October), pp. 569–587.

Derrick's (1884): *Hand-Book of Petroleum*, Derrick Publishing Company.

Hidy R. and Hidy M. (1957): *Pioneering in Business: History of the Standard Oil Company* (of New Jersey), Harper and Brothers, New York.

Langstroth C. and Stilz W. (1899): *Railway Co-operation*, University of Pennsylvania series in Political Economy and Public Law, No. 15.

Lloyd H.D. (1881): *The Story of a Great Monopoly*, The Atlantic, March.

McLaurin J.J. (1896): *Sketches in Crude Oil*, Harrisburg, PA.

Nevins A. (1859): *John D. Rockefeller: Study in Power*, one volume abridgement by William Greenleaf, Charles Scribner's Sons, New York.

Proceedings of the Special Committee on Railroads (1879): Appointed under a Resolution of the Assembly to Investigate *Alleged Abuses in the Management of Railroads Chartered by the State of New York*, The State of New York.

Rockefeller J.D. (1933): *Reminiscences of Men and Events*, Doubleday, Doran & Company, Inc., Garden City NY.

Tarbell I.M. (1904): *The History of Standard Oil Company*, Brief Version, Chalmers D.M. (Ed), Dover Publications. Reprint 2015.

Williamson H.F. and Daum A.R. (1959): *The American Petroleum Industry, 1859–1899 The Age of Illumination* (Vol. 1), Northwestern University Press.

5

From Monopoly to Competition (Oil Markets Going Global)

Quiet Before the Storm

Standard Oil achieved most of its goals by 1880s when it became synonymous with the American oil industry. In the process, it exerted its control and stability over prices that Rockefeller always craved for. As Fig. 5.1 shows, oil prices fell and hovered around $1 per barrel and their volatility was substantially reduced throughout the period of the Standard Oil dominance. Setting their own price certainly helped.

As the trust consolidated its position in the American refining industry, it was increasingly aware of the importance of the overseas outlets for its products. Between 1865 and 1866, total petroleum exports doubled (Fig. 5.2) and continued the exponential trend into the early 1880s. For this reason, as early as 1866, John Rockefeller's younger brother William moved to New York to take charge of this growing market. The more the American oil production grew, the more the foreign 'sink' for their product became important. From 1895, Standard Oil might have been setting the price at which they bought domestic crude oil, but some of their plants, such as Bayonne refinery, exported almost all of their product overseas.[1]

It was these marginal product barrels, mainly kerosene, sold in relatively competitive markets of Europe and elsewhere that were driving profits and increasingly influencing the oil price in America. Standard Oil might have been a price maker at home, but it had to accept the going market price for kerosene overseas. The main competitor was Russia, which was soon to become the largest oil producer in the world.

© The Author(s), under exclusive license to Springer Nature Switzerland AG 2021

A. Imsirovic, *Trading and Price Discovery for Crude Oils*, https://doi.org/10.1007/978-3-030-71718-6_5

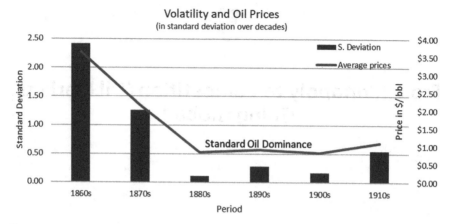

Fig. 5.1 Standard Oil monopoly and Oil Price & Volatility (1860–1920) (Calculated from data the BP Statistical Review of World Energy data)

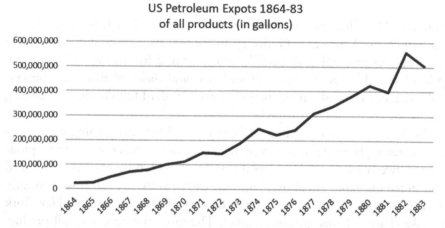

Fig. 5.2 Total US Petroleum Exports 1964–1983 (*Source* Derrick's Handbook)

'Beyond the Sea a Chicken May Be Bought for a Farthing, But It Costs a Pound to Bring It Home[2]'

For Russia, kerosene was an ideal source of illumination. The country was rural and poor. Just like in the early days of the American oil industry, oil was relatively easy to find, but difficult to transport to the refinery and even harder to deliver the product to the consumer. The Russian vast expanse and harsh climate made this problem even harder. The oil-rich region of Baku[3] was cut off from the Black Sea by a mountainous region and the river Volga, the main bloodline into the country would freeze in the winter. This made the product easy to move in the summer when it was not needed. In the dark and cold winter months, when it was most needed, it could not be transported. In the early days of kerosene use, it was cheaper to import American illuminants into Russia, than to transport their own, abundant and cheap one: '... *Tiflis, up to within a few weeks of the opening of the Baku railway, drew her supply of lamp-oil from America, a distance of more than 8,000 miles, in spite of countless millions of gallons of petroleum running to waste 341 miles from her doors. For years America literally controlled the entire petroleum market of Russia*'.[4]

Despite prolific finds around the Caspian region,[5] Russian oil industry really started to take off only after 1873, when the Tzar 'liberalised' the industry by abolishing the policy of granting[6] monopoly on oil production. This was helped by the lifting of the excise duty on oil and kerosene in 1877, on the advice of the great chemist and the father of the periodic system of elements, Dimitri Mendeleev, who also dabbled as an oil consultant.[7] This resulted in an oil rush and booming production, which, from 20,000–25,000 tons in the 1870–1872 period suddenly jumped to 64,000 tons in 1873 and continued exponentially to over 200,000 in 1876–1877.[8]

The real force behind the transformation of the industry came from the industrious Nobel brothers. Following their father Emmanuel, who invented the torpedo, Alfred invented dynamite and Ludwig and Robert reshaped the Russian oil industry. Ludwig, the youngest brother was a particularly able engineer, working for a while as a blacksmith. Nobels' involvement in the oil business seemed to have happened by chance, when Robert went to Baku, looking for walnut wood, used for rifle stock manufacturing in their ammunition factory. Helped by his brother's capital, Robert decided to build a small refinery and compete with 120 other small plants there.[9]

One of their first investments was a crude oil pipeline from the wells to their refinery in Baku. The Nobels then brought drillers from the United States to produce oil in 'Pennsylvania fashion' The result was an efficient operation, bringing cheap and plentiful oil supply by pipeline to a well-organised refining plant. Their constant striving for improvement and efficiency soon resulted in the first development of continuous distillation in 1880, well before it was adopted in America.[10] Just like Rockefeller, the Nobel brothers realised that the key missing link to the operation was an efficient, integrated transportation system from the well, via refinery, to the end-user.

Ingenious Ludwig designed a cistern-steamer himself, using a complex system of watertight compartments and soon had them built in his native Sweden.[11] Carrying about 750 tons of kerosene, they were quick to load and unload into smaller, shallow draught barges, sailing from Astrakhan on the

Caspian up the river Volga into the Russian interior. Further investments were made in bulk rail transportation using hundreds of own built tank cars, loading and storage facilities, wharves, and other infrastructure, all incorporated in 1879 in the Nobel Brothers' Petroleum Production Company, with headquarters in St. Petersburg. Not unlike Rockefeller's New York headquarters, Nobels' central office run a sleek logistical operation which, with the help of the telegraph, enabled them to know, at any point in time, the position and volume of goods in any part of the country and abroad.[12]

This state-of-the-art organisation ensured that the brothers held a monopoly on kerosene distribution in the country. From this point, it was just a matter of time before the Nobels not only squeezed Standard Oil out of Russia (see Fig. 5.3), but also expanded their sales into the continent and eventually Britain.

The new, expanding oil industry was not missed by a wealthy banker, Baron Alphonse de Rothschild, who invested very early in several oil-related companies, including the Baku to Batumi railway, a key link to the Black Sea and the Mediterranean. Acting as a trader as well as an investor, he signed contracts with small refiners in Russia, built a canning and casing plant in Batumi which cut the original distance to Europe via the Volga river by some 1,500 miles, and shipped the product efficiently as far as Asia. Avoiding stepping on Nobels 'toes' inside the Russian trade, the Rothschilds established their own export monopoly via the Southern route. They formed The Caspian and Black Sea Company (known as 'Bnito')[13] in 1884 and quickly became the biggest kerosene exporter from Russia.[14]

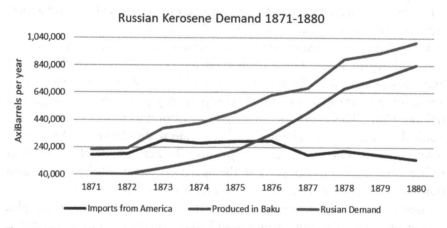

Fig. 5.3 Russian kerosene demand 1871–1880 (Calculated from data in Marvin [1891, p. 302])

Growing Competition and the Oil Market Goes International

In 1898, thanks to large inflows of foreign capital, Russia became the world's largest oil producer (see Fig. 5.4). Plentiful oil flowing from 'fountain' wells or 'gushers',[15] cheap labour and proximity to the now well connected, domestic market made Russian kerosene a formidable competitor to the American product. In 1883, the railway link between Batumi and a Black Sea port of Tbilisi was completed, opening the doors to the world via the Mediterranean. The immediate impact of Russian competition was in 1885, when its kerosene quickly undercut American imports in the Eastern Mediterranean to such an extent that Standard Oil allowed its own marketing agents to supply their customers with the Russian product.[16] That very same year, there was some dissatisfaction with the quality of the American product in the UK, which the Nobel brothers skillfully exploited to enter the UK market.[17] Both Nobels and Rothschilds strengthened their positions by forming companies and exclusive distributers in the country. As a result, the share of Russian kerosene in the UK market increased from 2% in 1884, to 39% only four years later.[18]

The Standard management realised that selling the product on 'Free on Board'[19] (FOB) basis put the company at a disadvantage in any negotiations with the two prominent families. In the very same year, it set up a wholly owned distribution subsidiary in Britain, Anglo-American Petroleum Company. On the continent, for language and legal reasons, Standard

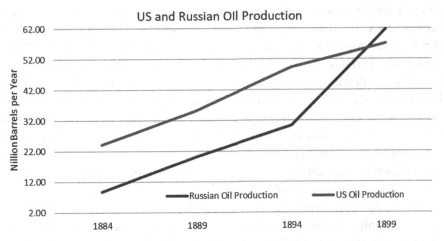

Fig. 5.4 Oil production of America and Russia (1884–1899) in Millions of barrels per year (Calculated from data in Williams and Daum [1959, p. 633])

focused on absorption and affiliation of local companies such as DAPG,[20] formed in Germany in 1890.

The competition was in full swing in the early 1890s and attempts to reach a lasting agreement among the competitors repeatedly failed. It was not for the lack of trying, but neither player had sufficient market power to negotiate an amicable market sharing agreement: Russian exporters were still somewhat fragmented and even Standard Oil faced some competition from the US independents.[21] In 1993, Standard did reach an agreement with the Rothschilds in the UK and in 1996 with the Nobels in Germany by leasing their distribution systems but selling the Russian product. However, this agreement lasted only four years, when the Rothschilds decided to re-enter the British market with a newly formed Anglo Caucasian Oil Company.[22]

'Marcus's Coup'

1890s Asia, not unlike a century later, was a large, undeveloped energy market with huge growth potential. A large and growing population, primarily rural had no access to gas or electricity, making kerosene the obvious source of illumination. But there, as well in Europe, Russian product had a competitive advantage: The 'Orient' was about 30 days sailing with the vessels of the day from Batumi, compared to over four and a half months from the eastern coast of the United States.[23]

This is where another family of traders stepped in: 'Marcus Samuel & Co', established in 1834, specialised in trading with the Orient. The family shipped textiles, tools, machinery, and cans of kerosene to the East and brought back rice, flour, sugar, and other commodities.[24] Over the years, they developed a wide network of agents and contacts throughout the region. With demand for kerosene picking up, Marcus Samuel started thinking of shipping it in bulk. Following a visit to Baku in 1890, where he saw Nobels shipping kerosene in bulk instead of tin cans, he came up with an audacious plan to do the same, but on ocean-going vessels. For the plan to work, he would have to solve a number of major problems and solve them simultaneously: get a stable supply of kerosene, have a fleet of large and safe, ocean-going ships allowed to use the Suez Canal, ensure continuous supplies and a large network of storage and distribution facilities throughout Asia.[25]

The Rothschilds were receptive to these bold ideas and offered Marcus a 10-year supply contract. The plan was kept secret in fear of Standard Oil reaction, but it became obvious following the launching of a 5,000-ton steel steamer 'Murex' in 1892. The vessel was a novel design, with many safety features which gave it a 'first-class risk' rating by Lloyds of London and ensured permission of the Suez authorities to use the channel. In August of the same year, it crossed the Suez, fully laden with Russian kerosene.

The product was packaged on arrival, in branded, bright red, 'Shell oil' tins where it was locally distributed. Throughout Asia, tin cans were used for roofing huts, lamps, cooking utensils and so on and was even more valuable than kerosene. Local packaging also meant that the tins were not rusty on arrival (as Standard oil blue cans were, having endured months of shipping) and soon, bright red roofs of towns and villages in the region were the best promotion the company could hope for their product. An ingenious tank-cleaning system of the vessels, ensured safe, bulk 'back haul' transportation[26] of products such as rice, flour, and sugar, fully utilising the vessel and ensuring great trading profits.[27] Astonishingly, the whole deal was tied up with relatively limited funds: Marcus managed to obtain kerosene from the Rothschilds on deferred payment terms as just as he did ships, while the local agents invested their own funds in storage and distribution.[28] As soon as the operation commenced, it started paying for itself. Samuel and his company not only staged a 'coup', but a true revolution in oil transportation and trading. He clearly showed how trading can add value to the world.

In 1893 in order to reduce his own risk in the whole operation, Samuel formalised it as a 'Tank Syndicate', including his brothers, seven Far Eastern agents and a prominent London shipbroker, Fred Lane. The syndicate was essentially a predecessor of the Shell Trading and Transportation company, which then was formally incorporated in 1897.[29]

It took the involvement of two other traders, before the Royal Dutch Shell was formed in a shape that we can recognise today.

Two More Traders in the Orient

Samuel realised that his 'Tank Syndicate' was vulnerable in the Asian market: on one hand, it depended on Rothschilds' oil supply and on the other, it was facing competition not only from Standard Oil but also from new market entrants with own production in the 'East Indies'. The syndicate did find its own source of oil in Balikpapan, Borneo, but it was a heavy type of crude, far from ideal for kerosene manufacture.[30]

One of the companies producing oil in the region was the Royal Dutch, which started production in Sumatra as early as 1880s and launched a well-capitalised operation there, including a refinery, railroad, pipeline, and a harbour in 1890.[31] In charge of the operation was J.B.A. Kessler, previously employed as a trader and partner in a Dutch trading firm with over a decade of experience in the Asia. Kessler was responsible for getting the whole operation going, as well as marketing the product through several contracted agents under a brand name 'Crown Oil'. Early on, Kessler recognised that the Royal Dutch had a cheap source of oil and labor but a weakness in marketing where it was competing with the well-established rivals such, Shell Trading and Standard Oil. He persuaded one of his colleagues, another trader and a subagent of the Netherlands Trading Company, Henri Detering, to join the operation in 1896. Detering was to play a pivotal role in the company, flowing Kessler's tragic and premature death four years later.

The young, growing oil industry in Asia was fluid, involving a number of players,[32] all of which had weaknesses: Standard Oil was a well-funded and established operation but, in spite of several attempts, had no oil production and refining in the region.[33] Shell Trading had a sleek and efficient trading and marketing operation based on cheap Russian oil, but the geopolitics of the country[34] were always a threat to their security of supply. Royal Dutch had cheap and efficient production and manufacturing, but poor distribution and marketing. Some sort of merger and concentration of market power seemed inevitable and a series of contacts and negotiations between all the involved parties went on for almost a decade.[35] Like all business interactions, they depended on personal relationships and trust as much as on economic and business logic. The correspondence among the Standard Oil management clearly pointed to Royal Dutch being the main prize of any amalgamation in Asia: '*Given the company's progressive management, ample financial means, and influence with the Dutch government… neither Russian nor American competitors with their kerosene carried from a distance could meet the new force of Royal Dutch in the oil industry of the East.*'[36]

In the end, this proved correct. Stubborn Standard Oil failed to woo Royal Dutch on its own terms and Shell Trading eventually achieved the amalgamation with the company in 1906. However, it had to accept a humiliating 60:40 division of the newly formed company, in favour of the Dutch entity, with Detering in charge.[37]

Roughly around the same time, another investor and speculator made his mark in the history of oil. William Knox D'Arcy who got incredibly rich in the gold rush in Australia in the late 1880s, invested most of his proceeds in a concession from the shah of Persia to drill for oil in the country.[38] With a smart appointment of G. B. Reynolds, an engineer with experience in drilling in Sumatra and good contacts in the British government,[39] oil was eventually found in 1908. A year later, the Anglo-Persian Oil Company was formed.

The shares were heavily oversubscribed in the new venture that which would eventually become British Petroleum (BP).

The turn of the century saw intensified market competition: New sources of oil were found in the United States, attracting fresh entrants and demand for petroleum products significantly shifted in favour of mobility and manufacture, rather than illumination. The very beginning of the twentieth century in America saw substantial new discoveries of oil in the Gulf of Mexico, Mid-Continent, Illinois and California. The output in the first two decades increased at an astonishing rate of about 45% per annum.[40]

Growing demand kept the oil prices steady, while the introduction of a rotary drill and increased use of the science of geology[41] significantly increased productivity: In the Gulf area, wells of over 1,000 feet were being drilled in days with a record depth of 1,065 feet drilled in just 32 hours.[42] It resulted in gushers such as the legendary Spindletop well which, in four years, produced over 30 million barrels of oil and started the Texas oil boom of 1901.[43]

The companies that traced their roots to this find included Gulf Oil and Texas Company[44] (originally Texas Fuel Company, later better known as Texaco). Californian production consisted mainly of heavy grades of oil, but the lack of local coal supplies created a business around fuel oil or even direct oil burning for steam. Larger companies emerging were Union Oil of California (Unocal), Associated Oil Company (an offshoot of the South Pacific Railway) and Standard Oil of California. A late entrant into this regional market was also Shell Oil.[45] The power of the independent producers and refiners also grew from the early 1890s and the Producers' Protective Association, formed in 1891 (later Producers' Oil Company) and Producers' and Refiners' Company, formed in 1893, grew into a new challenger, the Pure Oil Company, incorporated at the end of 1895.[46] With integrated operations, all of these companies proved fierce competitors to the Standard offspring, not only in America but also abroad.

Tectonic Shifts

The first decade of the century saw a major shift in the use of petroleum, caused by the widespread application of internal combustion engines both for power and mobility and adoption of electricity for lighting.

High energy density and low flash point of gasoline, making it easy to carry the fuel and start the engine, making it perfect as a transportation fuel.[47] The first cars were actually electric, but their range limitation was then as in the early twenty-first century, a familiar problem.[48] Mass production of automobiles by Henry Ford in 1908 opened the floodgates for exponential growth in gasoline demand. In the United States, car registrations went from 8,000 vehicles in 1900 to 305,950 in 1909 and over 6.5 million in 1919.[49] The introduction of cord tires, electric self-starters, and expansion of surfaced roads greatly facilitated this trend. Not only did gasoline and fuel oil[50] demand pick up significantly, but so did the need for lubricants for all of these machines.

Henry Ford started his career with the Edison Illuminating Company where he was a chief engineer in 1893.[51] While the history of electric lighting went back to the early nineteenth century, it was Edison who successfully commercialised it as a full package, with integrated and reliable power supply, transmission and metering.[52] When the alternative current (AC) electric system enabled transmission of power over long distances and the invention of converters made use of the existing direct current (DC) infrastructure, the use of electricity seriously took off.

The result was a fall in the use of kerosine and exponential growth in the use of gasoline, fuel oil and lubricants. At the turn of the century, kerosine made up over half of the value of all the petroleum products refined in the United States. By 1919, gasoline was over 55%, fuel oil about 25% and kerosene and lubricants under 11% of the value each.[53]

Tectonic changes in petroleum demand and growing competition at home and abroad were unfolding at the same time as political pressures in the United States to curb the oil monopoly of Standard Oil.[54] As it often happens in litigation and politics, years of legal and political battles came to a head with the 1911 Supreme Court decision to dissolve the trust.[55] Of course, the decision was a couple of decades too late: the heyday of Standard Oil was in the 1880s, when it controlled over 90% of the oil production and almost 95% of all the refining in the country. When the trust was dissolved, it owned just over 60% of each activity.[56]

Dissolution redistributed shares of over thirty constituent companies from the trust back to the shareholders. For a while, it changed little in the overall behaviour of the separated entities which naturally continued to avoid direct competition. The biggest of these would become major oil companies in their own right: Standard Oil of New Jersey (or Esso), would eventually become Exxon, and Standard Oil of New York (Socony) would eventually become Mobil. Almost 90 years later, under different competitive market forces, the two would merge again (into ExxonMobil) in 1999. Standard Oil of California would go it alone as Chevron.[57] The others later became household names such as Marathon (The Ohio Oil Company), Amoco (Standard

Oil of Indiana), ARCO (merged Atlantic and Richfield companies), Conoco (Continental Oil Company) and others, which would eventually disappear forever in an endless vortex of mergers and spin offs.

The changes would culminate in the First World War. The intensity of the fighting in the war could never have been possible without mechanisation and oil that powered it. The strategic importance of oil in the mobility of the armies would make the commodity one of the ultimate goals (or 'The Prize'[58]) in the World War Two.

The importance of oil as a strategic commodity was clear to the governments and their intervention in the industry would not only continue, but also intensify with the subsequent events such as: The British government purchase of 51% of British Petroleum (Anglo-Persian Oil company) in 1913, The 'Texas Railroad Commission' intervention in the market in the 1930s; The birth of OPEC and nationalisations in 1960; The wars in the Middle East; Imposition and the eventual lifting of the US oil export ban in 1973 and 2015 respectively and many others.

After the war, government involvement and the post-imperial nature of the international relations resulted in oil markets being largely controlled by the national champions of the US, Britain and France, an oligopoly of the oil 'majors'.[59] Aside from being vertically integrated, these companies were also integrated 'horizontally' to ensure maximum control of the market and profits. Oil was carefully supplied from various geographic areas at the lowest possible cost and to ensure that supply and demand were balanced, and prices were kept stable. Such integration enabled the supply of oil to be fine-tuned to the prevailing demand for end products, thus ensuring political as well as market stability.

Notes

1. In 1899, 74% went into exports. Hidy and Hidy (1957, p. 234).
2. Russian proverb, taken from Marvin (1891, p. 276). Most of the early Nobel brothers' history in oil is drawn from this source.
3. The region, rich in oil was even mentioned by Marco Polo: '*To the north lies Zorzania, near the confines of which there is a fountain of oil which discharges so great a quantity as to furnish loading for many camels. The use made of it is not for the purpose of food, but as an unguent for the cure of cutaneous distempers in men and cattle, as well as other complaints; and it is also good for burning. In the neighboring country no other is used in their lamps, and people come from distant parts to procure it.*' http://public-library.uk/ebooks/60/81.pdf, p. 35.
4. Marvin (1891), p. 276.

5. 'On the eastern shores of the Caspian Sea, twenty thousand such wells, all of them quite shallow, existed in 1868.' Henry J. T. (1873, p. 170).
6. The monopoly was, of course sold.
7. '*He frequently consulted the government and private business, and one of the topics was oil industry… Mendeleev, as the consultant of a government commission, made in 1876 a trans-ocean trip to Pennsylvanian oil refineries. After he got acquainted with modern state of art and taxation system (summarised in Mendeleev D. Oil Industry in the Northern-American State Pennsylvania and in Caucasus, 1877.) he advised the government to cancel the excise-duty for the kerosene and oil. His advice was accepted in 1877, and the industry revived next decade. With this new experience (combined with his early experience at Caucasus oil plants in 1863, he helped his disciple Ragozin to build in 1879 a perfect oil refinery close to Yaroslavl. One scientific output of this period has been his hypothesis of 1877 about the mineral origin of oil…*' Babaev (2009, p. 11).
8. Marvin (1891, pp. 237–238).
9. Ibid., p. 280.
10. Williamson and Daum (1959, p. 263).
11. The first in a series of these steamers was 'Zoroaster', the forerunner of all the modern oil tankers.
12. 'The central place chosen for this operation was Orel, which is conveniently situated in Middle Russia fordistribution in the most populous districts. Here the reservoirs were made to hold 18,000,000 gallons ofburning oil at the time, and with the oil station, the sidings, and the repairing shops for the tank cars, coverseveral hundred acres of ground. Four other large depots were erected at Moscow, St. Petersburg, Warsaw, and Saratoff. Scattered between these, and between the Baltic and Black Sea on the one side and Germany and the Volga on the other, were twenty-four smaller depots. In this manner, in the summer the sixty oil trains run from the Volga to the twenty-six depots in every part of European Russia, including Poland and Finland, filling up the reservoirs; and in winter they change their base of operations from Tsaritzin to those depots, and convey the oil to the various intermediate railway stations where a demand exists for kerosene. No barrelling is carried on by the firm. They sell the oil by the train-load to the petroleum dealers in provincial Russia, who bring their own barrels to the railway station, and carry it away in this form to their stores.' Marvin (1891, p. 289).
13. Russian initials for: "Batumskoye Neftepromyshlennoye i Torgovoye Obschestvo" (literally translated: 'the Batumi oil and trading company').
14. Hidy and Hidy (1957, p. 134).
15. Ibid., p. 509.
16. Williamson et al. (1963, p. 662).
17. One of the pioneers in the British petroleum industry, Boverton Redwood actively encouraged English importers to turn to the Russian imports. Ibid., p. 647.
18. Ibid., p. 648.

19. In FOB sales, the title to the goods passes at the loading port.
20. Deutsch-Amerikanische Petroleum-Gessellschaft.
21. Producers Oil Company later renamed Pure Oil Company in 1895 also had sizeable operation in Germany.
22. Ibid., pp. 653 and 659.
23. Ibid., p. 259.
24. See Howarth (1997). Chapter 2. Most of the material on the origins of the company is from this source.
25. Ibid., p. 36.
26. Saving half the freight cost by avoiding for the vessel to return empty.
27. Ibid., p. 37.
28. Williamson and Daum (1959, p. 666).
29. Howarth (1997, p. 47).
30. The operation was a family affair, and the drilling was supervised by his cousin, Mark Abrahams. Ibid, p. 45.
31. Williamson and Daum (1959, p. 670).
32. The expansion of the oil trade originally followed the well-established historical trading patterns in the region. For a fascinating research into these patterns and actors involved, see Hussin (2007).
33. Standard was frustrated by the Dutch in being able to obtain production concessions. Establishing a refinery in Japan also ended up in a failure. See Hidy and Hidy (1957, p. 259).
34. There were rumors of a possible nationalization of the industry by the Russian government.
35. Ibid., p. 502.
36. Ibid., p. 265.
37. Howarth (1997, p. 71).
38. See Longhurst (1959, p. 19).
39. The story of the concession is fascinating, and D'Arcy had a fair share of luck. Lord Fisher, a big proponent of the use of oil to power the navy was appointed the First Sea Lord at the Admiralty in 1904. Just as D'Arcy was running out of funds and was negotiating the sale of the concession to the Rothschilds, the Oil Committee of the Admiralty introduced him to Burmah Oil with an intent to form a syndicate which would develop oil in Persia and ensure the security of oil supply to the British navy. Ibid., p. 24.
40. Williamson et al. (1963, p. 19).
41. With the president Theodore Roosevelt, the resources of the nation becoming a matter of public interest with The Geological Survey and the use of science in the government gaining more prominence. See https://pubs.usgs.gov/circ/c1050/first.htm.
42. Williamson et al. (1963, p. 30).
43. See Talman (1919, p. 20).
44. Williamson et al. (1963, p. 203).

45. Shell's entry into California was driven by the mentioned concern about the security of supply. Ibid., p. 28.
46. See Tarbell (1904, pp. 170,177 and 181).
47. Energy density of gasoline is about 33 MJ/l and flash point −40C. Smil (2017, p. 249).
48. Even compared to the modern lithium-ion battery, gasoline is about 100 times denser: https://www.aps.org/publications/apsnews/201208/backpage.cfm#:~:text=Gasoline%20thus%20has%20about%20100,typically%2060%2D80%20percent%20efficient.
49. American Petroleum Institute (1959, p. 82).
50. At the time, the term 'fuel oil' included all the fractions heavier than kerosine. In today's speak, it included heavy diesel, heating oil and residual fuel oil.
51. Rhodes (2018, p. 229). Chapter 15 of the book is a good summary of the history of automobile.
52. Smil (2017, p. 259).
53. Williamson et al. (1963, p. 23).
54. Between 1904–1906 alone, there were at least 20 major state suits against the company. See Hidy and Hidy (1957, p. 683).
55. The charge was violation of the first two sections of the Sherman Anti-Trust Act of 1890. Williamson et al. (1963, p. 10).
56. Ibid., pp. 6–7.
57. In 2020, ExxonMobil and Chevron seriously discussed a merger: https://www.reuters.com/article/us-chevron-m-a-exxon-mobil-idUSKBN2A00T5.
58. Hence the name of the book 'The Prize' by D. Yergin (1991).
59. Marvin (1891, p. 475).

References

American Petroleum Institute (1959): *Petroleum Facts and Figures*, 9th Edition.
Babaev E. (2009): *Dmitriy Mendeleev: A Short CV, and A Story of Life*, http://www.chem.msu.ru/eng/misc/babaev/papers/139e.pdf.
Henry J.T. (1873): *The Early and Later History of Petroleum*, Jas. B. Rodgers Co. Printers, Philadelphia.
Hidy R. and Hidy M. (1957): *Pioneering in Business: History of the Standard Oil Company* (of New Jersey), Harper and Brothers, New York.
Howarth S. (1997): *A Century in Oil, The Shell Transport and Trading Company 1897-1997*, Weindenfeld & Nicholson, London.
Hussin, N. (2007): *Trade and Society in the Straits of Melaka*, NUS Press, Singapore.
Longhurst H. (1959): *Adventure in Oil, Story of British Petroleum*, Sidgwick and Jackson Ltd.
Marvin C. (1891): '*The Region of Eternal Fire*, W.H. Allen & Co. Ltd.

Rhodes R. (2018): *Energy, A Human History*, Simon and Schuster.

Smil V. (2017): *Energy and Civilization, A History*, The MIT Press.

Talman C.F. (1919): *The Story of Oil*, The Mentor (The Scientific American), Department of Science, Serial Number 189, October 15.

Williamson H.F. and Daum A.R. (1959): *The American Petroleum Industry, 1859-1899 The Age of Illumination* (Vol. 1), Northwestern University Press.

Williamson H.F., Andreano R.L., Daum A.R. and Klose G.C. (1963): *The American Petroleum Industry* (Vol. 2), Northwestern University Press.

6

Governments and Oil Markets

Governments Get Involved

As 'the Allies floated to victory on a sea of oil',[1] the strategic importance of the commodity became so obvious it would dominate its history ever since. From the British perspective, the timing of the government intervention was very fortunate: only two weeks after the resolution to buy a controlling share in the Anglo-Persian Oil Company was passed in the British parliament in June 1914, Archduke Franz Ferdinand was assassinated in Sarajevo. Within weeks, The Great War was to start. The company's Abadan refinery in Persia was so important to the British war effort that the employees were forbidden to join the active service in the army, under the pretext that it was a munition factory.[2]

While most of the post-war period was dominated by strategic and political government involvement in the oil markets, the British government's acquisition of the controlling share in the Anglo-Persian was primarily driven by commercial reasons.[3] The company was willing to supply the navy with a large long-term contract (some 40 million barrels of oil over 20 years) at favourable prices,[4] but it was in serious financial difficulties. Anglo-Persian company required advanced payments which, in case of a default, would be a problem for the government. This was an issue not only for the navy but the Exchequer too. Arranging pre-payments to a company with large government ownership made better commercial sense. This was especially true given other suppliers, such as Royal Dutch Shell, would not sign any fixed price deals for longer than two years, expecting oil price rises over time.[5] However, this

© The Author(s), under exclusive license to Springer Nature Switzerland AG 2021
A. Imsirovic, *Trading and Price Discovery for Crude Oils*,
https://doi.org/10.1007/978-3-030-71718-6_6

partial 'nationalisation' would send a strong message across the globe that oil may be too important to leave to business.

As the United States was entering the First World War, its government legislated two new bodies: The Petroleum Advisory Committee (later the National Petroleum War Services Committee), supervised by the Oil Division, a part of the Fuel Administration and the Office of Price Administration (OPA), within the Office for Emergency Management to administer prices.[6] The administration's task was to direct the petroleum industry activity during the war, including production, distribution, and pricing. This increased government involvement in the oil industry was to continue after the war.

Sluggish drilling activity, coupled with growing demand,[7] resulted in sharp increases in oil prices (see Fig. 6.1) during the war. Revolution and nationalisation of the oil industry in Russia did not help the tightening market. Concerns regarding the future of oil supply grew more vocal, sparking one of the earliest 'Peak Oil' debates.[8] Again, centre stage in the debate was taken by the government in the form of Senate and the Federal Trade Commission inquires, all of which were concerned with future availability of oil in the country.[9] This, in turn, was to trigger further government involvement in securing foreign oil supplies and imposing import tariffs in order to protect domestic industry.

Then, as in later 'Peak Oil' narratives, there was no shortage of oil. Incentivised by high prices, the drilling activity increased. In the decade between 1920 and 1929, proved reserves doubled.[10] Eventually, this would result

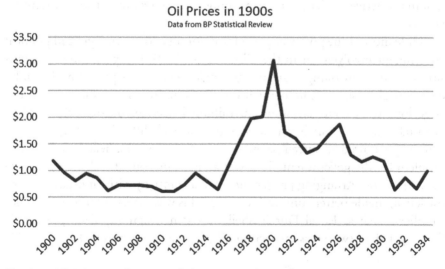

Fig. 6.1 Oil Prices at the turn of the century (Data from BP Statistical Review of World Energy)

in a flood[11] of oil and low prices, changing the pro-interventionist narrative to conservation and 'waste' prevention.[12] This was particularly true in 1930 when the economic calamity and continued production pushed local wellhead prices in Texas to only 13 cents per barrel. Gas stations were reduced to offering inducements such as free chicken to try to lure in customers.[13] In response, the state government called in the National Guard to enforce production rationing, administered by the Texas Railroad Commission (TRC[14]). But, under a banner of reducing waste, the TRC's system actually encouraged it. Like any cartelised quota system, it limited production from large, cheap wells and helped expensive and inefficient ones. Prorationing and production quota enforcement eventually failed, due to cheating. But not before it caught the eye of Venezuela—and, in effect, the TRC's quotas became the blueprint for the current OPEC production mandate system.[15]

Moguls and Mandarins[16]

In the meantime, the American companies were hard-pressed to look for oil abroad. Some of the earliest promising oil regions were in Mesopotamia, under Turkish control at the turn of the century. On the advice of one shrewd Armenian, Calouste Gulbenkian,[17] Turkish sultan, Abdul Hamid transferred the most promising acreage to his personal account and approved a concession to be held by the Turkish Petroleum Company (TPC, eventually to become the Iraq Petroleum Company or IPC). Half of the company shareholding was owned by the Central Bank of Turkey (including Gulbenkian's share and a British syndicate, led by no other than D'Arcy of Anglo-Iranian) and the rest equally owned by a subsidiary of Royal Dutch Shell and Deutche Bank.

At a conference in the British Foreign Office in March 1914, the British and German governments muscled into the arrangements forcing the Anglo-Persian (D'Arcy syndicate) share to 50%, with German and Royal Dutch Shell equally dividing the remainder (Gulbenkian getting 5% share contributed equally by the British and Shell interests). The salient point of agreement was a self-denying clause, prohibiting the contractual parties from producing oil in the Ottoman Empire other than through the TPC. After the war, the German interests were given to the French government, following the San Remo agreement in April 1920.[18]

The 'Foreign Office' accord angered the American counterparts who saw it as imperial and discriminatory. After the war, Americans saw the world through an equal, non-exclusive, and competitive, 'open door' lens. At least until they got in. This clash of world views between the former allies would dominate the Middle East affairs for another decade.

Under pressure from the oil industry (later formally establishing the American Petroleum Institute or API[19]), the US State Department actively supported the American oil companies in the region and their negotiations for a share of the TPC. The only truly private party in the whole affair was Mr. Gulbenkian. Even though the 'self-denying' clause was potentially violating the antitrust laws of the land, the US companies accepted it anyway, primarily spurred by a very large oil find in October 1927. Similarly, the British overlooked the inaccuracy of the Middle East map presented by the French[20] and a red line demarcating the area in which the self-denying clause would apply was accepted. After six years of difficult negotiations, the 'Red Line Agreement' was finally signed in the summer of 1928. The American companies[21] secured an equal (23.75%) share, the same as the British, French, and Royal Dutch Shell interests. The remaining 5% private share was with Mr. Gulbenkian, later frequently referred to as 'Mr. Five Percent'.

Towards the International Cartel

Having argued for an 'open door' policy for almost a decade, and having obtained a fair share, the American oil companies happily helped firmly shut it. This time, the concentration of market power was not only overlooked, but actively encouraged by the participating governments. This was particularly true after the Second World War from which the old colonial powers emerged economically weak, encouraging the US policymakers to expand its strategic and commercial interests to secure a dominant role in the Middle east. This role was recognised by Britain in the 1944 'Anglo-American Oil Agreement', which was perhaps the first attempt by governments to regulate petroleum markets at a global level. While it was eventually relegated to a mere 'memorandum of understanding',[22] it guaranteed the 'open door' policy in the regions under British control, particularly in today's Iran, Iraq, Kuwait, and Bahrain.

The Bahrain concession was eventually developed by the Standard Oil of California (now Chevron) with some strong 'arm-twisting' from the US Department of State.[23] The prize was plentiful and cheap oil pouring from the ground, conveniently only 10 miles away from the sea. The Standard Oil of California was outside the 'Red Line' agreement and thus a threat to the TPC monopoly. As the company had no outlets for oil in the Far East, it approached Texas Company (Texaco) to cement global ambitions of both and form a joint venture, Caltex in 1936. Texaco would sell half of its marketing operations east of Suez in return for half of California Standard's Bahrain and Saudi concessions, creating outlets for Bahrain oil and potentially increasing competition.

In order to 'stabilise' the new supply of oil, the 'Red line agreement' had to be amended or simply broken. The biggest obstacle to resolving the legal aspects of the agreement was the sheer embarrassment all the involved parties would face if the details of the monopoly arrangements were made public. As a result, the breaking up of the combination dragged on until 1948 when the agreement was finally cancelled and the relationships among the partners continued under the 'Heads of Agreement' signed in November that year.[24]

Other important new finds were in Saudi Arabia, where the legendary Max Steineke, a Standard California geologist discovered Abqaiq field in 1938, followed by Ghawar, the largest oil field in the world.[25] There, Standard California and Texaco, together with Standard of New Jersey (later Exxon) and Socony (later Mobil), jointly set up the Arabian American Oil Company (Aramco) as well as the Trans-Arabian Pipeline Company (TAPCO). In Kuwait, the concession was controlled by Gulf Oil (later also Mobil) and Anglo-Iranian (later BP). In Qatar, the partners were the same as in the IPC (Iraq), and so on.

The mechanisms for controlling these large petroleum reserves were ingenious, generally based on various common 'rules' such as Average Program Quantity (APQ) in Iran, the 'Five Sevenths' rule in Iraq and the 'Dividend Squeeze' in Saudi Arabia.[26] In a nutshell, these and other rules were designed to restrict the production to the level that balances the actual demand, so the crude oil ends up in the integrated systems of the major oil companies or majors, with a minimal effect on markets and prices. In spite of the price wobble (See Fig. 6.2) in the early 1930s, caused by the Great Depression and newfound oil discoveries, the cartel of international oil companies retained control of the global market and the new Middle East supplies in particular.

For example, Gulf Oil with a 50% concession in Kuwait ended up with excess volumes of oil which could not be absorbed in its own system. Therefore, in 1947, it agreed to sell a large volume of crude oil to Shell (in 1958 this agreement exceeded 400,000 barrels per day). Rather than sell the oil at a fixed price,[27] the two companies simply agreed to share the total profits resulting from the whole vertically integrated operations of production, transportation, refining and marketing. The companies avoided competition, especially in the Far East, where most of the Middle East oil was marketed. Effectively, the arrangements made sure there was no competition, no markets

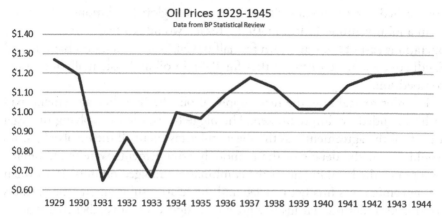

Fig. 6.2 Oil Prices 1929–1945 (Data from BP Statistical Review of World Energy)

and no prices for crude oil in the region, other than what the majors decided it to be.[28]

The Second World War further illustrated the strategic importance of oil. The US oil requirements towards the end of the war were telling: '*In less than two months, the United States Fifth Fleet burned over half a billion gallons of fuel oil. At the height of fighting on the western front, the Army Air Corps alone used fourteen times the total amount of gasoline shipped to Europe for all purposes between 1914 and 1918*'.[29]

After the war, the European Recovery Program (ERP) of 1948, popularly known as 'Marshall Plan', was partly designed to cement the dominant position of the US companies in the strategically important Middle East[30]: "*In addition to its profit potential, due to low production costs, the Middle East was the natural supply source to Western Europe and Japan. Control over the region, thus, would give the US influence over the economic and military policies of almost all the major participants in World War II*'.[31]

Joint ventures and shared ownership did not involve only the Middle East. They extended to marketing, refining and transportation in the Far East, South America, Europe, Canada as well as the United States.[32] While one can plausibly argue that vertical integration helped companies reduce costs and achieve economies of scale, there is absolutely no doubt that most of the horizontally integrated activities were a blatant abuse of monopoly power. For example, the mentioned Gulf–Shell agreement explicitly restricted Gulf from access to the Far East markets and provided penalty clauses (lower volumes and realised prices) in such cases.[33] At the same time, Anglo-Persian joint venture with Gulf Oil in Kuwait could supply the Gulf's share from either Iran or Kuwait in seller's option, with an explicit contractual clause that this crude oil would not be used to 'injure' the other's marketing position in India or anywhere else.[34] On top of the contractual agreements to limit competition, the global pricing arrangements certainly made sure discrimination is complete.

Discriminatory Pricing

One of the key characteristics of the global petroleum market before the beginning of the Second World War was a relatively stable contribution by the United States of just about over 60% of the global production.[35] As the country was a major producer and exporter of oil and petroleum products, it was only natural the key global pricing point would be the US Gulf (USG).[36] This meant the oil and products sold anywhere else in the world traded at some premium over the USG price (so-called 'US Gulf Plus' pricing), normally equal to the cost of shipping from the Gulf to the point of sale. The 'free on board' (FOB)[37] Gulf price was assessed daily by an independent publication, Platt's Oilgram. It was based on scarce market information, a price quotation (as a range, high and low) often only one company, possibly a major.[38] Having a single pricing point, regardless of where the oil was coming from was highly advantageous to the oil majors as it prevented 'harmful' competition. As they owned most of the global shipping and chartered most of the rest, the shipping cost assessment might have been questionable as well.[39]

After the war,[40] following the conservation efforts within the United States and a drive to produce oil outside the country, output in Venezuela picked up, especially after 1935 (see Fig. 6.3), but this only reinforced the USG-centric price. The real challenge to the prevailing pricing system came after the Middle East production picked up and started flowing to Europe, and eventually to the United States. The issue of discriminatory pricing actually started during the war, in 1944, when the British Auditor General complained about being charged bunker prices for the Royal Navy, based on very high USG prices plus some non-existent 'phantom freight' to the Middle East, for the product refined from cheap Iranian oil in the Abadan refinery.[41] Such complaints resulted in the creation of a second pricing point in the Persian Gulf. The idea was to use USG FOB prices and simply 'post' them as Persian Gulf FOB prices.

Even this newly agreed price parity was a rip-off by the Majors. The cost of production in the Middle East was far lower than in the United States. According to a Congressional hearing,[42] it cost about 40 cents (including a

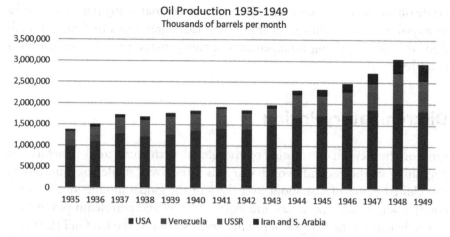

Fig. 6.3 Oil production 1935–1949. Thousands of barrels per month (Using data compiled from The Select Committee on Small Business, US Senate 1952, pp. 444–449)

21 cent royalty) to produce oil in Saudi Arabia and only 25 cents (including 15 cents royalty) in Bahrain, compared to the $1.05 price charged to the US Navy. The majors were making lots of money from selling Middle Eastern oil to their own governments, from the concessions they obtained with their very help.

Changing oil flows always impact pricing structures and the increase in the Middle East export to Europe and eventually to the United States itself, gradually dented the 'dual Gulf Plus' pricing. Given that most of the oil shipments to Europe after 1948 were financed by the European Cooperation Administration (ECA) as a part of 'Marshall Plan', the pricing structure also invited public scrutiny. The spirit of the plan was to supply overseas oil to Europe, and under the 'dual' US/Persian Gulf pricing system, the Middle East oil was landing there at higher prices, costing the US government far more. Under pressure from ECA, the oil majors then amended the formula to equalise the prices at the point of delivery into the United Kingdom (UK). Using the US Maritime Commission (USMC) estimated freight rates, shipping cost from the US Gulf to the United Kingdom was added to the FOB US Gulf price and cost of shipping there from the Middle East was then subtracted, reducing the FOB Persian Gulf price in the process.[43]

In 1948, the imports of the Middle East crude into the United States started to grow (from 600,000 barrels in April to 4 million barrels in December). Using the 'dual base' formula, realised sales price for the Middle East oil in Europe was far higher than the one for the US oil. To avoid further embarrassment, the majors simply shifted the equalisation point from the UK to New York. The 'Gulf Plus' effectively became 'Gulf Minus'.[44] This adjustment, however, would have resulted in a large fall in the oil price FOB Persian Gulf (as the shipping cost was deducted from the price). To prevent this fall in price, the Majors unilaterally decided to apply the prevailing spot, rather than the usual USMC shipping rates, as the spot rates were about 35% lower. This tweak gave them a much higher FOB Persian Gulf price of $1.75 rather than $1.30 per barrel, when using the USMC rates.[45] It did not end there. As the spot rates for shipping picked up in 1951 and reached a level good 50 per cent over the USMC assessment, the majors simply refused to reduce their FOB Persian Gulf Price and kept it unchanged at $1.75[46] (according to the adjusted formula, it should have been $0.85).

This tweak netted majors much higher delivered prices for the government-financed ECA sales to Europe. This blatant act of unilateral price-making was the clearest sign of market power firmly consolidated in the hands of the major oil companies. Under the excuse of the oil supply security, the governments of the US, Britain and France helped create an international oligopoly. As one observer wrote: '*In the long run, private companies might find profit in activities that worked against what government authorities considered to be national interests... some bemoaned the anti-competitive tendencies of consolidation in the Middle East, none was willing to make more than half-hearted attempts to alter affairs.*'[47]

The governments did not only help, but actively encouraged it. When appalling living conditions of the workers at Abadan refinery[48] started brewing a revolt in Iran, under the leadership of a British-installed, puppet monarch Reza Shah, both Britain and the United States saw it as an existential threat to the post-war political and economic order. Iran was a key supplier of oil to the American troops in the Korean war and Eastern Europe was already under the Soviet Communist yoke. A popular and democratically elected prime minister, Mohammed Mossadegh was trying to obtain better terms for the country and its people which, under the paranoia of the Red Scare[49] was enough for the United States and Britain to foment a coup in 1953[50] and reinstate the deposed monarch, soon turned dictator.[51] The oil started to flow again from Iran, but this time under a consortium of oil majors.[52] With intense pressure to increase the oil production in the country, only such a consortium could ensure that this was done in an orderly fashion, without disrupting the global oil market. It was yet another display of the interdependence of governments and majors with their global monopoly market power.

The Majors Charge

By the 1950s, the seven major oil companies, often referred to as 'Seven Sisters',[53] with the help of their respective governments, achieved global market dominance in all aspects of the oil business. This control was exercised through direct or indirect control of concessions, joint ventures of corporations and their affiliates, long-term contracts and marketing agreements as well as information sharing, contractual and informal, via interlocking directorships.

In 1949, the majors controlled 65% of the world reserves (82% of reserves outside the United States and 92% outside the US, Russia, and Mexico); produced 95% of oil in the Eastern Hemisphere and 99% of the oil from the Middle East; owned 77% of the global refining capacity outside the US and Russia, as well as two-thirds of the privately owned tanker fleet and pretty much every single, important pipeline outside the United States.[54]

The beating heart of the cartel was the 'Pool Association' between the biggest players, Standard Jersey (now Exxon Mobil), Anglo-Persian (now BP) and Royal Dutch Shell. Signed by Teagle, Detering and Cadman, larger-than-life leaders of the respective companies, during a grouse shoot in Achnacarry in Scotland in September 1928, this agreement originally set to optimise the joint resources in order to minimise cost.[55] An example of such optimisation would be Anglo-Persian company supplying of oil from Iran to the United Kingdom. If Shell is supplying a similar type of oil to its Italian affiliate from a location closer to the UK, it may be cheaper for Shell to supply the Anglo-Persian UK affiliate, while the latter could supply Italy, given shorter distance and thus lower cost. This kind of optimising arrangements are mutually beneficial and very common to this day, among refineries supplying petrol stations from various locations in the country.

However, the 'Pool Association' agreement was far more sinister than that. The very first 'Governing Principle' of the 'Pool' affirmed: '*The acceptance by the units of their present volume of business and their proportion of any increases in future consumption*'.[56] In effect, the companies agreed to accept the existing market shares and avoid any competition aimed at increasing them it. The 'As Is' agreement, as it is often referred to, did not just apply to the three companies, signatories of the contract, but to all the 'groups' operating in the countries outside the United States. It clearly implied that the three companies had a significant influence over their peers. All the volumes of oil and shipping were assigned to 'pools' in terms of quotas and in accordance with the 'As Is' agreement. If oil could not be exchanged between different geographic areas in order to minimise costs of delivery, the prices at which it

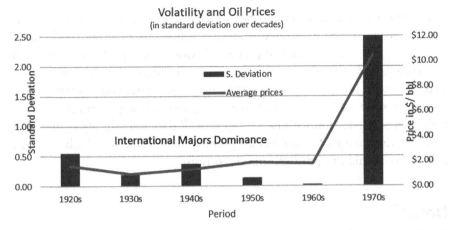

Fig. 6.4 International Oil Majors dominate the market (Data from BP Statistical Review of World Energy)

was exchanged within the 'group' were based on the 'Gulf Plus' system, thus avoiding any price competition. Figure 6.4 shows that the system worked. In spite of the war, the prices were rather stable.

What is more, all the oil volumes would be handled by the cartel's administrative agency, making sure that no purchases from outsiders are made. If sales had to be made to outsiders, the price would not be more favourable than to the cartel members. The agency would also calculate and enforce 'stabilised' freight rates on the basis of information provided by the cartel members, eliminating a very important aspect of volatility of delivered oil prices. The arrangement was to apply outside the United States only, to avoid any antitrust action. While the articles of the 'Pool Association' were never quite fully applied in practice, especially the 'administrative agency' and 'allocation plans', it continued to be seen and widely used as a declaration of objectives of the 'Seven Sisters'.[57] Given the details of the cartel arrangements agreed at Achnacarry, is not surprising that in 1952, John Sparkman, The Chairman of The Committee on Small Business asserted that: '*Today the power of the international oil companies is so vast that it invites its own abuse.*[58]'

The cartel of oil majors abolished a market in any real sense of that word. The 'US Gulf Plus' prices, analysed in any of their incarnation, were based on the scarce trade indications, often involving only one company, likely one of the majors. When the formula did not suit them, they simply 'posted' prices that did. Rockefeller would have been impressed.

In any case, the posted prices were primarily applicable to the intercompany transfers (including affiliates) and the tax positions with the producing as well as their respective governments. Caught between the Department of

Justice antitrust suit of 1953 and State Department push for energy security, the US majors probably steered a middle course, maximising profits while not raising any eyebrows in the process.[59] Most of the profits were made in the refining and marketing of the petroleum products, and the posted prices were far more important to the revenues of the producing countries. The producers were kept in the dark regarding the industry operations within their own countries and with rare exceptions,[60] they were simply rentier land-lords, at the mercy of neo-colonial political arrangements which they had neither economic nor political muscle to resist.

Notes

1. Much used phrase by Lord Curzon, taken here from Longhurst (1959, p. 54).
2. Ibid., p. 54.
3. Most economic historians agree that, prior to 1920s, Britain did not have an oil policy other than to secure cheap source of supply for the navy. For a review of the literature on the topic, see Gibson (2012).
4. Kent (1993, p. 54).
5. Ibid., p. 44.
6. Williamson et al. (1963, p. 268).
7. Ibid., p. 300.
8. 'Peak oil' narratives are flawed by definition. Proven reserves are resources that can be economically exploited using existing technology. Therefore, they are a function of price and technology, both of which change over time. So, the proven reserves are not a constant but a variable and change over time. We shall come back to this topic in later chapters. For an overview of various views, approaches and debates, see Mills (2008, ch. 2, p. 11) and Lynch (2016, p. 7).
9. Feis (1944, pp. 4–5). Also see Williamson et al. (1963, p. 300).
10. Williamson et al. (1963, pp. 302–304).
11. Not for the first time, 'Peak Oil' creed was followed by a flood. For more on this theme, see Lynch (2016).
12. President Coolidge created the Federal Oil Conservation Board with the oversight of reserves, technology and production. See: 'The Federal Oil Conservation Board Public Hearing' (1926).
13. See Adelman (1972, p. 43).
14. TRC was formed in 1891, originally to regulate the railroads. Texas was the largest producing (and a swing) state, hence the importance of TRC as a leader, although other states had similar arrangements. See: https://www.rrc.state.tx.us/about-us/history/.
15. See Imsirovic (2020a).
16. After Kent (1993) book with the same title.

17. Gulbenkian visited Baku back in 1888 and wrote a book on the subject, even though he never set a foot in Iraq. He was even offered a sole concession for £15,000, which he declined (and regrated for the rest of his life); see Lonhgurst (1959, p. 82).

18. Originally African and Eastern Concession Ltd would become Turkish Petroleum Company (TPC) in 1912 and Iraq Petroleum Company (IPC) in April 1929. The R.D. Shell subsidiary was Anglo-Saxon Petroleum. See Select Committee (1952, p. 48). Most of the information on the subject is from this source, pp. 47–67.

19. The American Petroleum Institute was established later, on March 20, 1919 to represent the interests of the oil and gas industry. However, it traces its beginning to World War I, when Congress and the domestic natural gas and oil industry worked together to help the war effort. See: https://www.api.org/about#tab-origins.

20. The French government created a state-owned company, Compagnie Française des Pétroles (CFP), as a vehicle for their national interests.

21. In the form of Near East Development Corporation, eventually equally shared between the Jersey Standard and Socony—later Exxon and Mobil respectively or ExxonMobil.

22. For a full narrative related to the agreement, see Stoff (1981, pp 69–70).

23. Select Committee (1952, p. 73, footnote 14).

24. Ibid., p. 105.

25. For an interesting, personal account of the discovery, see Al-Naimi (2016, pp. 16–22).

26. For an excellent study of price discrimination by major oil companies in the Middle East see Leeman (1962, pp. 19–30). For a simple description of the rules to control production, see Sampson (1988, p. 145).

27. There was no market and no price discovery mechanism other than estimating 'netback' orthe value of products refined from a barrel of the crude.

28. Of course, it can be argued that such a large sale was not possible precisely because of the lack of markets and prices, but that only reflects the extent to which the oil production in the Middle east was carved out by the Majors.

29. Stoff (1981, p. 63).

30. '*Roughly 10% of Marshall Plan funds were allocated to oil and oil products alone, more than 70% of which was supplied by only three US companies: Standard Oil of New Jersey (48.8%), Caltex (14%) and Socony-Vacuum (9.2%)… ECA Act of 1948, which stipulated that 'the procurement of petroleum and petroleum products…shall to the maximum extent practicable be made from petroleum resources outside the US', 70% of the oil supplied through the Marshall Plan came from Latin America and the Middle East (roughly 35% apiece).*' Miller (2018, p. 367). It seems that the US Majors were also a source of opposition to the refinery expansion in Europe. Ibid., p. 368.

31. Ibid., p. 361.

32. For full details of the companies as well as their affiliates, see Select Committee (1952, p. 30) and especially Chart 14.
33. Ibid., p. 139.
34. Ibid., p. 131.
35. Frankel, P. H. (1969, p. 114).
36. There was also a pricing point for exports of oil from Romania, FOB Constantsa, but volumes were rather small and subject to the country's changing export tax regime. Ibid., p. 146, endnote 16.
37. FOB sale excludes shipping and insurance cost.
38. Select Committee (1952, p. 352).
39. Ibid., p. 353, Footnote 7.
40. During the war, most prices were government controlled. In the United States, the Office of Price Administration (OPA) was established within the Office for Emergency Management of the United States government by Executive Order 8875 on 28 August 1941 and lasted until the end of the war.
41. Select Committee (1952, p. 356).
42. Ibid., p. 357.
43. Ibid., p. 362. USMC rates fluctuated less than the prevailing sport market rates.
44. See Adelman (1955, p. 48).
45. Select Committee (1952, pp. 364–369).
46. See BP Statistical Review 1951 (it is the name of the file to be found on the BP website, even though the company was still officially called Anglo Iranian). It says: *'The introduction towards the end of the 1950 by Socony-Vacuum of a published price list for the Middle East crude oils has been further extended for the 1951… The prices are those generally practiced at present by all other companies although so far nobody has followed Socony in actually publishing its own price list'*, pp. 5–6.
47. Stoff (1981, p. 73).
48. 'Wages were fifty cents a day. There was no vacation day, no sick leave, no disability compensation. The workers lived in a shanty-town, called Kaghaz-abad, or paper City, without running water or electricity…' Kinzer (2003, p. 67).
49. The Communist threat.
50. An excellent account of the events can be found in The New York Times (2000).
51. *'The world has paid a heavy price for the lack of democracy in most of the Middle East. Operation Ajax taught tyrants and aspiring tyrants there that the world's most powerful governments were willing to tolerate limitless oppression as long as oppressive regimes were friendly to the West and to Western oil companies.' That helped the political balance in a vast region away from freedom and towards the dictatorship.'* Ibid., p. 204.
52. The seven Majors (see endnote below) and French CFP.
53. The seven Majors are often referred to as 'Seven Sisters' and included five American and two European companies: Standard Oil Co. New Jersey (later Exxon

and ExxonMobil), Standard Oil Co. of California (later Chevron), Socony-Vacuum (later Mobil and then ExxonMobil), Gulf Oil Corp. (later Mobil and ExxonMobil), Texas Company (or Texaco, later Chevron Texaco and then only Chevron), Anglo-Iranian Oil Co. (later BP) and the Royal Dutch-Shell.

54. Select Committee (1952, pp. 23–29).
55. Ibid., p. 199.
56. Ibid., p. 200.
57. Ibid., p. 210.
58. Ibid., Preface, p. VI.
59. The Department of Justice started an antitrust suit in 1953 which was, under political influence, watered down and dragged out, at the end, making very little impact. For more details regarding this view, see Adelman (1995, p. 49).
60. Mexico was one. It was the very first producing country to nationalise its oil industry in March 1938.

References

Adelman M.A. (1955): 'Concept and Statistical Measurement of Vertical Integration', in *Business Concentration and Public Policy*, Princeton University Press for National Bureau of Economic Research, Princeton.

Adelman M.A. (1972): *The World Petroleum Market*, The Johns Hopkins University Press.

Adelman M.A. (1995): *The Genie Out of the Bottle, World Oil Since 1970*, The MIT Press.

Al-Naimi A. (2016): *Out of the Desert: My Journey From Nomadic Bedouin to the Heart of Global Oil*, Penguin.

Federal Oil Conservation Board (1926): *Public Hearing*, May 27, 1926, Office of Board, Washington, DC.

Feis, H. (1944): *Petroleum and American Foreign Policy*, Food Research Institute, Stanford University.

Frankel P.H. (1969): *Essentials of Petroleum, A Key to Oil Economics*, Chapel River Press, Andover, Hants.

Gibson, M.W. (2012): *British Strategy and Oil, 1914-1923*, PhD thesis, http://theses.gla.ac.uk/3160/1/2012gibsonphd.pdf.

Imsirovic A. (2020a): *The US Should Avoid Repeating Past Mistakes*, Petroleum Economist, April 2.

Imsirovic A. (2020b): 'Chine and Asian Oil Benchmarks: Where Next?', *OIES Forum*, No. 125 (September), p. 33.

Kent M. (1993): *Moguls and Mandarins, Oil, Imperialism and the Middle East in the British Foreign Policy, 1900-1940*, Franc Cass & Co. Ltd.

Kinzer S. (2003): *All the Shah's Men*, Wiley, Hoboken, NJ.

Leeman W.A. (1962): *The Price of Middle East Oil: An Essay in Political Economy*, Cornell University Press.

Longhurst H. (1959): *Adventure in Oil, Story of British Petroleum*, Sidgwick and Jackson Ltd.

Lynch C.M. (2016): *The "Peak Oil" Scare and the Coming of Oil Flood*, Praeger Publishers.

Miller N.Y. (2018): *The United States, Britain and the Marshall Plan: Oil and Finance in the Early Post-War Era*, Economia e Sociedade, Campinas, Unicamp. IE, https://doi.org/10.1590/1982-3533.2017v27n1art12.

Mills M.R. (2008): *The Myth of the Oil Crisis*, Praeger Publishers.

Sampson A. (1988 ed.): *The Seven Sisters*, Cornet Books.

Select Committee on Small Business, US Senate (1952): *The International Petroleum Cartel*, Staff Report to the Federal Trade Commission submitted to the Subcommittee on Monopoly of the Select Committee on Small Business, US Senate, Government Printing Office, Washington, August 22.

Stoff M.B. (1981): 'The Anglo-American Oil Agreement and the Wartime Search for Foreign Oil Policy', *The Business History Review*, Vol. 55, No. 1 (Spring), pp. 59–74.

The New York Times (2000): *Secrets of History: The C.I.A. in Iran -- A Special Report*, April 16, https://www.nytimes.com/2000/04/16/world/secrets-history-cia-iran-special-report-plot-convulsed-iran-53-79.html.

Williamson H.F., Andreano R.L., Daum A.R. and Klose G.C. (1963): *The American Petroleum Industry* (Vol. 2), Northwestern University Press.

7

From One Cartel to Another

The World of Oil in the 1950s

After the war and especially after 1950, the oil industry witnessed growing demand, production, and revenues. Large discoveries of cheap oil in the Middle East during the 1920s and 1930s were ideally placed to take advantage of this growth. In just over 20 years, global oil consumption grew over sixfold (see Fig. 7.1), demanding new refinery capacity, more oil tankers for transportation and petrol stations for distribution of fuels. The integrated oil industry, which was previously confined to the US, took off in the rest of the world, transforming people's lives, industries, and whole countries. What is more, the extent of this growth was such that it started to change our planet. The surge in human activity, facilitated by fossil fuels, generally referred to as 'The Great Acceleration'[1] is the most convincing starting point of the 'Anthropocene'[2] and it can be dated back to 1950s.

The oil majors were in a good place. They controlled the largest oil reserves in the world in, located in Venezuela, the Persian Gulf and Indonesia. Oil producing countries needed their expertise and integrated outlets for the oil. They needed the 'Sisters' to fine-tune the supply of oil from various producers to match the overall global demand, without 'disruptive' price competition.

The majors did not always have it their own way. The economic shock caused by the Great Depression decimated years' worth of demand. Oversupplied markets for oil pushed the majors to take a hard stance towards Mexico and ultimately led to nationalisation of the oil industry there in 1938.[3] On the eve of the Second World War, stung by the Mexican experience, the US

© The Author(s), under exclusive license to Springer Nature Switzerland AG 2021
A. Imsirovic, *Trading and Price Discovery for Crude Oils*,
https://doi.org/10.1007/978-3-030-71718-6_7

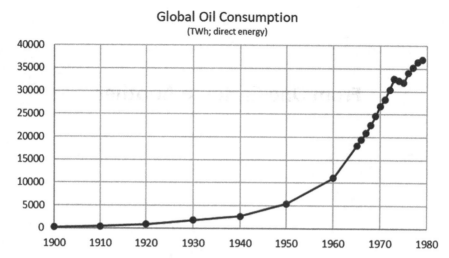

Fig. 7.1 Global Oil Consumption in TWh (*Source* Author from data in https://ourwor ldindata.org/energy)

government helped draft the Venezuelan Hydrocarbons Law of 1943 and acknowledged a 50/50 split in profits from the concessions there. Despite this radical increase in the producing country share, continuing good concession terms helped the local subsidiary of Jersey Standard earn 42% return on assets.[4] Most importantly, nationalisation was averted and the cheap supply oil for the Allies was assured. After the war and under pressure of the Cold War, similar concessions were given to the Middle East producers: Saudis in 1950, Kuwait 1951, Iraq 1952, and Iran in 1954, following a coup, a year earlier.[5]

In spite of these concessions, companies continued their symbiotic relationship with the producing countries, and this was well observed and supported by the Saudi Minister of Petroleum, Sheikh Yamani: '*Nationalization of the upstream (production) operations would inevitably deprive the majors of any further interest in maintaining crude oil-price levels. They would then become mere offtakers buying the crude oil from the producing countries and moving it to their markets in Europe, Japan, and the rest of the world. In other words, their present integrated profit structure … would be totally transformed. With elimination of their present profit margin of, say, 40 cents a barrel from production operations, the majors would … shifting their profit focus downstream to their refining and product-marketing operations. Consequently, their interest would be identical with that of the consumers – namely, to buy crude of the cheapest possible price*'.[6] Even if the producing countries could sell all the oil themselves, they had no way of controlling the supply and price.

Consuming country governments, and the US government in particular, needed the major oil companies not only to keep the supply of oil stable and affordable, but they also used them as an instrument of their foreign policy. Under a real or perceived threat of Communism, the policy started to develop after the war, with the goal of supporting pro-Western governments through economic growth, and a steady, affordable supply of oil. This was to be achieved through a dominant role of the American companies in the world trade. This required the highest level of the state to work closely with large companies.

For example, in response to the Saudi demands for higher revenues, the US National Security Council allowed the oil companies income tax paid to be creditable against the US income tax liability.[7] This was soon applied to all the oil companies operating overseas. Thus, the Oil Majors could happily agree to the producing country demands for higher revenues in the knowledge that the cost could be passed on to the US taxpayers.[8] At the same time, the government of the day could avoid the inconvenience of asking the elected legislators in Congress for any additional funds. The companies would take care of appeasing some rulers (generally the Shah of Iran) by increasing output, while limiting it elsewhere (often Iraq), thus balancing the market and ensuring stable prices. The Shah would buy American weapons 'to keep his country safe from Communism',[9] supporting the US military industry, eventually balancing the books.

Thus, the concessions made to the producing countries were, in effect, not made by the majors, but by the US government and paid by the US taxpayers and consumers of other industrial nations.[10] To facilitate this oil balancing function,[11] the American Majors were explicitly exempt from the antitrust sanctions by the US Justice Department: '*This foreign policy initiative was perceived by the US National Security Council as being so important as to require the sacrifice of the American antitrust laws as they applied to the international oil*'.[12]

Continued demand growth helped everyone. Producing country revenues and company profits continued to grow.[13] More production could be accommodated, and profits could be channelled into new investments. Most importantly, there were few 'outsiders' to upset this relationship. Posted prices were just numbers, primarily used to calculate the producing government taxes, with little real relationship to exchange values. As Morris Adelman observed[14]: '*... after 1959, no posted price number has any meaning as a price. It can serve only as an interim figure for calculating the per barrel tax*'. There were no real markets,[15] no meaningful prices and no price volatility to worry about.

As is generally the case, the government intervention in the markets had unintended consequences. The 'subsidised' foreign oil started to make its way into the United States and the country became a net importer in 1948. The government pressured the major oil companies to keep the imports down voluntarily, in order to protect the domestic industry. It did not work and in 1959, on the grounds of national security, the government established a Mandatory Oil Import Program[16] which, in its numerous incarnations was to last for many years.[17]

This cosy relationship between companies and producing governments contained the seeds of its own destruction. The US government abandoned free markets. At home, the Texas Railroad Commission (TRC) supported the small domestic producers and prices and abroad, the US government abdicated the supply and balancing function to the majors. It never developed any alternative institutional framework[18] for handling the strategic commodity at the international level. When this cosy arrangement with companies and producing government started to crumble, the US government did not have a plan 'B'.

New Kids on the Block

While the existing oil producers such as Venezuela and Iran were pushing for higher production and revenues, new state-owned refineries, with no integrated supply arrangements, begun to appear on the scene. These were large scale importers in countries such as Italy, Japan, India, Brazil, Argentina, and others. They would tender for the cheapest oil available in the market and make the awards public. For example, in 1954, Standard Oil California (later Chevron), won a supply contract to Petrobras, Brazil's state-owned company with a new refinery in Cubatao. Being long oil in the Middle East, Californian Standard offered to supply the Arabian Light crude oil at a discount to the posted price.[19] Transparency, one of the key characteristics of any functioning market, started to creep in. Previous recorded deals became a measure of the market value. This 'market value' was gradually eroding, below the posted prices.[20]

At the same time, low taxes favouring foreign investments[21] and large profits of the oil majors were attracting newcomers, smaller 'independent'[22] oil companies. A new round of concessions in Venezuela in 1957 attracted US independents such as The Sun, Phillips, and Sinclair which soon produced about 10% of the country's output.[23]

In the same year, the National Iranian Oil Company (NIOC) pioneered a new approach to granting concessions, this time offshore, setting up a 50/50 joint venture with Agip, a subsidiary of the Italian state-owned company 'Ente Nazionale Idrocarburi' (ENI). A year later, they set up another similar joint venture with a US independent, Amoco (much later bought by BP). In 1957, Saudi Arabia also signed an agreement with the Japanese Petroleum Trading Company (JPTC) for exploration and production in the offshore part of the Neutral Zone.[24] The onshore section of the Zone was awarded to another US independent, Getty Oil a few years earlier. Similar deals were signed in Kuwait. These newcomers, such as J.P. Getty paid producing countries more for concessions and offered higher royalties.[25] Despite paying a lot more, Getty still made a fortune.[26] It did not go unnoticed among the producers.

In 1956, the French[27] discovered oil in Algeria and started production under very favourable terms.[28] By the end of the War of Independence in 1962, the country was supplying 40% of all the French oil imports. Unhappy with the terms with the French, the first Algerian prime minister, a revolutionary leader Ahmed Ben Bella, set up a national oil company, SONATRACH[29] and pressed for a new agreement—The Oil and Aid Accord of 1965. This treaty increased the tax reference price, income tax (to 55%), eliminated tax deferrals and generally provided better terms for the Algerian government.[30] Having signed a favourable joint venture agreement with Getty Oil, the government was to become one of the leading hawks in pressing the oil companies for better concession terms.[31]

Following the Iranian crisis in the early 1950s and the closure of the Suez Canal during the 1956–1957 Suez crisis, Libya with direct access to the Mediterranean became of interest to oil companies. In Libya, the 1955 Petroleum Law offered a large number of smaller concessions and stricter terms for exploration than the existing producers. At the same time, it offered very generous tax terms, which attracted a large number of operating companies, many of them without integrated refinery systems. The terms allowed for the price discounts versus posted price (which were prevalent at the time), to be deducted from the gross revenue in arriving to the taxable income.[32] By 1957, some sixty concessions[33] were awarded, involving among others, the Oasis[34] group of US independents, Occidental, Conoco, Bunker Hunt and later a major, Jersey Standard (Exxon).

More than half of the Libyan production ended up in the hands of companies that had no integrated systems in Europe and hence no outlets for the oil. They left the 'balancing of the market' and consistency of posted prices[35] to the majors and sold their oil at the best price they could get, driving the prices down. In 1956, BP and Shell[36] found oil in Nigeria, opening West Africa as a new oil frontier. Some majors, such as crude-short Shell and Jersey Standard (Exxon) welcomed the new finds which provided more diversified supplies, away from the Persian Gulf.

Russian production also started to take off, with volumes growing annually at 14% in the 1950–1963 period, eventually reaching over 4 million barrels per day. Exports to the 'free world' picked up after 1955 at just over 100,000 barrels and reached almost a million barrels per day in 1965.[37] By the end of the 1950s, the USSR became the second-largest producer in the world, after the United States, and produced a volume of oil that could compete with the Middle East. Italian ENI was one of the first companies to start importing cheap Russian oil from the Urals region into Italy, undercutting prices set by the oil majors.[38]

With the US import quota system protecting the domestic oil producers in place,[39] many independents were 'stranded' with oil which had to find markets elsewhere. These 'newcomers', not unlike the shale producers in the 2010s, were keen to get the oil out of the ground and sell it as soon as possible, securing a quick return to their investment, thus putting pressure on prices. Lower spot[40] market prices meant higher discounts relative to the posted prices (used for tax reference), and higher effective tax rate. The majors were losing money, market share and the ability to balance the market and keep prices stable.

Tax, Markets, and the Birth of the Producers' Cartel

The integrated structure of the industry was crumbling. In 1946, nine oil companies operated in the Middle East. By 1970, this number reached 81.[41] In the 1960–1965 period alone, the oil majors' share of the European refining capacity fell from 67 to 54%. This intensified competition in the products markets, reducing the refinery margins and putting further pressure on oil prices. The growing competition for oil concessions between the Majors and the 'independent oil companies', coupled with falling oil prices, put increasing pressure on the relationships between the oil-producing countries and the Majors.

At the same time, a new breed of populist leaders emerged in some of the producing countries: Gamal Abdel Nasser in Egypt, Muammar al-Qaddafi in Libya, Houari Boumediene in Algiers, Abdullah Tariki in Saudi Arabia, and Perez Alfonso in Venezuela. Apart from being well educated, they shared strong anti-colonial, left-leaning, and nationalist feelings. The Algerian President argued for the producing countries to lead the 'Third World' towards more equitable and just global world order.[42]

Better terms offered to producers by the 'newcomers' in the oil markets made it very clear that the 'old' terms agreed with the Majors were a bad deal. While the old colonial powers in the 1920s picked one producing country at a time, offering them meagre returns, competition among the oil companies now meant that the established producers could pick one company at a time, demanding better terms and getting them (see Fig. 7.2). This process picked up at the 50/50 profit sharing and gradually moved on towards participation and eventually, nationalisation.

This was a revolutionary period, a decade marked by the Suez crisis, anti-colonial movements, Sputnik and Cuban revolution.[43] The years between 1958 and 1960 were equally revolutionary in the oil market. In 1958, in Iraq,[44] a group of officers overthrew the British installed monarchy and established a republic. A year later, a revolution in Venezuela removed a military dictator and elected a democratic government. The country increased taxes on the oil industry to almost 70%.[45] The confidence of smaller nations and ex-colonies was growing, and oil prices were falling. The producers were still thinking about oil, but this time collectively.

At the First Arab Petroleum Congress in Cairo in 1958, there were two bombshells.[46] The first one was a presentation by Arab economists that the 50/50 profit-sharing arrangements with oil companies were nothing of the

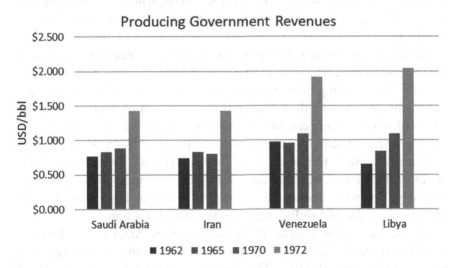

Fig. 7.2 Producing Government Revenues in USD per barrel. (Calculated from the United States Tariff Commission [1973, p. 40])

sort. They calculated that, on top of equally shared oil price of $1.60 a barrel, oil companies made a further 20 cents a barrel on transportation, about $1 on refining and $2 on marketing. That prompted the Director-General of Saudi Petroleum Affairs, Sheikh Abdullah Tariki, to demand more Arab refineries and an all-Arab pipeline in order to participate in these additional profits.

The second bombshell was a presentation by an American legal advisor to the Saudi Arabian Directorate of Petroleum and Mineral Affairs, M. Hendryx. His paper titled: 'A Sovereign Nation's Legal Ability to Make and Abide by a Petroleum Concession Contract' argued that the producing countries were entitled, under the US, British and French law, to change or cancel any existing concessions which were not in the best public interest of those countries. The producers clearly had grievances about the existing arrangements and now they potentially had a legal justification for changing them. The newly acquired confidence of the producing nations was in full swing and their expectations were high.

Another document that came from the Congress was an unofficial 'understanding' of representatives from S. Arabia, Kuwait, Egypt, Syria, Iran, and Venezuela, so called 'Maadi Agreement'.[47] This 'pact' might have been a wish list, but clearly stated the aspirations of the producing nations: to increase their share of oil revenues, support prices (on which tax revenues were based), be consulted before any changes are made in posted prices, increase the refining throughput inside the producing countries, establish national oil companies and coordinate production policies through a commission that was to meet annually. While it had no legal consequence, 'Maadi Agreement' was a road map for everything the producing nations would strive for in the decades to come.

The oil companies and their governments failed to grasp the significance of these developments. Spot markets continued to trade well below the posted prices, resulting in companies paying effectively higher rates of tax.[48] The majors started to reduce their postings. Most importantly, they did so unilaterally, without any consultation with the producing countries, sovereign states, severely impacted by these actions.[49] Early in 1959, BP cut postings and got away with it. In August, Jersey Standard (Exxon) announced a further cut in posted prices, but this time there was a strong reaction. The very same day, Venezuela banned all the sales of its oil at large discounts. The 'aspirations' of the Mehdi Pact turned into a decisive action.

On the 14th of September 1960, Venezuela, S. Arabia, Iran, Iraq, and Kuwait met in Baghdad and set up the Organisation of the Petroleum Exporting Countries (OPEC). The agreement was short and to the point[50]: '*The principal aim of the Organization shall be the unification of petroleum policies for the Member Countries and the determination of the best means for safeguarding the interests of Member Countries individually and collectively'.* The agreement recognised the finite nature of oil and its importance to the development of producing countries, as well as their vulnerability to its price fluctuations. It proposed a unified and opened (to new members) front in formulating production agreements and energy policy in general. It demanded that: '*Oil Companies maintain their prices steady and free from all unnecessary fluctuations ... to restore present prices to the levels prevailing before the reductions...*' It proposed: '*That Members shall study and formulate a system to ensure the stabilisation of prices by, among other means, the regulation of production...*'. Finally, it proposed regular consultations and the establishment of the secretariat responsible for the organisation and administration of the organisation.

A year later, in Libya, Jersey Standard (Exxon) posted the price for Brega crude below those for East Mediterranean grades of crude oil. This resulted in a lower tax for the country and angered the Libyan government. Within a few months, Libya also joined OPEC.[51]

The Dumb and the Blind

What is striking is that all these events were happening in a climate of a complete disconnect between the producers on one side and the foreign companies (and their governments) on the other.[52] OPEC demands for high and stable posted prices revealed a complete naivety and lack of understanding of the prevailing market conditions at the time.[53] The Majors, on the other hand, revealed an equal degree of arrogance, and a lack of empathy for their main partners, producing nations.[54] The US government and its allies, living under the spell of the Cold War, had neither ability nor will, to help the companies, which continued to make large profits.[55] (also see Fig. 7.3).

At the heart of the problem was the oil pricing structure that ceased to make any sense. The Majors could no longer balance the market by rationing supplies. Therefore, they could not keep prices fixed. Instead, spot trades dictated them. The Majors lost their market power and the ability to be price makers. Having tax payments based on the posted prices, producing companies faced volatile production revenues. With the arrogance of those who believe they are still in charge, they just followed the market, unilaterally cutting posted prices, simply passing on the problem to the producing nations. Having no other integrated assets such as transportation, refining or

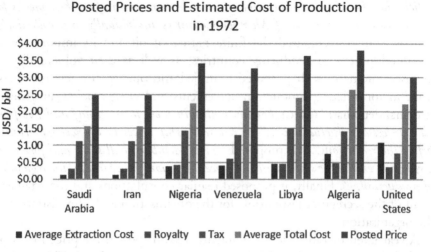

Fig. 7.3 Estimated Costs of Production and Posted Prices (Calculated from the United States Tariff Commission [1973, p. 24])

marketing to hedge falling revenues, the producing countries, highly dependent on oil income, were left at the mercy of the market (through posted price adjustments). The market was winning.

If the Majors could not stabilise the market, OPEC members believed, they could do it. The very act of setting up their own organisation gave them a strong sense of empowerment and control over the most important resource they possessed. One of the signatories of the original Baghdad agreement, and one of the key founding fathers of OPEC, Venezuelan oil minister, Perez Alfonso believed he knew how to do it. A careful student of the US oil industry and the Texas Railroad Commission in particular, he saw it as a blueprint for an OPEC production (quota) rationing system.[56] This view was shared by his 'brother in arms', Saudi minister Al-Tariki, who also trained at the Texas Railroad Commission.[57]

While the members of the organisation had legitimate rights to control the destiny of their own resources, demands for higher and stable prices through an orchestrated (quota) rationing system clearly point to a desire to form another cartel. The ultimate goal was to replace the cartel of major oil companies, unable to balance the market anymore, by another cartel of producing nations, which they beleived could.

The ex-Deputy Secretary-General of OPEC, Fadhil al-Chalabi spelt this thinking very clearly: '*If left entirely to free market forces, without any intervention in supply regulation, the oil industry would be susceptible to a high degree of price volatility. Without ensuring an even-handed balance between supply and demand, the oil market would be chaotic and subject to price wars among the producers, each endeavouring to protect its own share in the world oil market, regardless of the extent to which the price fell...*'.[58] From the other side of the fence, the impression was exactly the same: '*From the point of view of the producing countries, OPEC has done nothing more than substitute a producing country cartel for the system administered by the companies with the support of the United States and its major allies during the decades of the Fifties and Sixties*'.[59]

The only problem was that OPEC had no means to function as a cartel. At least, not for a while. The first decade of its existence achieved very little. OPEC needed oil companies, the majors in particular, with their still large share of transportation, refining and marketing. Even if the producers could legally change or cancel the prevailing production agreements (bravely assuming that Hendryx's legal arguments were correct), they had no capability to 'go it alone'. The OPEC members were a diverse group of countries with political differences and varied affiliations.

Francisco Parra, the ex-Secretary-General of the organisation, who was very much involved in this period, called the early years of the organisation a 'resounding failure'.[60] The oil companies kept calm and carried on. The majors kept OPEC countries competing for productivity gains. While the market was oversupplied, they used their integrated system to control it as much as they could. In the United States, TRC made sure spare production capacity was available if needed. In this unstable situation, posted prices remained remarkably stable. OPEC achieved very little. It would take a decade before 'The Genie (finally got) Out of the Bottle'.[61]

Notes

1. Steffen et al. (2015). They argue that: '*... of all the candidates for a start date for the Anthropocene, the beginning of the Great Acceleration is by far the most convincing from an Earth System science perspective*'. Abstract.
2. Anthropocene is the Earth's most recent geologic time period in which most of the earth systems have been influenced by humans.
3. Demand shock caused by the Great Depression caused the market to crash. A flood of cheap oil poured out of Venezuela and exacerbated already tense relationship between the companies and the Mexican government. A hard line taken by the companies led to a surprise nationalisation of 1938 and creation of Petroleos Mexicanos (PEMEX). See Magueri (2006, pp. 48–49).
4. The State Department's Herbert Hoover Jr. helped draft it. As the 50/50 profit split was linked to prices, it was not achieved before 1948, the same year when the Jersey Standard subsidiary, Creole, achieved 42% return on its assets. The

50% government take was stipulated a minimum, important point with major consequences a decade later. See Parra (2004, pp. 14–16).

5. As a result of the turmoil in Iran between 1940 and 1953, the industry ended up being nationalised in 1951 with the National Iranian Oil Company (NIOC) as the caretaker. Anglo Iranian changed name to British Petroleum 1954. These events will be discussed in more detail later as the implications of these events have rippled down to this day.

6. Report to the Committee of Foreign Relations, United States Senate by the Subcommittee on Multinational Corporations (1975, p. 11).

7. Ibid., p. 2.

8. In 1950, Aramco paid the US $50 million in taxes. In 1951, it paid only $6 million. Report to the Committee of Foreign Relations, United States Senate by the Subcommittee on Multinational Corporations (1975, p. 85).

9. *'The Shah intended to maintain a standing army of five divisions and, in order to pursue that goal, 40 percent of the government's budget was earmarked for military spending'.* See Garavini (2019, p. 47).

10. A former Deputy Secretary General of OPEC, Fadhil Chalabi, quotes Sheikh Yamani, in conversation with the Shah of Iran where the Shah claims that the Americans were 'all for higher oil prices' and if Yamani did not believe him, he should: 'Go and meet Henry Kissinger'. Chalabi (2010, p. 247).

11. This balancing function based on anticipated production and allocated quotas was not dissimilar to the one used by Texas Railroad Commission (TRC). Eventually, it was also to be adopted by OPEC.

12. See Ibid., p. 2.

13. By 1960, the Majors were achieving the return to investment of nearly 100% per annum. See Parra (2004, p. 40).

14. Adelman (1995, p. 55).

15. Outside the US, where it was tightly controlled by the Texas Railroad Commission.

16. See the United States Tariff Commission (1973, p. 4).

17. Ibid., p. 4.

18. A free market would have been an obvious choice.

19. It was a delivered price, so the amount of discount was not exactly clear. See Parra (2004, p. 73).

20. This erosion would be temporarily interrupted by the 1956–1957 Suez crisis.

21. In 1973, Exxon paid an effective tax rate of 11.2% on earnings of $2.98 bn, Mobil 5% on earnings of $783 million and Texaco 3% on earnings of $1.32 bn. See the Report to the Committee of Foreign Relations, United States Senate by the Subcommittee on Multinational Corporations (1975, p. 13).

22. The term loosely means companies 'other than the majors'. In the USA, these were: Amoco, Sohio, Conoco, Atlantic Richfield (Arco), Occidental, and some others. By and large, they emerged from Texas, which, in 1960 produced some 39% of US oil. Libya was a steppingstone for Amerada (Hess), Continental, and Marathon. Occidental took off in Russia and Getty in S. Arabia and later

Iran. In Europe, 'independents' included French Total (CFP) and Elf, Italian Agip (ENI), Belgian Petrofina and others. For an excellent narrative, See A. Sampson, chapter 7, 'The Intruders'.

23. Parra (2004, p. 75).

24. In the Saudi share of the N. Zone. The Zone is an undefined area of just under 6,000 sq. km between Kuwait and S. Arabia, to be equally shared by both countries. A vestige of the British imperial past, it was established by Uqair Convention of December 1922.

25. A. Sampson pp 157. In Saud Arabia, Getty made a $9.5 m down payment and offered higher royalties for exploration and production in the Neutral Zone, between S. Arabia and Kuwait. Getty was later bought by Texaco, which in turn, was 'merged' with Chevron.

26. *'J. Paul Getty became a billionaire after negotiating a series of oil leases with Saudi Arabia and Kuwait starting in 1949. He soon was being widely reported as the richest man alive.'* Where the Getty family fortune came from, CNNMoney, April 1, 2015.

27. The French national interests were led by CFP and CREPS plus some private companies. See CIA (1970, p. 2).These were later to be merged into 'Elf'. In 2003, Elf was to merge with 'Total'.

28. The Evian Accord of 1965 assured the government take of only 29 cents per barrel compared to 75–90 cents in the Middle East and South America at the time. CIA (1970, p. 4).

29. SONATRACH stands for Société Nationale pour la Recherche, la Production, le Transport, la Transformation, et la Commercialisation des Hydrocarbures.

30. CIA (1970, p. 5).

31. Ibid., p. 7.

32. The terms were out of line with the rest of the Middle East producers. The ex-Secretary General of OPEC, F. Parra claims the terms were '... generous to the point of absurdity...'. Parra (2004, pp. 76, 78).

33. See CIA (1986, p. 7).

34. The Oasis Group (originally the Conorada Group) was a Libyan consortium composed of three U.S. independent oil companies: Amerada (Amerada Hess), Continental (ConocoPhillips), and Marathon. Later, Shell was to take a share as well.

35. Jersey Standard (Exxon) insisted on consistency of tax reference prices, paying Libya far more tax than independents until 1961 when the 1955 Law was amended. Parra (2004, p. 78).

36. The first successful well drilled at Oloibiri by Shell D'Arcy 1956. The following year, it changed ownership and name to Shell-BP Petroleum Development Company of Nigeria Limited. See: https://www.nnpcgroup.com/NNPC-Bus iness/Business-Information/Pages/Industry-History.aspx.

37. Data from the National Petroleum Council Report (1964, pp. 18, 29, 74, 101).

38. USSR was also undercutting the prices sold to the rest of the Soviet bloc, by a large margin. In 1955, it sold oil at an average of $2.16 to the 'free world',

while selling it to its 'satellites' at \$3.38. This margin would increase into early 1960s. Ibid., pp. 7, 109.

39. See Chapter 6.

40. Normally referred to as arm's-length or third-party deals in the trade.

41. D. Yergin, p. 531.

42. The expression of this political thinking was the establishment of the Non-Aligned Movement in 1961. Algeria was an active member, together with almost 2/3 of the other UN member countries. The movement fought for: 'the national independence, sovereignty, territorial integrity and security of non-aligned countries... against imperialism, colonialism, neo-colonialism, racism, and all forms of foreign aggression, occupation, domination, interference or hegemony as well as against great power and bloc politics' (as later distilled by F. Castro in his adopted, Havana Declaration of 1979).

43. In 1952, Nasser led the 1952 overthrow of the monarchy, nationalised Suez Canal and prevailed in the subsequent crisis. In 1955, in Bandung, Indonesia, an Afro–Asian Conference met to promote Afro-Asian economic and cultural cooperation and to oppose colonialism or neo-colonialism by any nation, leading later to the establishment of the Non-Aligned Movement. Sputnik was launched in 1957, showcasing how advanced the Communist regimes can be. Cuban revolution won in 1959, overthrowing the corrupt, pro-American regime and setting up a Communist one on the American doorstep.

44. The political and cultural climate of Baghdad of the 1950s is well described in Chalabi (2010, pp. 12–13).

45. See Parra (2004, p. 89).

46. This section is mainly based on the Chatham House (1959) paper, 246–253.

47. Often referred to as: 'Gentlemen's Agreement' of Maadi', after the meeting at the informal meeting at the Maadi Yachting Club, Cairo. See Rubino (2008, p. 174). Parra refers to it as 'Mehdi Pact', See Parra (2004, p. 94). Most signatories had no authority to commit to the agreement, so a clause was inserted to emphasize that the signatories were agreeing in their personal capacities only.

48. This was not the case in Venezuela, where companies were taxed on the 'realised' prices.

49. Ambitious development plans have led both S. Arabia and Iran to the verge of bankruptcy, just at the time of cuts in posted prices and severe falls in their oil revenues. See Garavini (2019, pp. 117 and 119).

50. See the United Nations Treaty Series (1962, pp. 248–252).

51. Indonesia also joined in the same year. Qatar joined a year earlier.

52. The extent of the disconnect at the time is beautifully portrayed by Rubino (2008), in particular in chapter 6, 'OPEC's Midwife' and especially on p. 182: 'The dramatis personae were not very well known to each other'.

53. Tariki in particular did not seem to understand the intensity of the competition from the new producers, asking in 1959: 'Why couldn't the oil companies curtail production and thus strengthen prices?' Ibid, p. 193. In 1958, Tariki was asking journalists about oil pricing, workings of Aramco and US policies! Ibid., p. 143.

54. '... *these men worked in 'ivory towers' with a few key personalities dominating the boards... There was just a small cabal of people who made decisions, either collectively or individually... The US majors, particularly, 'were arrogant and naive'...'* Ibid., p. 178.
55. A study by A. D. Little, commissioned by OPEC in 1962 found 1956–60 company returns on net assets to be 66%. See Parra (2004, p. 100).
56. Ex-Secretary General of OPEC, Francisco Parra, reflects on the political realities of such system in the early days of OPEC. See Parra (2004, pp. 100–103).
57. Garavini (2019, p. 95).
58. Chalabi (2010, p. 36).
59. Report to the Committee of Foreign Relations, United States Senate by the Subcommittee on Multinational Corporations (1975, p. 2).
60. Iranian government continued to push for increased production as a means of achieving higher revenues. Their representative at the OPEC meetings, Reza Fallah was known as the 'BP Delegate to OPEC' and at one stage in 1962, the Shah was ready to pull out of the organisation. See Parra (2004, pp. 103–104 and 106).
61. Name of the book by Adelman, M. (1995).

References

Adelman M.A. (1995): *The Genie Out of the Bottle, World Oil Since 1970*, The MIT Press.

Chatham House (1959): 'The First Arab Petroleum Congress', *The World Today*, Vol. 15, No. 6 (June), pp. 246–253, Royal Institute of International Affairs.

Chalabi F.J. (2010): *Oil Policies, Oil Myths*, I.B. Tauris & Co. Ltd. London.

CIA Intelligence Memorandum (1970): *Algeria: The Importance of the Oil Industry*, Directorate of Intelligence, October 1970.

CIA Intelligence Assessment (1986): *The Libyan Oil Industry: Dependence on Foreign Companies*, Directorate of Intelligence, January 1986.

Garavini G. (2019): *The Rise and Fall of OPEC in the Twentieth Century*, Oxford University Press.

Magueri L. (2006): *The Age of Oil, The Mythology, History and Future of the World's Most Controversial Resource*, Praeger, Westport, Connecticut.

National Petroleum Council Report (1964): *Impact of Oil Exports from the Soviet Block, Supplement to the 1962 Report*, MPC, March 19, Washington.

Parra F. (2004): *Oil Politics, A Modern History of Petroleum*, I.B. Taurus Co. Ltd.

Report to the Committee of Foreign Relations, United States Senate by the Subcommittee on Multinational Corporations (1975): *Multinational Oil Corporations and the US Foreign Policy*, January 2, US Government Printing Office, Washington.

Rubino A. (2008): *Queen of the Oil Club*, Beacon Press, Boston.

Steffen W., Broadgate, W., Deutsch L., Gaffney O. and Ludwig C. (2015): 'The Trajectory of the Anthropocene: The Great Acceleration', *The Anthropocene Review*, January 16.

United Nations Secretariat (1962): *Agreement Concerning the Creation of the Organization of Petroleum Exporting Countries (OPEC)*. Done at Baghdad, on September 14, 1960, United Nations Treaty Series UN Resolution No. 6363, https://treaties.un.org/doc/Publication/UNTS/Volume%20443/volume-443-I-6363-English.pdf.

United States Tariff Commission (1973): *World Oil Developments and the US Oil Import Policies*, A Report Prepared for the Committee on Finance, US Senate, TC Publication 632, Washington, DC.

8

Producers and Companies: Transfer of Power

First a Stalemate

OPEC was probably an inevitable result of the political needs and ideas of the time. As early as 1955, the Asian-African Conference in Bandung[1] recognised the '*vital need for stabilizing commodity trade in the region*', ... *collective action be taken by participating countries for stabilizing the international prices of and demand for primary commodities through bilateral and multilateral arrangements... unified approach on the subject*' and a need to: '*diversify their export trade by processing their raw material, wherever economically feasible...*'.[2] This was to be achieved through economic cooperation, technical assistance, and the establishment of a Special United Nations Fund for Economic Development (later United Nations Conference on Trade and Development or UNICTAD).

Following this reasoning, establishing OPEC was a way of liberating the oil resources of producing countries from the yoke of the foreign neo-colonial control. The organisation was an expression of oil producers' sovereign right to manage their own resources and align it to the needs of their economic and social development, rather than the needs of consuming nations.

This line of argument was reinforced at the UN Conference on Human Rights on 14 December 1962, giving: '*... inalienable right of all States freely to dispose of their natural wealth and resources in accordance with their national interests, and on respect for the economic independence of States.*[3] In particular, article 4 of the resolution explicitly addressed the issue of nationalisation: '*Nationalization, expropriation or requisitioning shall be based on grounds or*

© The Author(s), under exclusive license to Springer Nature
Switzerland AG 2021
A. Imsirovic, *Trading and Price Discovery for Crude Oils*,
https://doi.org/10.1007/978-3-030-71718-6_8

reasons of public utility, security or the national interest which are recognized as overriding purely individual or private interests, both domestic and foreign. In such cases the owner shall be paid appropriate compensation, in accordance with the rules in force in the State taking such measures in the exercise of its sovereignty and in accordance with international law… where the question of compensation gives rise to a controversy, the national jurisdiction of the State taking such measures shall be exhausted. However, upon agreement by sovereign States and other parties concerned, settlement of the dispute should be made through arbitration or international adjudication.[4]

OPEC was also planned to be a vehicle for stabilising and supporting oil prices and maximising oil revenue of its members, by means of restricting output.[5] Its major objective was economic: the overall output of the member states was to be jointly controlled in order to maintain prices above a competitive level. By doing so, the producing country elites would also achieve the goal of consolidating and legitimising their political power. OPEC was originally conceived to become a cartel. Only this time, it was an international cartel of producing nations.

Historically, hardly any cartel has even been perfect. Successful cartels need[6]:

1. Homogenous product, or product to be easily differentiated into a small number of classes.
2. No existing direct substitutes,
3. Concentrated production among few players,
4. Significant barriers to entry, ideally with a commodity reserves concentrated in few geographic regions,
5. A cartel must be able to balance the supply,
6. Legal framework within the member countries must allow for collusion.

In 1960, OPEC did not satisfy points 4, and especially point 5. As we shall see, after 1970, it did satisfy most of the requirements for a successful cartel.[7]

From the perspective of the market power, the 1960s were a period of stalemate[8] between the old oil cartel of oil companies and the aspiring one of the producers. Originally, the oil companies avoided negotiating with OPEC, fearing the anti-trust litigation.[9] The producers continued to depend on the companies in all aspects of the oil business and settled for moderation and negotiation rather than unilateral action. The consuming governments, and the US government in particular, also continued to rely on the oil companies to represent their foreign policy interests.[10] Given the United States was a

large oil producer itself and less affected by higher foreign prices, it could: '...
appease the producing nations, buying popularity with someone else's money.[11']

The 'stalemate' was reinforced by the internal politics in some of the
key producing countries such as Iraq, Iran, Saudi Arabia, and Indonesia.
In 1963, the Iraqi dictator, General Qassim was assassinated and another
one, General Arif took over. In Indonesia, in 1966, General Suharto took
over from Sukarno. In Saudi Arabia, in 1964 the Crown Prince Faisal overthrew his brother King Saud. The Shah of Iran was busy with his 'White
Revolution' as well.[12]

The extent of reforms needed in most of the producing countries was
best illustrated by the fact that Kuwait became independent only in 1961,
Nigeria established its first department of Petroleum resources only in
1963[13] and King Faisal officially abolished slavery in Saudi Arabia only
in 1962.[14] Also, many of them were busy implementing new ideas about
economic development.[15] New ways of thinking about economic development became prominent at the time. Economists and technocrats, Prebisch
and Myrdal (Myrdal won a Nobel in 1974 with von Hayek) rejected the
ideas of neo-classical economics and argued that poor countries, sticking to
their comparative advantage of exporting primary products would stay poor
forever. They argued for developing countries to industrialise as quickly as
possible. Such policies needed massive investments and made oil-producing
countries inclined to negotiate and cooperate rather than wage war with
the oil companies. The leading revolutionaries within OPEC, Perez Alfonso
and Abdullah Al-Tariki were not there for much longer.[16]

As a result, the fourth OPEC conference in Geneva in 1962, passed relatively unambitious resolutions, focusing on higher share of revenues by the
eliminating royalty expensing, marketing allowances and demanding a return
to the earlier, higher posted prices (this demand was soon dropped, given
weak market conditions).[17] Maximising output remained their key objective for oil-producing governments.[18] Throughout the 1960s, the OPEC
acronym was not especially familiar to the reading public (See Fig. 8.1) and
the organisation would remain relatively anonymous in the English speaking
world until 1970.

War, Nationalism, and Ambition

The aims of the organisation became far more focused towards the end of
the decade. Various debates and ideas during this period were given direction
at the Vienna Conference in June 1968. Francisco Parra, who played a key

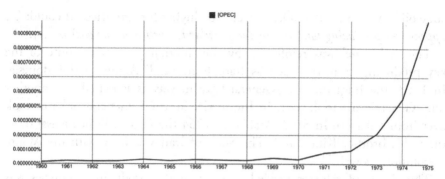

Fig. 8.1 Frequency of OPEC mentioned in English 1960–1975 (Generated by Google Ngram Viewer: '[OPEC]', in English)

role as Secretary General at the Conference, emphasised three (out of nine) agreed principles as presented in The Declaratory Statement of the Petroleum Policy[19]: Each government was to draw detailed plans for implementing the best conservation practices, producers themselves were to establish basis for the posted prices and most importantly, acquire a maximum degree of participation possible from the oil companies, using the argument of 'changing circumstances' (recall Hendryx at the First Arab Petroleum Congress in Cairo in 1958 discussed in Chapter 7). According to Parra: '*The implementation of the principles… would of course transfer control over most key aspects of the concession-holding companies to the governments of the host countries*'.[20] Fadhil Chalabi, described these principles, incorporated in Resolution No. XVI.90[21]: '*… the most influential factor in shaping the future of the oil industry and oil policies… reaffirming the right of the OPEC countries to exercise permanent sovereignty over their hydrocarbon resources… was instrumental in heralding a fundamental change in the oil industry and in oil companies' policies*'.[22]

It is hard to disagree with these comments, especially as the section of the Resolution concerning 'Posted Prices or tax Reference Prices' clearly and explicitly states that setting these were to pass into the domain of the oil producers[23]: '*Such price shall be determined by the Government and shall move in such a manner as to prevent any deterioration in its relationship to the prices of manufactured goods traded internationally… such price shall be consistent, subject to differences in gravity, quality and geographic location, with the levels of posted or tax reference prices generally prevailing for hydrocarbons in other OPEC Countries and accepted by them as a basis for tax payments*'.

It is important to emphasise the section of the article referring to prices '*as a basis for tax payments*'. This was not a direct attempt to control prices at which oil was changing hands in the marketplace. OPEC did not have the means to do so, although the Resolution point regarding '*government … to draw detailed plans for implementing the best conservation practices'* conveyed an intention to use production rationing as a means to controlling prices. The ultimate goal was to stabilise oil revenues. This function was carried out by the companies. They became tax collectors.[24]

The negotiated tax rate, applied to the posted price, plus the cost of production effectively set the floor to oil prices.[25] Since the oil companies simply passed on the cost to the consumer, the price of oil and therefore the price of oil products would increase every time the producers increased the tax rate. In Europe, import and other duties were a large part of the price of the final product. Given the very high domestic prices, any large tax increase by the producing countries, translated in relatively small increase in product prices.[26] So, the consuming countries did not mind modest producer tax increases, as long as the security of supply was guaranteed.

From the tax point of view, the use of posted prices was problematic. As long as the spot market continued to trade below posted prices, all was well for the producers as their tax revenue was protected. The companies passed a higher posted price on to the consumers and calmly carried on producing and 'collecting taxes'. When the spot market started trading above the posted prices, the producers experienced an effective tax cut. This poorly designed system, under the onslaught of genuine post-colonial ambitions, nationalism, rivalry, and war,[27] created a chaotic atmosphere of subsequent declarations, meetings, and agreements, only to be broken months or even days after they were made. Most of the 'horse trading' between the producers and companies were essentially tax revenue negotiations.

The 'Resolution 90' of the June 1968 Conference had another important element: it asked for maximising producer 'participation; The idea of participation goes back to the First Arab Petroleum Congress in Cairo in 1958 (see Chapter 7) as an additional way of increasing revenues of the producing countries. Following the war and the Suez crisis of 1967, there was a strong nationalist rhetoric and demands for nationalisation of foreign assets throughout the region. The Saudi oil minister, Sheik Yamani saw participation as a moderating alternative to nationalisation. This became especially important after the 1968 military coup in Iraq, with Ba'athist radical general Al-Bakr in power. With Saddam Hussein soon a Vice-President, Iraq started own oil production in north Rumaila with Soviet help. The following year another military coup put Colonel Muammar Gaddafi in power in Libya. The same year, Peru nationalised the assets of the International Petroleum Company operating there. In 1971, Venezuela set 1983 as a date for expropriating all concessions in the country.[28]

Revolution

The new Libyan government immediately demanded a large, retroactive increase in posted prices. They picked on the weakest company, Occidental, highly dependent on the country's production for its oil supply. To show the seriousness of their intent, Libya almost halved the company's production quota. Following the closure of the Suez Canal in 1967 and a deliberate Syrian sabotage of the Trans-Arabian pipeline, the Mediterranean market suddenly lost some 800,000 barrels of daily supply.[29] High shipping rates (due to the canal closure and longer voyages for the oil tankers) exacerbated the already tight oil market. Occidental had no choice but to capitulate[30] and, to collect the retroactive funds, the Libyan government increased the tax rate to 55% for all the oil companies. Soon, this tax rate was offered to pretty much all other producers: Iran, Saudi Arabia, Kuwait, Iraq, Nigeria, and the Gulf Sheikdoms. The supposedly equitable, 'fifty-fifty' split in revenues was in tatters. Soon, the Algerians were to go a step further and increase their posted prices unilaterally.

The 1970 OPEC conference in Caracas agreed to a 55% tax rate for all the members but it did not last long as Venezuela soon increased tax to 60%. Early in 1971, Libya unilaterally increased its posted prices further. In a half-hearted effort to try and slow the avalanche of the leap-frogging demands, the US Department of Justice issued 'Business Review' letters, allowing the American companies to negotiate together with OPEC, insulated from the anti-trust legislation.[31] The companies tried to reach a comprehensive, five-year agreement with producers by giving further concessions in Teheran, in February 1970. Even though it included an anti-leap-frogging article, it was soon to be dead in the water, due to further Libyan demands. Almost exactly a year later, another 'comprehensive' agreement was signed in Tripoli, conceding further increases in posted prices. With the US government making it clear the security of supply is the only issue of their concern, the company negotiators were essentially a road-kill; run over time after time, by new demands. By now, even the Saudis had started using threats of nationalisation and shutting production in order to get their demands.[32] As Morris Adelman predicted: '*The crude oil price can go much higher before it reaches the monopoly equilibrium or point of greatest profit*'.[33]

With rising inflation and falls in the value of the dollar,[34] the producers increasingly turned to the goal of protecting their dollar-based revenues (in real terms, oil prices were falling, especially in the late 1960s, (see Fig. 8.2) and seeking increased share in participation. Originally, participation was only a way to collect more tax or increase the government share in the

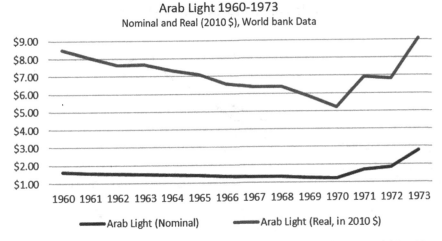

Fig. 8.2 Arab Light Real (in 2010 dollars) and Nominal prices (Data World Bank)

proceeds from the produced oil. The Saudi oil minister always favoured it rather than outright nationalisation, fearing that without the horizontally integrated structure of the oil companies, national oil companies (NOCs) would be selling into a void, causing a price collapse.[35] However, the rising prices undermined the argument for participation. The calls for nationalisation as the only way to master their own resources by the 'progressive' OPEC members such as Libya, Algeria, and Iraq were getting louder.

Participation meant the oil continued to be produced by oil companies, but the government share of the 'participating oil' was normally sold back to the companies. With rising spot prices, the price of this 'buy-back' oil also became contentious. Since posted prices were only a formal, bilateral way of setting tax take between the companies and governments, they were meaningless in terms of the 'market value' of oil. The higher the spot market went, the higher the producer demands were. Early 1970s were a sellers' market for oil. The producing government realised that, in such a market, they could easily sell their own oil, without the help of the companies. Buyers were knocking on their doors, especially targeting this 'government' oil, seen as more secure under the prevailing political climate.

Soon, some of these issues fell by the wayside as well. Revolutionary Algeria nationalised the oil industry in 1971. In January 1972 in Geneva, the company negotiators agreed to OPEC demand to link the posted prices to the price of gold, but Libya then rejected it. By the end of the year, Libya nationalised BP assets in the country.[36] Soon, it also decreed 51% government participation to all the other companies. In June of the following year, Iraq nationalised the IPC.[37] In October 1973, Arab–Israeli war started.

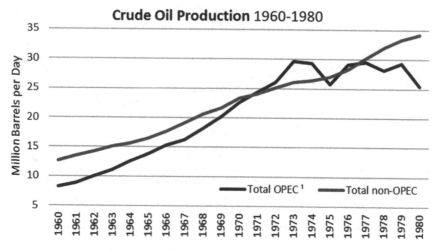

Fig. 8.3 World Crude Oil Production 1960–2009 (Data from EIA—Energy Information Administration)

The war caught the consuming countries off guard. Europe and Japan were highly dependent on the Middle east supplies and OPEC supplies began to dominate the global market (see Fig. 8.3).

While the US produced well over 10 million barrels a day (mbd) in 1973, it also imported almost 6 mbd.[38] American production was falling, and excess capacity soon disappeared. In case of a major supply disruption, it was in no position to help its allies. Behind a wall of protectionism, the American oil prices decoupled from the rest of the world (see Fig. 8.4). The US policies of conservation, import, and pricing had a significant impact on the country's production and the global market as a whole and need to be explained in more detail.

Oil Production and Price Regulation in the United States

In Chapter 7, we discussed the early 'Peak Oil' theories, which emerged in the 1920s. They encouraged the 'conservation' movement and more government intervention in the industry. Following the Great Depression of 1929 and subsequent collapse in demand in prices, these voices grew louder, with a real intent to prevent competition and protect producers by supporting prices. In 1935, the major producing states developed a system of market demand rationing and signed the 'Interstate Oil Compact'[39] to conserve oil and gas. Under this agreement, they were permitted to produce only a specified

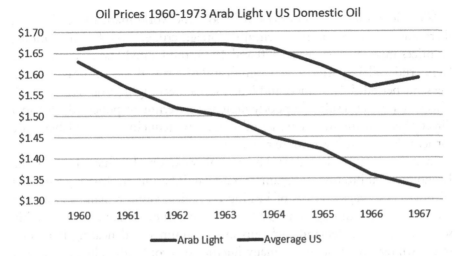

Fig. 8.4 US Domestic and Middle East oil prices

percentage of 'basic maximum allowables', which was an estimated maximum efficient rate of production. However, artificially high domestic prices soon faced growing cheap foreign imports and to protect the domestic industry, in 1959, President Eisenhower established the Mandatory Import Program.[40] The programme set volumetric limits on the crude oil and product imports, decoupling the local oil prices from the international markets.

However, in 1970, the United States production peaked anyway and two years later, the conservation agencies of the producing states set the 'allowables at 100 per cent. The United States had no longer any spare oil capacity. Between 1956 and 1967, domestic reserves hardly changed and the reserves to production ratio fell significantly. Most importantly, drilling activity fell by over 40 per cent.[41] Instead of addressing the legal and institutional problem of the 'rule of capture' which did result in waste,[42] indiscriminate rationing of oil production across all the wells protected small and inefficient ones, at the expense of large and efficient wells, significantly increasing production costs for the same level of output: '... *incentives to find and develop new oil fields have been reduced by market demand prorationing, the process which generates new prospects has been drastically curtailed... The combined effect of reduced drilling, lower success ratios and lower average discovery sizes has been to reduce total U.S. discoveries.*'[43] Such a bizarre incentive system could only survive with additional government intervention in the form of import quotas. The fact that the country's excess capacity disappeared was, in a perverse way, a success of the rationing system, precisely designed to do so.[44]

With domestic wellhead prices well above the world market (see Fig. 8.4), there was a pressure to import cheaper, foreign crude.[45] As the international oil prices increased between 1970 and 1973, the United States was the only large crude oil importer which significantly increased net imports. During the same period, UK, France, and Japan saw a meaningful drop in imports.[46] This was a direct result of a poorly designed government policy which had a direct effect on the international oil market by reducing the available spare capacity. Sadly, there was more to come.

In August 1971, President Nixon embarked on the first phase of the Economic Stabilization Program to combat inflation by freezing virtually all prices and wages. Prices of heating oil and gasoline remained frozen at mid-1971 levels throughout 1972. Given that these products were highly seasonal (gasoline demand picks up in the summer and heating is needed in the winter), their prices normally fluctuated accordingly. The price freeze, however, removed the incentive for refiners to produce additional volumes of products, and shortages began to develop.

In the next phase of the Program, a Price Commission was established, tasked with regulating prices. In phase three, the Price Commission was abolished, and the Cost of Living Council was expanded to administer the Program. There was an immediate and large increase in prices[47] and this phase was terminated in June 1973 and replaced with a sixty-day price freeze.[48] With rising global crude oil prices, and an inability to pass the higher costs onto consumers, the refiners were discouraged from importing additional crude, contributing to the existing product shortages.

In December 1975, President Ford signed the Energy Policy and Conservation Act,[49] so dense that it was termed '99-page filibuster'.[50] The key provision of the act is a separation of the United States production into 'old' oil (oil produced at or below the average monthly volume of September to November 1975) and 'new' oil (oil produced in all new wells as well as the additional production from the old wells).[51] This policy seriously discouraged production of 'new' oil and the total domestic production declined from 9.2 mbd in 1973 to 8.3 mbd in 1975.

Europe and Japan were not much better. Indigenous and high-cost coal industry was under a severe attack from cheap oil. In the UK, in just five years, between 1967 and 1972, the share of coal in the energy use fell from 59 to 40%, while the share of oil increased from 39 to 46%.[52] The governments were trying to dampen the social impact of this transition through imposition of subsidies and import taxes and supporting the national champions of the oil industry.[53]

In conclusion, energy policies of the key consuming nations significantly distorted price signals giving wrong incentives to both domestic producers and consumers, exacerbating the perception of shortage of oil.

The Takeover

It is impossible to disentangle oil from politics and the war of 1973 accelerated the events which were already under way. On October 16th, at a meeting in Kuwait, OPEC unilaterally increased the government take on the main Saudi grade, Arab Light, essentially setting a higher posted price for the grade and proclaiming that the organisation would be the sole arbiter of prices.[54] The arduous process of price negotiations with companies was finished. OPEC took over the responsibility of administering oil prices. But did they have the ability to become the price-makers?

With the United States support for Israel, the pressure among Arab producers was growing to use oil as a political weapon. Two weeks following the Kuwait meeting, the Arab states announced escalating production cuts and divided countries into 'preferred', 'neutral' and 'embargoed'. The United States and Netherlands were embargoed.[55] The complex operation of rationing was left to the Aramco partners[56] and they complied.[57] Under the threat of nationalisation, the four oil companies embargoing their own country.[58] While the production cuts[59] and higher prices were very real, the embargo soon proved to be unworkable. Being a relative homogeneous commodity, oil was relatively easy to swap and substitute for oil from a different source. The embargo lasted less than six months. It almost certainly caused huge operational problems in terms of shipping and deliveries, but the real impact was on the market sentiment. The consuming nations were frightened.[60]

On the other hand, producers were not just high on confidence, but also awash with oil revenues,[61] enabling them to 'conserve' production if they so wished, but also to acquire the operating company assets. In January, Kuwait followed the Libyan example and acquired 60% of Kuwait Oil Company at 'net book' value. Abu Dhabi and Qatar followed, and, by the end of 1974, the Saudis agreed, in principle, a 100% takeover of Aramco.

While OPEC effectively took control of the posted prices for oil, without the help of oil companies, it had no mechanism for rationing production to balance the market. There was no liquid, organised, and transparent spot market for oil yet. Arab Light grade of crude oil[62] sold by Saudi Arabia and well accepted by most refiners around the world became the reference point or benchmark for all the other grades of oil (see a close relationship with similar quality crudes, Iranian Light, and Iraqi export grade in Fig. 8.5). All the other grades of oil with different qualities would adjust their prices to the agreed Arab Light posting, by applying quality differentials, reflecting their relative refining value.

OPEC had no clear rules and mechanisms for setting the posted prices and quality differentials[63] and squabbles were a norm. To resolve these problems, in 1978, OPEC set up a Ministerial Long Term Strategy Committee as well as a Committee of Experts, headed by the Saudi Oil Minister Yamani.[64] OPEC might have been started setting the posted prices, but they had to learn how to do it. They were 'making' (posted) prices, but they were not 'price makers' yet.

In the meantime, as long as the oil demand grew and market remained tight, everything was fine. OPEC could simply continue increasing prices to the levels markets would bear. Around the same time, most producers were beginning to worry about how long their oil would last. Among them, an accepted narrative was that oil was way too cheap; it was being wasted by burning and would not last very long. Therefore, the price of oil can only go up and it should be conserved. This generally accepted view needs further explanation.

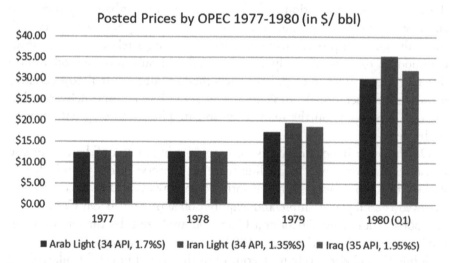

Fig. 8.5 Selected Posted Prices by OPEC (Data from the CIA International Energy Statistics Review [1980])

Peak Oil (Again) and Record High Prices

In 1970s, fears regarding a general resource depletion, re-emerged.[65] In 1972, a hugely influential study, 'The Limits to Growth' was published and argued: *''The earth's crust contains vast amounts of those raw materials which man has learned to mine and to transform into useful things. However vast those amounts may be, they are not infinite. Now that we have seen how suddenly an exponentially growing quantity approaches a fixed upper limit, the following statement should not come as a surprise. Given present resource consumption rates and the projected increase in these rates, the great majority of the current important non-renewable resources will be extremely costly 100 years from now'.*[66]

In spite of some sensible voices warning about the fallacy of this idea of scarcity,[67] the took hold in pretty much all social circles, the most important being the policy makers both in producing and consuming countries (see Fig. 8.6). Robin Mills drew a great parallel about this recurring[68] 'resource scarcity' paranoia: *'... consider... a leading economist, supported by even more famous colleague, has proposed that the energy supply of the greatest country in the world is in imminent decline... He predicts a future of energy deficits, industrial collapse, and national decay. His ideas are taken seriously enough to induce the country's leader to reduce the national budget accordingly. The date was 1865, the economist was William Jevons, and his supporter was political thinker, John Stuart Mill, the nation was Britain, the leader was renowned Prime Minister William Gladstone, and the fuel was coal'.*[69] The idea took hold within OPEC was that oil was finite, it would soon run dry, and should not be sold off too cheaply. It was wrong.

As a result, most producing countries[70] started setting ceilings on their production in this period. Most importantly, Saudi Arabia instructed Aramco to set a ceiling of 8.5 million barrels a day (mbd) for a number of years.[71] The

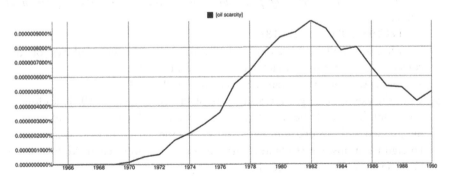

Fig. 8.6 'Oil scarcity' mentioned in British English press (between 1965 and 1990) in Ngram Viewer, Google

mix of this prevailing mind-set, the Iranian revolution of 1979 (temporarily halting the country's oil production) had a predictable effect: panic[72] and sky-rocketing prices (see Fig. 8.5).

The events took producers completely by surprise, as Parra explains: '... *OPEC had been transformed from a loose confederation of price administrators into a confused and divided cartel of production restrictions*'.[73] In spite of the agreed posted prices, some producers raised them again unilaterally.[74] In this respect, there was little organisation or unity. It could only be called greed. But the market was going only one way-up. OPEC was not controlling the market, it was riding it.

Coupled with the ill-imposed production ceilings, the sudden loss of the Iranian barrels (some 5 mbd between October 1978 and January 1979[75]) forced a number of companies, who were now effectively only just third-party buyers, to look for lost barrels elsewhere. They rushed into the spot market. The rising sport market was a bonanza for the cartel. But it was a party that would bring a major hangover.

Notes

1. Arab delegation was particularly well represented at the conference, including the Saudi Price Faisal and Egypt's President Gamel Abdel Nasser.
2. The Final Communiqué of the Asian-African Conference, Economic cooperation, section A.
3. UN General Assembly resolution 1803 (XVII) of, "Permanent sovereignty over natural resources", 14 December 1962, p. 1.
4. Ibid., p. 2.
5. As discussed in Chapter 7, the Article I.3 of the September 1960 Baghdad agreement explicitly states: '*That Members shall study and formulate a system to ensure the stabilisation of prices by, among other means, the regulation of production...*'.
6. See LeClair (2000, pp. 16–18).
7. Growing demand and geopolitical factors helped a lot. Policies of the consuming nations were a factor too as we shall discuss.
8. There was still plenty of drama. See Garavini (2019, Ch. 3).
9. Until the exemption by the US ministry of Justice in January 1971, leading to the establishment of the 'London Policy Group' or 'London Club' of companies, tasked with negotiations with OPEC. See the Report to the Committee of Foreign Relations, United States Senate by the Subcommittee on Multinational Corporations (1975, pp. 128–129).
10. '*The system managed by the American multinational corporations was successful in carrying out American foreign policy during the 1950s and 1960s.*' Report to the

Committee of Foreign Relations, United States Senate by the Subcommittee on Multinational Corporations (1975), p. 121.

11. Adelman M. A. (1973, p. 89).

12. Possibly just a 'myth' legitimising Shah Reza's monarchy. See Ansari (2001, p. 2).

13. Nigerian government did not have a single map of all granted concessions! Ibid., p. 168.

14. For a good overview, see Garavini (2019, pp. 131–144).

15. See Puntigliano and Appelqvist (2011, p. 43).

16. Both remained revolutionaries at heart. King Faisal replaced Tariki with much more moderate Ahmed Zaki Yamani in 1962. The 'red sheik', as Tariki was often referred to, remained vocal with his extreme views and had a major influence (as an official advisor) of the Algerian and Libyan government views. Alfonzo left Venezuela in 1966 and wrote a fair bit on oil policy, development, conservation and environment.

17. Royalty expensing' was inclusion of the 12.5% royalty payment withing the 50/50 profit sharing arrangement (where it was meaningless, being simply lumped in the 50%). Marketing allowances were tax deductible, and this was ended, boosting the tax return. See Garavini (2019, p. 133).

18. In 1968, The Shah of Iran was pressing the companies hard to install a production capacity of 5 mbd in his country. Report to the Committee of Foreign Relations, United States Senate by the Subcommittee on Multinational Corporations (1975, p. 116).

19. Parra (2004, p. 111).

20. Ibid., p. 112.

21. OPEC Secretariat (2012, p. 8).

22. Chalabi (2010, pp. 45, 46, 47).

23. OPEC (1968, p. 1184).

24. '*Most precise of all was Sir Eric Drake, the chairman of BP, who called the companies a "tax collectingagency," for both producing and consuming country governments.*' Adelman (1973, p. 79).

25. '*The producing nations cannot fix prices without using the multinational companies. All price-fixing cartels must either control out-put or detect and prevent individual price reductions, which would erode the price down toward the competitive level. The OPEC tax system accomplishes this simply and efficiently. Every important OPEC nation publishes its taxes per barrel; they are a public record, impossible to falsify much. Outright suppression would be a confession of cheating. Once the taxes are set by concerted company-government action, the price floor of taxes-plus-cost is safe, and the floor can be jacked up from time to time, as in early 1971, or early 1972, or by "participation."* Ibid., p. 87.

26. '*The average price in Europe of a barrel of oil products in 1969-70 was about $13 per barrel... If the new tax rates were doubled, say from $1.50 to $3 per barrel at the Persian Gulf, a straight pass-through into product prices would be an increase of only 10-14 percent*'. Ibid., p. 86.

27. The political fever of the period peaked in the Six Day War of the 1967, when Egypt, Syria and Jordan suffered a comprehensive defeat to Israel, causing the closure of the Suez Canal which was to last to 1975 with consequences for the oil market (discussed later in the chapter). The war and its aftermath raised the political profile and role of Saudi Arabia.
28. Garavini (2019, pp. 181–186).
29. Report to the Committee of Foreign Relations, United States Senate by the Subcommittee on Multinational Corporations (1975, pp. 121–122). Most of the historical narrative for this period uses this excellent source.
30. Occidental asked both the US government and other majors for help but got none. Director of fuels and energy at the U.S. State Department, James Akins thought that the Libyan demands were reasonable. Ibid., 124.
31. The US Secretary of State and his deputy, James Irwin essentially went along with the producers and particularly the Shah of Iran. Ibid., pp. 130–131.
32. A threat by Prince Saud and Sheik Yamani, Ibid., p. 138.
33. Adelman M. A. (1973, p. 86).
34. In August 1971, the Nixon administration ended the dollar convertibility.
35. Ibid., p. 88.
36. 'On December 7, 1971, the Government of Libya announced on the Tripoli radio that it had nationalized the assets of the British Petroleum Exploration (Libya) Ltd. in retaliation for Great Britain's failure to prevent Iranian occupation of Arab islands in the Persian Gulf.' Winthrop (1972, p. 541). The completion took roughly another year.
37. For a personal account of the event, see Chalabi (2010, pp. 92, 93).
38. Data from CIA (1980, p. 9).
39. DOE/EIA (1980, p. 1).
40. Before that, a voluntary programme was in place.
41. The ratio fell from 12.1 to 10.1. and reserves stayed just over 30 billion barrels. See Erickson (1970, pp. 28, 30, 32).
42. For a discussion on the 'rule of capture', see Adelman M. A. (1972, p. 43).
43. Ibid., pp. 33, 39,41. Erickson argues that, in the economics speak, the policies shifted the oil supply curve to the left.
44. The rationing system was originally designed to reduce the excess supply of oil and support prices.
45. An earlier study by McKie and McDonald (1962) concludes: '*Until recently, the relatively high prices which encouraged "conservation" of marginal oil in known deposits also encouraged discovery of new deposits. In the last few years, the growth of imports and the increasing cut-backs of production in relatively new domestic pools have combined to discourage new exploration.*'
46. Between 1973 and 1977 US net imports increased from 6.02 to 8.56 mbd, Japanese net imports fell from 5.55 to 5.44 mbd; French from 2.60 to 2.22; Italian from 2.09 to 1.94 and the UK imports fell from 2.34 to 1.09 mbd, respectively. CIA (1980, pp. 9, 10).

47. The increase was especially large for heating oil, just as it was used most. The reason was that January price increases permitted the industry to pass on cost increases that had accumulated in the previous 17 months. See DOE/EIA (1980, pp. 2–4).
48. In the same year, import quotas were replaced with tariffs.
49. https://www.iea.org/policies/7402-act-11245-the-energy-efficiency-and-conser vation-act.
50. Blair (1976, p. 355).
51. This is simplified. Various additions, limitations and allowances can apply.
52. Using figures from Odell (1986, pp. 120–121). Odell covers Europe in Ch. 6 and Japan in Ch. 8 of this excellent book.
53. Ibid., p. 144.
54. See Garavini (2019, p. 203).
55. Report to the Committee of Foreign Relations, United States Senate by the Subcommittee on Multinational Corporations (1975, p. 145).
56. A reminder that the US majors, partners in Aramco were: Standard Oil of New Jersey (Exxon), Socony Vacuum (Mobil), w Standard California or SoCal (Chevron) and Texaco (later 'merged' but in reality, taken over or by Chevron).
57. Aramco actually welcomed the cutback as they were struggling with technical problems of increasing the capacity at the time. Ibid., pp. 163–165.
58. Their argument was that outright nationalisation would be even worse both for them and the country.
59. A good analyses of the cuts and price increases is in Adelman (1955, p. 109).
60. Ibid., p. 113. One of the consequences of the 1973 events was the creation of the International Energy Agency in November 1974: 'with a broad mandate on energy security and energy policy cooperation. This included setting up a collective action mechanism to respond effectively to potential disruptions in oil supply. The framework was anchored in the IEA treaty called the "Agreement on an International Energy Program," with newly created autonomous Agency hosted at the OECD in Paris.' https://www.iea.org/about/historyAnother one was the creation of the Strategic Petroleum Reserve, included in the Energy Policy and Conservation Act signed by President Ford in 1975. https://www.energy.gov/articles/history-strategic-petroleum-reserve.
61. The value of oil imports to the US alone increased from $8.5 to $25.2 billion, in only one year, from 1973 to 1974. For the other major importers, it increased from $21.1 to $74.8 in the same period. Ibid., p. 151.
62. About 34 API and 1.7% sulphur.
63. Different grades of oil yield different shares and qualities of refined products. As the product prices fluctuate over time and seasons, differentials between different crudes change as well.
64. Parra (2004, p. 216).
65. It was discussed briefly in Chapter 6, in the context of growing demand in 1920s.
66. Meadows (1972, p. 66).

67. Probably the most eloquent explanation was written (published much later, following earlier writings by M. Adelman) by Adelman and Lynch (1995), p. 2: *These estimates of declining reserves and production are incurably wrong because they treat as a quantity what is really a dynamic process driven by growing knowledge. To know the limit to oil reserves and output, we must first predict future earth science and technology. This is impossible. Repeated attempts to do it have generated repeated bad estimates.*

68. As Adelman and Lynch say: 'A "repeating surprise" should be an oxymoron.' Ibid., p. 2.

69. Mills (2008, p. 2).

70. Venezuela, Kuwait, Iran, Abu Dhabi, and Saudi Arabia.

71. Parra (2004, p. 217).

72. An interesting, field of research in economics is 'Narrative Economics' with the Nobel Prize winner, Robert J. Shiller as one of the proponents. Following the research in psychology by Tversky and Kahneman, he elaborates it some detail in Shiller (2019, pp. 66–67). Further, a great illustration of how these experiences are spread using social networks are explained in a bestseller 'Connected'—see Christakis (2011, pp. 37–44).

73. Parra (2004, p. 220).

74. Kuwait, Abu Dhabi, Qatar, and Libya, all in February 1979.

75. Production recovered relatively quickly and in April 1979, it was over 4 mbd. From Adelman (1995, p. 170).

References

Adelman M.A. (1955): 'Concept and Statistical Measurement of Vertical Integration', in *Business Concentration and Public Policy*, Princeton University Press for National Bureau of Economic Research, Princeton.

Adelman M.A. (1972): *The World Petroleum Market*, The Johns Hopkins University Press.

Adelman M.A. (1973): 'Is the Oil Shortage Real? Oil Companies as OPEC Tax-Collectors', *Foreign Policy*, No. 9 (Winter, 1972–1973), pp. 69–107.

Adelman M.A. (1995): *The Genie Out of the Bottle, World Oil Since 1970*, The MIT Press.

Adelman, M.A. and Lynch, M.C. (1995): 'Fixed View of Resource Limits', *Oil & Gas Journal*, April 7, 1997.

Ansari AM (2001): 'The Myth of the White Revolution: Mohammad Reza Shah, 'Modernization' and the Consolidation of Power', *Middle Eastern Studies Journal*, Vol. 37, No. 3 (July), pp. 1–24.

Blair J.M. (1976): *The Control of Oil*, Pantheon Books, New York.

Chalabi F.J. (2010): *Oil Policies, Oil Myths*, I.B. Tauris & Co. Ltd. London.

Christakis F. (2011): *Connected*, Harper Press.

CIA (1980): *International Energy Statistical Review*, National Foreign Assessment Centre, November 25, 1980.

DOE/EIA (1980): *Price Controls - and International Petroleum Product Prices*, February.

Erickson E.W. (1970): 'Crude Oil Prices, Drilling Incentives and the Supply of New Discoveries', *Natural Resource Journal*, Vol. 10, No. 1 (Winter).

Garavini G. (2019): *The Rise and Fall of OPEC in the Twentieth Century*, Oxford University Press.

LeClair, M.S. (2000): *International Commodity Markets and the Role of Cartels*, 2015 Edition, Routledge, New York, NY.

McKie J.W. and McDonald S.L. (1962): 'Petroleum Conservation in Theory and Practice', *The Quarterly Journal of Economics*, Vol. 76, No. 1 (February), pp. 98–121.

Meadows D.H., et. al. (1972): *The Limits to Growth, A Report for the Club of Rome Project on the Predicament of Mankind*, A Potomac Associates Book.

Mills M.R. (2008): *The Myth of the Oil Crisis*, Praeger Publishers.

Odell R.P. (1986): *Oil and World Power*, Penguin Books.

OPEC Secretariat (2012): *General Information*, Organization of the Petroleum Exporting Countries, https://www.opec.org/opec_web/static_files_project/media/downloads/publications/GenInfo.pdf.

OPEC (1968): 'Guidelines for Petroleum Policy in Member Countries', *International Legal Materials*, Vol. 7, No. 5 (September), pp. 1183–1186, Cambridge University Press.

Para F. (2004): *Oil Politics, A Modern History of Petroleum*, I.B. Taurus Co. Ltd.

Puntigliano A.R. and Appelqvist O. (2011): Prebisch and Myrdal: Development Economics in the Core and on the Periphery, *Journal of Global History*, Vol. 6, pp. 29–52, London School of Economics and Political Science.

Report to the Committee of Foreign Relations, United States Senate by the Subcommittee on Multinational Corporations (1975): *Multinational Oil Corporations and the US Foreign Policy*, January 2, US Government Printing Office, Washington.

Shiller R. (2019): *Narrative Economics*, Princeton University Press.

Winthrop, G.H. (1972). Libyan Nationalization of British Petroleum Company Assets', *The International Lawyer*, Vol. 6, No. 3 (July 1972), pp. 541–547, American Bar Association.

9

The Producers' Cartel

OPEC Legacy

For over half a century, OPEC has been an important factor in the oil markets.[1] The initial goals set at the fringes of the First Arab Petroleum Congress in Cairo in 1958, in the 'Maadi agreement'[2] might have taken a good decade to reach, but by the end of the 1970s, the organisation was in charge of its own resources, output and prices. The pivotal, 1970 Tehran and 1971 Tripoli agreements[3] put OPEC in the driving seat and exposed the weakness of divided and competing oil companies.

The founding fathers of the organisation, Venezuelan oil minister, Perez Alfonso, and the Saudi minister Al-Tariki, were very clear in their intentions to create a new cartel, explicitly stating in the 1960, founding document: *'That Members shall study and formulate a system to ensure the stabilisation of prices by, among other means, the regulation of production...'.*[4] This proposal was only taken seriously in 1978, when OPEC set up a Ministerial Long Term Strategy Committee as well as a Committee of Experts, headed by the Saudi Oil Minister Yamani to study the problem. It took two years to prepare a Draft Declaration of Long-Term Policies for the 1980 Baghdad conference when the events around the Iran–Iraq war made it fall by the wayside.[5]

In the meantime, OPEC managed to put an end to the price declines of the 1960s, helped by growing energy demand and shambolic policies of the major consuming countries. Production and price controls in the United States did nothing to dampen the growing demand, and significantly reduced the incentives for the domestic industry to be efficient, competitive, and to grow.[6]

© The Author(s), under exclusive license to Springer Nature Switzerland AG 2021

A. Imsirovic, *Trading and Price Discovery for Crude Oils*, https://doi.org/10.1007/978-3-030-71718-6_9

Virtually all of the developed, consuming nations had policies designed to protect domestic energy industries, particularly coal and nuclear, so they did not see high oil prices as necessarily undesirable. During the 'Kissinger years',[7] high oil prices were seen as a way to beef up the military strength of the Gulf countries,[8] to act as a buffer against the Communist expansion, without the need for Congressional approvals.

The literature on the role of OPEC in the oil markets is vast. One point that most informed observers generally agree on is that OPEC evolved, following different strategies at different times.[9] The organisation is a collection of many, very diverse, independent states. As the circumstances changed, so did the organisation. It is precisely this evolving nature that ensured its survival for over 60 years.

Economic Models of OPEC Behaviour

In the 1970s, OPEC may have followed a 'Target Revenue Model'.[10] The idea is simply that the producers adjusted their output in line with their national budgetary needs. Even though it is still frequently used as a 'rule of thumb' in working out a price of oil which the individual members require to balance their books, the model does not seem to fit the data well for the subsequent periods.[11] In the first half of the 1980s, OPEC did behave as a cartel, setting production quotas in 1982. However, cartels are rather unstable structures,[12] subject to cheating by its members. It was Saudi Arabia, taking a role of a leader and a 'swing producer' that generally resolved this problem. As we shall see, this role was untenable in the long run, and the kingdom soon officially rejected it. However, the kingdom remained an undisputed leader of the organisation, using its excess production capacity to discipline other producers and balance the market.

Perhaps the most flexible, generic model of OPEC behaviour is the 'Limit Pricing Model'.[13] It focuses on the impact of demand changes on a cartel that follows a profit-maximisation strategy,[14] allowing for some high cost, fringe producers to co-exist while maintaining the price well above a competitive level. In a defensive mode of this model, higher cost producers are kept at bay using the cartel's excess capacity as a threat. If the fringe producers grow their market share to the extent that price stability is compromised, the cartel uses an offensive strategy and declares a price war. Given its low production cost, the cartel can force the price below competitors' cost of production, driving them out of the market. This model fits well with the events after

2014, especially during the demand shock of 2020 and we shall revert to it later.

Panic of 1979: Everything that Could Go Wrong, Went Wrong

Having taken over the control of its resources and achieving higher revenues, OPEC lacked any long-term strategy. In the late 1970s, its members unilaterally implemented various conservation measures, reducing their output. At the same time, the price controls in the United States discouraged domestic exploration and production, fuelling demand and imports. In 1972, the United States imported 29% of its oil consumption. In 1978, this grew to 43%.[15] The US excess production capacity disappeared. Oil consumers were increasingly dependent on the Middle East supplies.

In January 1979, the unpopular Shah of Iran left the country, leaving the Ayatollah Khomeini to fill in the political power vacuum and sparking a revolution. Overnight, the world lost five million barrels a day (mbd) of oil supplies. Even though exports resumed in March that year, it was less than half of the usual country's production. At the same time, Saudi Arabia cut its output from 10.5 to 9.5 mbd and then further, to 8.5 mbd from April through June. While this might have been part of a long-term conservation programme, it did not help.

In August that year, Nigeria nationalised the assets of British Petroleum (BP). A couple of months later, Libya announced a reduction of volumes for the contractual term customers, preferring to give them to other, state, and national oil companies. Algeria cut its term contracts by 20%. Abu Dhabi and Venezuela also reduced their term volumes. What is more, Saudi Arabia, Kuwait, Indonesia, Venezuela, Libya, Abu Dhabi, Algeria, Iraq, and the United Kingdom announced planned reductions in output and exports for the following year.[16] If OPEC wanted to be a reliable steward of the international oil market, it did not show it.[17]

In June 1979, the United States and six other major consuming countries met in Tokyo to address the situation. Their agreement was to avoid trading in the spot market in order to moderate prices. This was short-sighted advice for two reasons. Firstly, oil companies were entering into the spot arrangements because they had no choice. Secondly, avoiding spot trading resulted in lower imports (about 200,000 barrels a day in the case of the United States), creating domestic product shortages. The US government did halt purchases of oil for the Strategic Petroleum Reserve (SPR) but did not make any oil available from the reserve to prevent shortages.[18] Department of Energy (DOE) did offer 127,465 barrels a day of crude oil from the Elk Hills Naval Petroleum Reserve, later in the year. But this small volume made things only worse. The highest bid was $41 a barrel,[19] which gave OPEC further justification to increase official prices. The US government halted purchases of oil originating from Iran which made it even harder for the US importers to source oil in a tight market.[20] What followed was an atmosphere of supply insecurity[21] and even panic.[22]

Broken System and the Growth of the Spot Market

The new regime in Iran was the first to cancel all contracts with the US and European consortium members, but it was soon followed by Qatar and Dubai. Having lost the oil, the members of the consortium[23] were forced to cancel their contractual deliveries to third parties, driving buyers to the spot market.[24] Tightly controlled, vertically integrated structure controlled by oil companies was broken. Well-rehearsed, smooth operation and scheduling of oil deliveries by the majors was in tatters. Discrepancies between nomination dates, quantities, types, and location of crude oil purchased by refiners became an issue. To remedy these problems, long-term contract holders had to swaps and trade different types of oil among themselves.

Even though Iran's production picked up again, the new regime announced a production rationing programme.[25] The spot price kept rising, reaching almost $40 by the end of the year.[26] The official prices were slow to adjust and the Saudi price benchmark, Arab Light, officially reached only $22 a barrel, in the last quarter of the year.[27] For Aramco partners with preferential access to Saudi oil at official prices, it was a bonanza. A two-tier official price system developed, with little regard for market prices or their relative refining values. Greed came before any agreements. In May 1980, the Government Selling Price (GSP) for Arab Light, was $28 a barrel. At the same time, GSP for Iranian Light crude of similar quality was $35.37. High-quality Nigerian oil had a GSP of $35.29 a barrel.[28]

The panic caused by the events, and possibly more by OPEC's general attitude, resulted in a large build-up of oil storage, in anticipation of shortages.[29] In the absence of large and liquid futures markets, the only way to ensure future supply was by building physical stocks. This further exacerbated the shortage.[30]

Selling oil 'spot' was a way to achieve higher prices and even though OPEC members agreed in June 1979 to limit spot sales, high spot prices often proved to be too tempting. While Saudi Arabia, Venezuela, and Algeria refused to participate in the spot market, Iraq, Libya, and Nigeria used it frequently and Iran even used it exclusively for a while.[31] Among some OPEC members, market prices were cited as a reason to increase the official prices.[32] Ecuador even linked their long-term contracts to spot prices. Non-OPEC Peru did the same. The market took the lead, and OPEC was following.

With producers turning to the spot market, traders also gained access to oil. Traditionally, with limited access to the international crude oil supplies, traders were mainly involved in transacting petroleum products.[33] The United States was an exception where a number of very small oil trading companies sprang up as a means of circumventing the price controls.[34] Some of those traders, such as the infamous Mark Rich, grabbed the opportunity and allegedly built an empire trading sanctioned Iranian oil.[35] While officially hostile to the spot markets,[36] some OPEC members effectively facilitated its creation. In a remarkably short time, the share of spot trades rocketed, from less than five percent, prior to January 1979, to about a quarter, by November of the very same year.

Having broken the monopoly of the major oil companies and their integrated supply chains, OPEC did not substitute them with an alternative. The state of the organization in this period is best summarised by Parra:' ... *OPEC had been transformed from a loose confederation of price administrators into a confused and divided cartel of production restrictions*'.[37] But this was a confused cartel in a fundamentally strong market. A real test for OPEC was still to come.

More Trouble

Nationalisation of the oil industry in the producing countries in the turbulent years of the 1970s and the subsequent events had another, serious downside, which the experienced and moderate voices within OPEC understood very well at the time. As Chalabi put it: '... *the state takeover of the industry would sever the relationship between the host countries and IOCs, a severance that only served to motivate the IOCs into investing in new high-cost areas outside OPEC.*[38]' Faced with uncertainty, companies were already shifting their investment to politically less volatile oil regions in the 1960s. This resulted in large, but expensive to produce finds in Prudhoe Bay on Alaska's North Slope in 1967 and Ekofisk field in the Norwegian sector of the North Sea, in 1969.

Later, these and other new finds would have major consequences for stability OPEC.

In the second half of 1979, under political pressure from the United States, Saudi Arabia increased production to 9.5 mbd. At the same time, high prices and consuming government measures to reduce consumption dented demand. In the OECD area, demand fell from 41.8 mbd in 1979 to 38.5 mbd in just one year.[39] Early in 1980, the markets started to calm down and some cargoes even became 'distressed'[40] and traded below the official prices.[41]

The 1979 oil crises was followed by another shock. Iraq invaded Iran at the end of 1980, and prices spiked again over $40. This time, the demand was already severely damaged by earlier high prices. Between 1979 and 1982, the United States and Japanese demand alone fell by over 4 mbd[42] (See Fig. 9.1). This time, the OPEC members opened up the taps to cash in at these historically high prices. They were getting used to them. At a meeting in Qatar, in March 1982, Saudi Oil Minister Yamani expressed commitment to the government selling price of $34 a barrel.[43] To defend this price, in an environment of falling demand, OPEC had to cut production. Indeed, in the same year, at the conference in Vienna, the cartel agreed on a ceiling (so-called 'total allowable production'[44]) to be 17.5 mbd. Also, they agreed on maximum production quotas, allocated for each individual country.[45] For the first time ever, OPEC was trying to function as an efficient cartel.

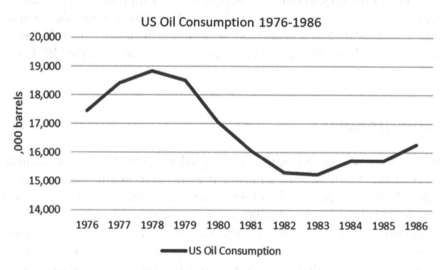

Fig. 9.1 US Oil consumption (thousand barrels a day) (*Source* CIA Energy Statistics Review [1987])

Even though the Long Term Strategy Committee was revived, the cartel had no long-term rationing plan. In particular, there was no agreed mechanism or formula to adjust the quotas in line with demand changes. Between 1981 and 1983, Iran's production was recovering and increased by over 2 mbd,[46] while the global oil demand fell by about the same amount.[47] Most member countries could not sell the barrels at their official prices and soon started selling at discounts to GSPs.[48]

North Sea production was also creeping up.[49] Sweet, high-quality North Sea barrels competed in Europe directly with the Nigerian grades of oil, and when the British National Oil Corporation (BNOC) dropped its selling price by $3 a barrel, Nigeria responded by an even greater cut of $5.5 a barrel. In a weak and falling market environment, OPEC prices were lagging behind the market. Only this time, they were struggling to sell the oil. At the same time, Britain, Norway, Mexico, USSR, and others would sell their oil at prices at which the markets would clear,[50] effectively setting the 'free market' price. Unable to control its exports, OPEC could not defend the prices they fixed. They were also rapidly losing their market share (Fig. 9.2). In response, in March 1983 in London, OPEC agreed to a substantial cut of $5 in their average official price.[51] Saudi Arabia took on the role of 'swing producer', effectively cutting their own production by the amount of excess oil in the market.[52]

Between 1979 and 1985, the world demand fell by a whopping 8.7 mbd. During the same period, non-OPEC production actually increased by over

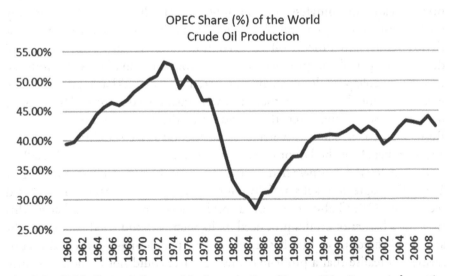

Fig. 9.2 OPEC share of the world oil production (*Source* EIA—Energy Information Administration)

5 mbd, resulting in the cartel output fall of almost 14 mbd![53] Most of the production decline came from Saudi Arabia which was forced to cut by 6.5 mbd in just four years. In 1985, the kingdom was producing only about 3.5 mbd,[54] losing probably $200 million each day from the forgone production.[55]

It was not sustainable. In July 1985, at a meeting organised by the Oxford Institute for Energy Studies (OIES), Yamani said that OPEC would have to defend their market share.[56] This was soon, officially confirmed at the Geneva Conference. Defending the price was out of the window. At the time, not everyone understood what this meant. Chalabi wrote: '*To my complete surprise, the Geneva Conference that year suddenly agreed that OPEC should declare its determination to acquire and defend a fair market share in conformity with its development requirements*'.[57] OPEC just declared a price war.[58]

The Price War

To regain their market share, the Saudis adopted a simple, but effective strategy. They offered their oil at prices based on prices of refined, petroleum product, so-called 'netback'[59] price, with an added discount.[60] The 'netback' price guaranteed refineries profit for every barrel they processed. It was hard to refuse such a deal. Buyers queued up.

Just a year later, the Saudis were pumping well over 5 mbd, and all the members of OPEC were producing as much as they wished. Official prices became meaningless, and the spot market fell below $10, before any quality discounts.[61] The problem with 'netback' prices was that it incentivised refiners to process oil at maximum rates, regardless of the actual demand for petroleum products. As they flooded the market with products, their prices collapsed. Refiners did not care, as the 'netted-back' price of crude which they bought, collapses too. They were guaranteed a profit. The oil price fall was so severe that even the President of the United States, George H. Bush, stepped in. He was worried about the 'oil price stability', a lobbying effort on behalf of the US producers, which was to be repeated in 2020.[62]

Eventually, the madness had to stop, and OPEC met in Geneva in August 1986. They agreed to substantially cut output to 17 mbd. Spot prices started recovering. OPEC also agreed on a fixed official price of $18 a barrel, this time for a basket of crudes produced by its members and fixed Arabian Light at a small discount to that basket price. Few people making these decisions seemed to realise that a profit-maximising cartel could not fix both quantity and price.[63]

The Saudi oil minister Yamani was against a return to fixed official prices and that, among other things, cost him his job. The Saudi king fired him later in the year. Chalabi, then a Deputy Secretary General of OPEC, claimed it was clear to him (and Yamani) that fixing a price would inevitably lead to the return of Saudi Arabia to the role of swing producer, but the $18 figure came directly from the Saudi King Fahd.[64]

Unsurprisingly, within a few months, the fixed price collapsed as some buyers, namely Aramco partners (Exxon, Mobil, Texaco, and Chevron) refused to lift oil unless they were given lower, market-related prices.[65] Eventually, Aramco reached an agreement with the partner companies to sell its oil based on prices of the internationally traded oil: sales to the United States were based on Alaska North Slope (ANS, later changed to the West Texas Intermediate crude oil or WTI), sales to Europe were based on Brent, and sales to Asia on the average of Oman and Dubai price assessments. Premiums and discounts were then applied to those benchmarks. It was made public in January 1988, and the rest of OPEC soon adopted it.

This is pretty much the international oil pricing system we recognise today.

A Clumsy Cartel?[66]

OPEC legacy will always be the anti-colonial struggle for sovereign control of their own resources.[68] However fortunate,[69] the organisation completed that task successfully. OPEC was naïve in thinking it could simply take over from the 'oil cartel' of majors. It had neither developed, integrated industry assets,[70] nor the know-how to control the international oil market and fix prices.

OPEC tried, but could not be a price maker. After a brief and painful period of attempted fixing prices, OPEC gave up, resigned to be a price taker, and remained so for the following three and a half decades. Highly dependent on oil revenues, majority of its members could not stomach the volatile swings associated with supply adjustments, necessary to maintain a targeted price. The cartel had to abdicate this function to where it belonged, to the free market. OPEC would continue to talk about 'fair' and 'target' price levels, desired 'price ranges', all thrown out of a hat, but these were nothing but a wish list, changed as soon as the market realities altered. As Fadhil Chalabi pointed out: *The only factor that unites OPEC's member countries with their diverse interests is their one common goal of an immediate short-term maximization of revenue.*[71]

This is not to say OPEC had lost influence in the market. For the oil market participants, it was and remained the proverbial 'elephant in the room'. During the last three decades, it maintained roughly 40% share of the global oil production. Many of its members retained discretion over resale and destination for their oil. These 'resale' and 'destination restriction' contractual clauses and different pricing formulae applied to different destinations were often taken as an indication of the cartel's monopoly pricing power.[72]

For many years, Asian customers bitterly complained about so-called 'Asian premium', an alleged higher price charged by the Saudis and OPEC in general, to this growing part of the world. After a careful study, it turned out to be fiction, sporadically caused by specific buying and pricing patterns in Asia, as well as the prevailing price structure.[73] It is often forgotten that the differential pricing[74] (applied to various destinations)[75] was originally proposed by the Aramco partners as a way of reflecting the fundamentals in different markets. Imposing destination restrictions has been an expression of market power, but on its own, it has meant relatively little. What is more, these remaining vestiges of market power are slowly disappearing.[76]

Saudi Arabia has heavily invested in creating and maintaining a sizable excess production capacity. This, expensive to maintain, safety buffer was used on occasions to balance the market and discipline the other producers, maintaining Saudi leadership status within the organisation. It has been a source of Saudi (and therefore OPEC) market power.[77] That buffer served very well during the brief 'Iraq' war of 1990–91. As Iraqi and Kuwait export ceased, Saudi exports swiftly increased by almost 2.5 mbd,[78] calming the markets. However, it did not help in the subsequent downturn and by 1998, the talk was about the orgnization's demise.[79]

At the turn of the century, the rising economic power (coupled with massive energy inefficiency) of Asia and China in particular helped. However, even 5 mbd of spare capacity[80] proved ineffective (see Fig. 9.3) to prevent the price spikes of the early 2000s. By the end of 2004, the OPEC spare capacity virtually disappeared. Driven by surging demand, prices rocketed. OPEC members were clearly enjoying the windfall revenues to the extent that they actually cut output from November 2006.[81] The arguments for the OPEC support of high prices were that: 'OPEC's role is not to prevent oil prices from rising'... and that it was: 'Politically very difficult for OPEC to take action to lower prices'.[82]

There is some evidence the Saudi and OPEC spare capacity have had a dampening effect on the market volatility.[83] Equally, it is the evidence of the cartel's attempts to project market power. During the reigns of Rockefeller and the 'oil cartel' of majors, there was little volatility and the integrated industry functioned perfectly smoothly. But it did not mean the prices they

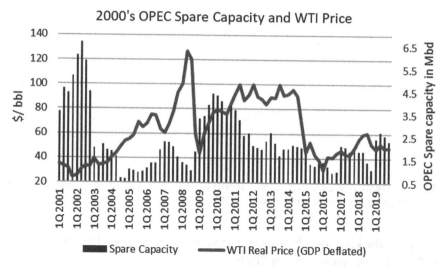

Fig. 9.3 OPEC spare capacity and WTI price, quarterly 2000–2020 (IEA data)

charged were fair. More importantly, there are other ways of stabilising commodity prices, without cartels. Perhaps the best way to reduce market volatility, both for producers and consumers, is to diversify away from their dependence on the oil, while relying on free trade and futures markets for managing the price risk.

Challenges

The extreme oil prices between 2005 and 2008 attracted new investments in a bundle of old and new production technologies, collectively known as 'fracking'.[84] This 'new' approach resulted in a massive increase in the US production: from just over 5 mbd in 2010, it exploded to over 12 mbd in 2019. Since the advent of OPEC, this was the most significant structural change in the oil and gas markets.

This phenomenon of a cartel (OPEC), accommodating a high-cost producers (US shale) can be analysed using the Limit Pricing Model.[85] It fits the events since 2014 fairly well, including the demand shock of 2020. Saudi Arabia used its excess production capacity primarily as a threat against any producer (weather OPEC member or not) eroding its market share. People have short memories, and, like any threat, it has to be credible. From time to time, Saudis have to make good on that threat. This move, from a defensive but threatening posture, to an offensive one, involving a price war, is very

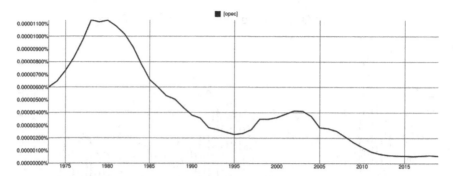

Fig. 9.4 Frequency of word 'OPEC' mentioned in the English speaking literature (Generated by Google Ngram Viewer: '[OPEC]', in English)

costly for the kingdom. However, it is very effective, as we have witnessed in 1986 and then again, early in 2020.[86]

In March 2020, frustrated by the growing non-OPEC market share, Saudi Arabia, declared a price war.[87] Coupled with the collapsing demand, due to the Covid-19 pandemic, the impact was so severe that, in April 2020,[88] Brent price closed below $10 and WTI went into a deep negative price territory.[89] If physical oil sales in the US market were based on only one day of pricing, sellers would have had to pay buyers a substantial amount of money for the privilege of having their oil.

The shock to all the producers, and indeed everyone in the industry was such that the Saudis managed relatively quickly to put together an alliance, so-called 'OPEC+'[90] and orchestrate an 'orderly'[91] global production cut some 7 mbd for several months. While the Saudi strategy worked remarkably well and propped up prices for at least for a period of time, it was a clear indication of OPEC's inability[92] to act alone in balancing the market. The role of the organisation in the global international markets has gradually diminished, at least as far as the public perception is concerned (see Fig. 9.4).

OPEC does not like being labelled as a cartel. For most of its history, it has not been an efficient one, but not for lack of trying. The official OPEC line is that: '*It aims at ensuring a balanced market and reducing oil price volatility in a manner that safeguards the interests of its member countries, ensures secure supply to consuming countries and a fair return to those investing in the oil sector… member countries rely on oil export revenues to satisfy the needs of their populations and finance their socio-economic development programmes*'.[93]

'Safeguarding the interest of its member countries' has been the cartel's priority, and so far, OPEC has done a better job than any other commodity cartel of nations in the world. Safeguarding everyone else's interest is the job of the free market.

Notes

1. This assertion is well supported by the empirical work: '*We find evidence that OPEC exerted substantial market power between 1986 and 2016, the period analysed in this paper.*' See Golombek et.al. (2018, p. 112). The only debatable issue is whether the impact has been short or long-term and the extent of its influence. For a view that the effect were mainly short-term and less significant, see Aguilera and Radetzki (2016, p. 4).
2. See Chapter 7.
3. See Chapter 8.
4. See the United Nations Treaty Series (1962, pp. 248–252).
5. Parra (2004, p. 238).
6. See Chapter 8.
7. Ibid.
8. In 2019, the UK courts were still dealing with disputes over a cancelled arms deal between UK and Iran: '… *British-Iranian relations has hit a new barrier after the high court in London ruled that the UK does not have to pay at least £20m interest on the £387m it owes to Iran over the cancelled sale of Chieftain tanks in the 1970s*'. https://www.theguardian.com/uk-news/2019/jul/26/court-ruling-over-tanks-debt-deals-new-blow-to-uk-iran-relations.
9. '*This also explains the failure of empirical studies to reach more concrete conclusions: Although some empirical models may fit the data quite well in specific time periods, they fail miserably in other time periods… Attempts to fit OPEC into one category have failed in the past and will most likely fail as OPEC's role continues to evolve*'. Fattouh and Mahadeva (2013), p. 440.
10. Associated with Ezzati (1976, p. 107). The OPEC price increases agreed at the Aby Dhabi conference in December 1978 were specifically designed to compensate for the falling value of the dollar. Therefore, they were set in line with the revenue needs of the producers. See Parra (2004, p. 220).
11. For an overview of the literature and evidence, see Fattouh and Mahadeva (2013, p. 9, Footnote 14).
12. Zweifel et al. (2017, p. 179).
13. See Bhattacharyya (2011, p. 347).
14. Marginal revenue equals marginal cost. The cartel has lower cost of production than the fringe.
15. Comptroller General of the United States (1980, p. 26).
16. Ibid., p. 13.
17. In Chapter 8, we listed six conditions for a successful cartel. The ability to balance the supply and demand is one of them. In 1979, OPEC could have

increased production (as it had spare capacity) but it had neither will nor an agreed mechanism to trigger such a decision.

18. Comptroller General of the United States (1980, p. 20).
19. For only 19,000 barrels a day. Ibid., p. 21.
20. DOE accepted the 'disadvantageous' implications of its sale. There were other policies in the highly regulated US market which contributed to an atmosphere of shortages. '*Both the DOE inventory target levels and the entitlement benefit for distillate imports were criticized as contributing to surplus demand and increased prices on the international spot market.*' Ibid., p. 24. Import ceiling was also set at 8.2 mbd but was not used in practice.
21. Ibid., p. 12.
22. Iranian occupation of the US Embassy in Teheran in November, US halting purchases of Iranian oil and a subsequent occupation of the Grand Mosque in Mecca did not help.
23. '*The major oil companies, Exxon, Texaco, Standard Oil Company of California (Chevron), Mobil, British Petroleum, Shell, and Gulf, lost access to an estimated 3 million barrels a day mbd of contract crude. Their combined role in international crude oil trade declined from about 55 per cent in 1978 to between 50 and 45 per cent by the end of 1979... British Petroleum, which among multinational oil companies in 1978 had the largest share of third - party sales (sales between unaffiliated companies), was deprived of bothits Iranian and Nigerian contracts in 1979. It therefore virtually terminated all its sales to other companies bythe end of the year. Exxon, one of British Petroleum's largest customers, began phasing out its own third–party sales. Mobil, Standard Oil Company of California, Shell, Gulf, and Texaco also reduced third - party sales, in varying degrees, in a chain reaction that multiplied its effects throughout the highly interdependent world oil industry*'. Comptroller General of the United States (1980, p. 14).
24. '*... many companies purchased expensive spot cargoes from producing countries expecting or hoping to obtain a Term contract... In other cases, the high – priced spot purchase was an explicit part of a specific term supply arrangement. In addition, some OPEC countries demanded and obtained spot – priced surcharges for a percentage of their crude oil sold under contract.*' Ibid., p. 15.
25. The wells were almost certainly damaged (probably deliberately) during the oil workers' strike and never quite recovered.
26. September spot price for Arab Light was $12.80, just over the official price of $12.70 and the spot price in February reached $21.80. Parra (2004, p. 220).
27. CIA (1980, p. 21).
28. Ibid., p. 21.
29. In the fourth quarter of 197, the OECD stocks were almost 10% higher than in the same period in the previous year. CIA (1980, p. 18).
30. Not unlike shortages of toilet paper during the 2020 Covid-19 pandemic.
31. See Parra (2004, p. 231).
32. Comptroller General of the United States (1980, pp. 16–17).

33. They started appearing in the early 1970s, particularly around oil hubs such as Rotterdam. They thrived in unregulated markets and even majors such as BP and Shell had affiliated trading houses, Anro and Petra, respectively. Bower (2010, pp. 42–43).
34. '... the "reseller boom," in which financiers in the oil market made phony trades in order to evade the spirit (and sometimes the letter!) of the price control rules'. See Murphy (2018, p. 2).
35. Copetas (1985, p. 115).
36. At the 55th OPEC Conference, it was agreed to limit spot transactions. See Parra (2004, p. 230).
37. Parra (2004, p. 220).
38. IOCs stand for International Oil Companies. Chalabi (2010, p. 95).
39. Hearing Before the Committee on Energy and Natural Resources (1983, p. 29).
40. Industry term for cargoes finding it hard to find a buyer.
41. Comptroller General of the United States (1980, p. 10).
42. US demand fell from 18.5 to 15.3 mbd and Japanese from 5.2 to 4.2 mbd. CIA (1987).
43. This is the OPEC agreed GSP for Arab Light (AL). They also announced cutting production by 1 mbd.
44. Note the resemblance with the 'allowables' used by the Texas Railroad Commission.
45. Saud Arabia was an exception and Iran never formally agreed. See Parra (2004, p. 278).
46. From 1.4 to 2.5 mbd. CIA (1986, p. 1).
47. Primarily due to a global recession.
48. Discounts can take many forms. Other than straight discounts to GSP, they can be provided through cheap freight, longer payment or credit terms, barter etc.
49. Between 1982 and 1983, UK production increased from 2.1 to 2.3 mbd and Norwegian production from 0.5 to 0.6 mbd. CIA (1986, p. 1).
50. This was a somewhat bureaucratic and cumbersome process and will be discussed in the next chapter.
51. The average price was reduced from $33.63 to $29.31. Ibid., p. 17.
52. Excess oil at the agreed, fixed, official price.
53. In 1979, total demand was 62.67 mbd and in 1985 it was 53.97 mbd. EIA data.
54. In 1981, Saudi production was just over 10 mbd. EIA data.
55. 6.5 mbd x about $30 a barrel per day.
56. From author's interviews.
57. Chalabi (2010, p. 203).
58. In terms of the Limit Price Model discussed in Chapter 8, the cartel was switching from a defensive to an offensive mode.
59. The price of oil was 'netted' back from the price of petroleum products.
60. The discount was 'well in excess of $1/B', According to Parra (2004, p. 287).

61. As Arab Light was the key benchmark grade, lower quality crudes such as Arab heavy, Iranian Heavy, Kuwait (heavy) oil were all trading below that price.
62. '*Donations from oil and gas interests accounted for a substantial portion of the more than $800,000 raised by Vice President Bush's political action committee in its first two months, according to the committee's first report, made public earlier this month by the Federal Election Commission*'. NY Times, August 19, 1985. In 2020, President Trump brokered a deal between OPEC and Russia in order to support the price of oil, above a competitive level. That much for 'free market'.
63. Facing a downward sloping demand curve, they can either fix price and adjust the output to support such price or fix the output and sell at whatever price that output would fetch.
64. Events are well described in Chalabi (2010, pp. 212–213).
65. Parra (2004, p. 289).
66. After Adelman (2001).
67. Ibid.
68. Mabro, R. (1975, p. 192).
69. As the chapter hopefully illustrates, OPEC was pretty inactive for a decade before the political events took its course and the organisation with it.
70. Exploration, production, transportation, refining, distribution, and marketing.
71. Chalabi (2010, p. 243).
72. Soglio, R. and Jaffe, A. M. (2000).
73. Doshi and Imsirovic (2013, p. 63).
74. This refers to different pricing formulas applied for sales to the US, NW Europe, Mediterranean and Asia. It will be discussed in the subsequent chapters.
75. Charging different prices to different customers is an indicator of monopoly power.
76. In 2021, Abu Dhabi will be leaving its official selling prices to the market and cancelling its resale and destination clauses when the new, ICE Murban exchange contract is launched. Other producers may follow. For more, see Chapter 14.
77. See Chapter 8 about the Limit Pricing Model of OPEC behaviour.
78. From about 5.7 mbd to over 8 mbd.
79. '*The Organization of the Petroleum Exporting Countries is dead. Saudi Arabia killed it. Now, OPEC is just a toothless zombie, attracting attention, but without having any impact on the living.* Anas Alhaji, https://www.anasalhajji.com/publications/the-death-of-opec.
80. For the whole of OPEC in 2002, EIA data.
81. At the meeting in Doha, in November 2006, they cut output by 1.2 mbd.
82. Allsopp and Fattouh (2008, p. 16).
83. See: https://www.oxfordenergy.org/publications/opec-at-60-the-world-with-and-without-opec/.
84. Fracking will be discussed in more detail in Chapter 13.
85. Mentioned in this chapter and discussed in Chapter 8.
86. For the events of 2020 in more detail, see Chapter 14.

87. 'Saudis Plan Big Oil Output Hike, Beginning All-Out Price War', Bloomberg, March 7th, 2020.
88. On April 21st, to be precise.
89. This particular event will be discussed in detail in a later chapter.
90. United front of 13 OPEC and about 10 non-OPEC producing countries, the most important in the latter camp being Russia.
91. Orderly in a sense that the pain of cuts was relatively evenly shared by all the participants.
92. One could argue that 'unwillingness' was a better word in this context, but the cost of acting alone would simply be prohibitive. More on this in Chapter 14.
93. Argus (2020, p. 3).

References

Adelman M.A. (2001): 'The Clumsy Cartel: OPEC's Uncertain Future', *Harvard International Review*, Vol. 23, No. 1 (Spring), pp. 20–23.

Aguilera R.F. and Radetzki, M. (2016): *The Price of Oil*, Cambridge University Press.

Allsopp C. and Fattouh B. (2008): *Oil Prices: Fundamentals or Speculation?* Bank of England, June 13, 2008 OIES.

Argus (2020): *Opec at 60: 'Road to Stability Long and Bumpy*, September 14, 2020.

Bhattacharyya S.C. (2011): *Energy Economics: Concepts, Issues, Markets and Governance*, Springer.

Bower T. (2010): *The Squeeze*, Harper Press.

Chalabi F.J. (2010): *Oil Policies, Oil Myths*, I.B. Tauris & Co. Ltd. London.

CIA Intelligence Assessment (1986): *The Libyan Oil Industry: Dependence on Foreign Companies*, Directorate of Intelligence, January 1986.

CIA (1980): *International Energy Statistical Review*, National Foreign Assessment Centre, November 25, 1980.

CIA (1987): *International Energy Statistical Review*, Directorate of Intelligence, November 27, 1987.

Comptroller General of the United States (1980): *Report to the Congress of the United States: The United States Exerts Limited Influence On The International Crude Oil Spot Market*, August 21, 1980.

Copetas A.C. (1985): *Metal Men*, Futura Publications.

Doshi T.K. and Imsirovic A. (2013): 'The 'Asian Premium' in Crude Oil Markets: Fact or Fiction?' in: Daoijong Z. (Ed), *Managing Regional Energy Vulnerabilities in East Asia*, Routledge. ISBN:978-0-415-53538-0, January, https://doi.org/10.13140/2.1.4053.6009.

Ezzati A. (1976): 'Future OPEC Price and Production Strategies as Affected by Its Capacity to Absorb Oil Revenues'. *European Economic Review*, Vol. 8, pp. 107–138.

Fattouh B. and Mahadeva L. (2013). 'OPEC: What Difference Has It Made?' *Annual Review of Resource Economics*, Vol. 5, pp. 427–443.

Golombek R., Irarrazabal A.A. and Ma L. (2018): OPEC's Market Power: An Empirical Dominant Firm Model for the Oil Market, *Energy Economics*, Vol. 70, pp. 98–115.

Hearing Before the Committee on Energy and Natural Resources (1983): 'World Petroleum Outlook – 1983', US Government Printing Office, Washington, DC.

Mabro R. (1975) 'OPEC After the Oil Revolution', *Millennium*, Vol. 4, No. 3, pp. 191–199.

Murphy R. (2018): *The Crazy Crude Oil Price Controls of the 1970s*, Institute for Energy Research Commentary, April 18.

Para F. (2004): *Oil Politics, A Modern History of Petroleum*, I.B. Taurus Co. Ltd.

Soglio R. and Jaffe A.M. (2000): *A Note on Saudi Arabian Price Discrimination*, The *Energy Journal*, Vol. 21, pp. 121–134.

United Nations Secretariat (1962): *Agreement Concerning the Creation of the Organization of Petroleum Exporting Countries (OPEC)*. Done at Baghdad, on September 14, 1960, United Nations Treaty Series UN Resolution No. 6363, https://treaties.un.org/doc/Publication/UNTS/Volume%20443/volume-443-I-6363-English.pdf.

Zweifel P., Praktiknjo A., and Erdmann G. (2017): *Energy Economics, Theory and Applications*, Springer.

10

Governments and Markets

From mid-1980s, OPEC abdicated the price-making function to the market. But the international oil market took some time to develop. A number of factors came into play to facilitate its development. High oil prices and resource nationalism in the producing nations incentivised exploration in new regions of the world. Production picked up significantly in Alaska, Mexico, Russia, and the North Sea.[1] With the established, vertically integrated channels of the oil industry broken, these new volumes of oil were spilling over into the marketplace, revealing the real market transactions, and prices. But the broken trade channels and excess oil were not sufficient for market to grow. The key additional ingredient was the government policy. As we are going to show in this chapter, Brent emerged as a premier international oil benchmark with the help of the UK fiscal treatment of the North Sea oil production and the liberalisation policies of the government of Margaret Thatcher.

North Sea: Exploration

The North Sea exploration goes back to 1930s, but it was discovery of the Groningen gas field in the Netherlands in 1959, that marked the beginnings of a serious increase in the exploration effort. The Permian rock, in which one of the biggest gas fields in the world was found, extended from Poland, through the North Sea to the British Isles.[2] The original search was all about

© The Author(s), under exclusive license to Springer Nature
Switzerland AG 2021
A. Imsirovic, *Trading and Price Discovery for Crude Oils*,
https://doi.org/10.1007/978-3-030-71718-6_10

gas. It was to change soon after the first significant oil find in the North Sea, in a dome-like geological structure, off the coast of Denmark in 1966. Three years later, the oil potential was confirmed after Phillips Petroleum discovered the giant Ekofisk field, in the Norwegian sector of the North Sea.

The additional incentives for oil companies to explore the North Sea came from the nationalisations of their assets in the producing countries. BP is a good example. After nationalisations in Libya, Kuwait, and Nigeria,[3] the Iranian revolution of 1979 was the last straw for the British major. It found itself short of oil. Much later, a senior BP manager admitted the focus of exploration on the North Sea was not a result of economics, but desperation.[4] Offshore technology of the period was primitive and there was no guarantee the technology used in the Gulf of Mexico would work in the roaring North Sea. Even if oil was found, there was no guarantee it could be produced.

Oil prices were still low in the late 1960s and drilling for the Forties field would never have started if it were not for an idle rig that was available and already paid for.[5] In those days, there was still a lot of luck involved in exploration. But BP was lucky, and a huge find was reported in October 1970. The search moved further North East of the Shetland islands. A year later, Shell and Esso[6] discovered Brent, one of the most iconic and largest fields in the world.[7] Ekofisk started production in 1971, Forties in 1975 and Brent in 1976. In 1981 the British Queen opened the Sullom Voe terminal, where Brent and Ninian crudes would be delivered and loaded. Eventually, the two would be co-mingled into one stream, Brent Blend.[8] The majors dominated the exploration and production effort and by 1984, almost half of the North Sea production was dominated by BP, Shell, Esso, and Statoil.[9]

Investments were astronomical. Development of the Forties field was fast approaching £1bn[10] in currency of the day. But, by 1975,[11] that one field alone would supply 25% of the UK demand[12] and following the 1973 price shock, the revenues could justify it. In 1975, oil price was $11.53 or $54.80 in 2019 money, and in 1980, the price was $36.93 or $114.27 in 2019 money![13] Once the initial investments were made, the operating costs were not so high in relation to the market price. In 1984, estimated cost for Brent was $2.20 and Forties only $1.30 a barrel.[14] By 1982, the UK production was over 2 million barrels per day (with Norway 2.6 million barrels per day), making the North Sea an important supplier of non-OPEC crude oil. But getting the right institutional framework for such production levels was not always easy.

UK Government Monopolies

After the Second World War,[15] the idea of greater government involvement in the economy was a norm. Professor of Energy Policy at Oxford, Dieter Helm wrote that: '*Until the 1980's, it was a conventional wisdom of the post-war years that markets are hopelessly inadequate in providing appropriate energy supplies. State-owned energy companies were deemed to be so natural that they were made statutory monopolies, and it was assumed that regulation was inevitable*'.[16] Competition was essentially illegal. Markets and were considered chaotic and good only for achieving short-term goals. For some reason, the short-termism and motivations of politicians were not questioned. Economic planning and government intervention were considered so 'normal' for both Labour and Conservative parties that Margaret Thatcher's 1979 manifesto barely mentioned privatisation.[17]

In such a planned economic structure, the energy sector was considered 'special', with a role best presented by the Leontief's input–output model.[18] In the simplest form of the model, the government would plan for a desired (or needed) level of economic development and production. Then, the planner would simply calculate the required energy input and costs.[19] Public corporations would manage a trade-off between efficiency and profit on one hand, and the general 'public interest' on the other. Protected from any competition, the government monopolies would face no risk in making long-term investment decisions as the cost would simply be passed onto the consumer.[20]

In the UK, the planning of the North Sea exploration and production (E&P) was controlled by two monopolies, the British Gas Council (BGC) and the British National Oil Corporation (BNOC).[21] BGC was a fully integrated company[22] with monopsony[23] power in purchasing gas and monopoly power in selling to its customers. After 1972, it was involved in transmission, and distribution of gas, and even the selling of appliances.

BNOC was concerned with the control of the offshore oil business.[24] One of the key roles for BNOC was to ensure the security of supply for the country. It was furnished with an option to purchase oil at a 'market' price. In reality, the security of supply function was never used, not even during the 1979 Iranian revolution. Later, BNOC also acquired exploration licences, providing it with 'participation' oil. It had access to oil from two other sources[25]: Royalties paid in kind or in cash, and third-party purchase contracts from small licensees who found it convenient to dispose of their oil through BNOC. By 1985, the government monopoly was a major oil player with over 800,000 barrels a day of oil at its disposal.[26] It moved this oil primarily through term contracts, based on its posted prices.[27] This arrangement of 'buying' oil and selling it back was designed to ensure the security of supply[28] and prevent transfer pricing where the companies are minimising tax. But BNOC role was rather ambiguous from the start: *'It was a classic confusion of producer, regulator, and agency of government'.*[29]

These contradictions made posting monthly 'term' prices a particularly difficult task. Colin Bryce, a trader at BNOC and later a successful 'Wall Street refiner' explains: *'We used all the methods available to set prices: Official OPEC prices, oil trades reported in spot markets as well as calculating gross net worth of oil using the spot petroleum product prices, which were readily available around the Rotterdam area'.*[30] Any deviation from market prices could result in unhappy buyers or sellers, arbitration, and trading losses. BNOC also had to follow the official government policy of the day which, in 1983, was to follow the official OPEC prices.[31] *'There were regular meetings and consultations with other producers, including the OPEC representatives'*,[32] says Ms. Liz Bossley, a trader at BNOC at the time. Clearly, there were times where BNOC was asked to follow conflicting objectives.

By fixing monthly prices, the Corporation was an integral part of the UK fiscal regime, which is the key to understanding the way the Brent market developed and operated.

Brent and the UK Fiscal Regime

The key components of the UK fiscal or tax regime, relevant to the oil industry were: Royalty (paid in cash or kind at the government option) based on field revenues, Petroleum Revenue Tax ('PRT') based on individual field profits and the Corporation Tax based on UK resident company profits. The upstream operations in the UK were subject to both PRT and Corporation Tax, while the downstream, including trading was exposed to the Corporation Tax only.[33]

After BNOC calculated monthly 'term' prices, they were vetted and approved by the British treasury. BNOC term prices were the basis for calculating the PRT.[34] The UK fiscal regime was an opportunity for the integrated oil companies, operating in the UK sector of the North Sea to refine either their own North Sea barrels or third-party barrels in order to optimise their tax bill.

Companies would compare the TRP set by BNOC to the prevailing spot market and then decide whether to take their own cargo into their refinery or sell it and buy a third-party cargo. When the market price fell below the TRP, (considering the transaction costs such as brokerage fees, financing, etc.) they would sell it and buy a substitute cargo from another seller, thus minimising their tax. As markets became volatile in the mid-1980s, they would frequently buy and sell cargoes, depending on the relationship of the market prices and TRP. At the end of the tax period,[35] they could declare the sales which correspond to their equity production and these would normally be the lowest prices achieved.

The upstream would lose money (or make less profit), due to lower sale price, but trading would gain an equivalent amount. Tax saving was realised because trading was taxed at the Corporation Tax rate, while the upstream was taxed at both PRT and Corporation Tax. In March 1987, this optionality was substantially reduced,[36] but not closed, when the Oil Taxation office (OTO) gave companies about 48 hours[37] to declare their sales. Regardless, some optionality remained, and it encouraged frequent buying and selling (often referred to as 'tax spinning'), over and above what would be expected in the course of the business.

For example, an integrated oil company producing only one cargo of oil per month may have five sales and four buys, making their net position zero. Forward sales that were not delivered were not considered by OTO to be valid physical transaction, further encouraging forward trades. If two companies had several mutual buys and sells, having nominated their lowest price sale as the equity transaction, they could simply settle the rest of the trades financially, through a 'book out'.

The first reports of short trades by BP and Conoco go back to 1981. In June that year, both companies sold oil into the US Strategic Petroleum Reserve (SPR). The BP sale of Forties was well below the BNOC official price (Reportedly, $1.75 lower than the May 1981 BNOC term price[38]) was one of the early signs of friction between BNOC and oil companies, exacerbated by the market declines.

The falling market of 1982 only encouraged short selling. One cargo of Brent in May that year reportedly consisted of a chain of 18 companies. Speculation added to the liquidity and managing all the inter-company trades became a priority. In January 1983, more Brent oil was sold than was available in the programme for the whole month. Realising the importance of the forward contract for their tax optimisation activities, Shell, Esso, and BP stepped up policing the unregulated market.[39]

In the same year, BNOC moved from using Forties to setting a Brent 'marker' price. The focus of spinning also gradually shifted to Brent, loading at Sullom Voe terminal. By 1984, most of the procedures for trading 15-day forward Brent were established and accepted in an informal and unregulated market. The market was concentrated, and the biggest lifters were the three majors, Shell, Esso, and BP, lifting 625 thousand barrels a day (kbd) or almost a half of the volume loaded from the Sullom Voe terminal in that year.[40] They were major buyers of both spot and term from BNOC as well. Given those volumes, they had strong incentive to 'spin' Brent cargoes and maintain an orderly and well-functioning market.

Spinning in Practice

One of peculiarities of the Brent forward market is the nomination procedure. Once the loading programme for a particular month is available (originally, for January loading, the operator[41] would publish it before the forward contract expires[42]), all the equity producers know their loading date ranges (say 15–17 January, if they have only one cargo). The equity producer is not obliged to inform their buyers which cargo they are going to allocate to them (they also may have purchases from other firms), until 15 days before the first day of loading (January 1st in our example). This is the origin of the name for the forward, 15-day Brent market, which later gradually widened to 30 days.[43]

In a weak market, prompt cargoes with loading dates would be worth less than forward,[44] cargoes. As a result, traders would not willingly keep them, and the nominations would be passed on down the chain. If the 'daisy chain' (as it was sometimes called) was long enough, it might not reach the end buyer in the course of the day. The nomination would be kept by whatever company received it by five o'clock (officialy, the end of work) that day. If such 'dated' cargo (cargo with nominated loading dates) was worth half a dollar per barrel less than an equivalent forward cargo, being stuck with a nomination would incur a loss of $250,000![45] At times, the cost may be even larger. As the nominations approached the five o'clock, the speed of nominations would accelerate, creating a frantic activity around the operations desks of the participating companies.

When I traded Brent in 1990s, we had several people designated for this duty, close to five o'clock. Sitting around the operations desk, they would have programmed speed-dials to selected counterparties on stand-by. As five o'clock approached, the whole trading floor would go quiet. If the operator's phone, designated to receive a nominations rang close to the cut-off time, they would all press their respective speed-dial buttons. The operator would speak aloud the received nomination (dates and cargo number[46]), and whoever got first through to the phone of another counterparty (which we had a sale agreed with), would hopefully pass on the same nomination. The company that did not manage to pass the nomination was stuck with the cargo. In the industry jargon, it was 'five o'clock. At times it was heart-stopping. Fridays were busiest as nominations for Saturday and Sunday would be made as well in the same day. Partly due to stress, we would normally go to the local pub most Fridays, soon after five o'clock.

Up until 1984, BNOC term or posted price was assumed to reflect the market and used for taxation. After the market volatility of the early 1984, OTO started using a calculated weighted average of BNOC, spot and other reported transactions. With abolition of BNOC in 1985, the term price became irrelevant. The fiscal incentive did not change though, and companies simply approximated the OTO calculation in order to determine if they should sell the equity oil to the market or keep it for their own refining system. For example, for a January cargo of Brent, OTO would normally average Brent prices between December 1st and January 15th. Companies would do the same and, towards the end of December, as the TRP was becoming more apparent, they would make 'spinning' decisions with increasing confidence.

In order to optimise tax, it was necessary to have a view on market and prices. Market coverage and analysis became critical and trading teams of companies such as Shell and BP came to play a very prominent role. Some of the best and brightest graduates ended up working in these teams for decades to come. They still do.

The final impetus to rebirth and growth of markets came from the new government dismantling the obstacles to its growth.

The New Philosophy: Liberalisation and Deregulation

Government heavy involvement using two monopolies was the UK oil and gas industry which the Conservative government of Margaret Thatcher inherited in May of 1979. At oil price of well over $100 a barrel in 2019 dollars,[47] they inherited a fortune. They could afford to experiment with new free-market-based policies of Milton Friedman and Friedrich von Hayek.[48] The government thinking was also influenced by views from the Institute for Economic Affairs (IEA), a free-market think-tank, which attracted policy-oriented economists such as Eileen Marshall,[49] Colin Robinson,[50] and others.[51] Their view was that the only government role in energy sector was to set up a legal framework for markets and let private companies freely operate within it.

Wider deregulation started in 1979 with abolition of exchange controls (capital and currency controls which were in place since 1939). In 1979, the government disposed of about 5 per cent of BP shares, reducing its share-holding to some 46 per cent.[52] In 1982, the London International Financial Futures and Options Exchange (LIFE) opened, attracting big American and Japanese banks to the City of London. Wider liberalisation[53] policies and the consequences for the finance industry, often referred to as the 'Big Bang',[54] simplified transactions, reduced costs, and created a trading boom in anything from financial securities to oil. Coupled with similar policies of the Regan administration 'across the pond' in the United States, it was a fertile ground for rebirth of markets.

In 1981, Nigel Lawson was appointed the Secretary of State for Energy and soon begun to put into practice views that government had no role in planning or balancing country's energy: '… *no industry should remain under state ownership unless there is a positive and overwhelming case for it doing so.*'[55] Lawson's first piece of legislation was the Oil and Gas (Enterprise) Act of 1982,[56] spinning out two upstream companies, Enterprise Oil and Britoil from the two monopolies and ending BNOC's and BGC's oil production activities. Both new companies were then privatised by the end of 1985. A good deal of their oil production went directly to the spot markets.

Just like the OPEC official prices, BNOC posted prices came under pressure after 1984, when the spot market kept leading the price fall, and rigid posted prices played a catch-up.[57] Customers started to withdraw from term contracts with BNOC, leaving the monopoly as a large, distressed seller in the spot market, losing money (it was buying oil at higher posted prices and selling it at much lower, spot levels). BNOC was forced to sell oil early to avoid being caught long with prompt, distressed cargoes. Having to cover the losses,[58] the government soon made it public it was abolishing the corporation.[59] There was no more 'term' or 'official', government-approved prices. Privatisation of the oil sector in the UK removed a rigid and bureaucratic government control of the producion exactly at the time when the oil markets were becoming turbulent and required flexibility.[60]

Trading Expands

In March 1983, the New York Mercantile exchange successfully launched its first crude oil futures contract. It was a WTI contract for a physical delivery of crude oil in storage in Cushing, Oklahoma.[61] It further encouraged arbitrage trades with the 15-day, forward Brent contract. At the end of the same year, the International Petroleum Exchange (IPE) launched its first futures Brent contract. It was also a contract with physical delivery, but in tank in the Amsterdam-Rotterdam-Antwerp (ARA) area. That attempt, as well as the contract two years later were unsuccessful. It was not before 1988 that a successful Brent contract took off the ground. It was an FOB[62] contract, complementary to the existing 15-day Brent forward market, with delivery at Sullom Voe terminal.[63]

The middle of the decade was a period of rapid expansion. The entry of Japanese trading houses (Sogo Shosha) such as Nissho Iwai and Marubeni, and Wall Street Banks (often referred to as the 'Wall St. refiners') such as Morgan Stanley and J. Aron, a commodities trading arm of Goldman Sachs,[64] increased their participation. In 1986, there were well over a hundred participants in the Brent market.[65] By the end of the year, the Wall Street banks made 33% of all the transactions,[66] introducing into oil trading products and strategies from the financial industry, making markets in options, spreads, arbitrage, cracks, partials, and 'mini' Brent contracts.[67] With the spot market in full swing, trading houses joined the feast with Phibro a trading company, becoming one of the top players in the market.[68]

One particular feature of the Brent market became very attractive to the top players: operational tolerance. The company that lifted a Brent cargo had the option to load it within 5% volume tolerance.[69] The company at the end of a Brent chain could nominate anywhere between 475,000 to 525,000 barrels, for a contractual volume of 500,000 barrels. Any optionality in trading is valuable and this one was very valuable for players with many buys and sells in the forward market. For example, if a company bought a forward cargo of Brent at $21 and sold it at $22 a barrel, the company would maximise the physical lifting, as they would make an additional $0.05 a barrel or a total of $25,000 for a full cargo.[70] Since big Brent players had many purchases and sales in any particular month, they could be in the same chain several times before keeping the cargo and declaring the volume tolerance of their choosing. If they could construct the chain in a way that they received low price purchases and high price sales, they could collect $25,000each time.[71] For this reason, top Brent players spent a great deal of time and effort on these operational matters, making additional profits from trading forward Brent. When I was trading the contract in London in the 1990s, a 15-day Brent operator of a major oil company was driving a Ferrari.

Trading whole forward Brent cargoes (originally 600,000 barrels) was not ideal for smaller players. This was where banks added value with a clever solution: a 'Partial Brent' market. It was probably conceived at a meeting of the Morgan Stanley (MS) traders in New York, late in 1987.[72] In the absence of a liquid futures contract in Europe (it was launched a year later), there was a need for smaller volumes trades in Brent, especially for hedging product cracks.[73] Forward 15-Brent was trading in full cargo sizes, and NYMEX WTI contract carried too much basis risk.[74]

The Morgan Stanley team devised a structure where the bank would quote bids and offers in 50,000 barrel (50 kb) increments, with the obligation for the parties either to reduce the position to zero or to build up to a full cargo by some agreed termination date. Two traders[75] were sent to Europe to market this product. Very quickly, ICI, Petronor,[76] LASMO,[77] Conoco, Enterprise, and a number of others took to this market. The success of the Brent partials market was probably a blueprint for the third and successful IPE futures contract in 1988.

While the expansion of trading was fuelled by the government's market-friendly policies, it was the English legal system that provided a solid foundation for the boom. The country had a long history of independent judiciary and compliance with the rule of law, inspiring business confidence. English common law was based on precedent, making it clear, predictable, and it was seen as fair. It respected the bargains made by parties involved, making it a solid basis for trade.

With the government monopoly structures dismantled, there was an increasing need for a transparent and liquid physical market as well. Transparency had to come from independent observers, and this is where the price reporting agencies (PRAs) again came to the fore.

Price Reporting Agencies

After the events of 1973 and especially 1979, PRAs became increasingly important, if not crucial to the functioning of the emerging markets. Unsurprisingly, the first PRA goes back to the beginnings of the oil industry and emergence of spot trading in the United States. Some of the first available price reports were published in the Derrick's Hand-Book of Petroleum and were used in the earlier chapters of this book. The first publications solely dedicated to prices and price assessments were attributed to Warren Platt, who established his 'National Petroleum News' in 1909, with an explicit aim of promoting transparency in the industry.[78] It was a very fortunate timing as the Standard Oil was broken up two years later, creating a need for price information. In 1923, he launched Platt's Oilgram, a short newsletter dedicated only to oil market and price information. It was sent to subscribers on daily basis. Platt's Oilgram's claim to fame was that its assessments were used by the oil majors to calculate the 'Gulf-Plus' formula.[79] It still publishes prices today under the ownership of Standard & Poor's (now S&P Global).[80] Platts started publishing its 'Crude Oil Market Wire' in 1978 and in the same year, Argus (now Argus Media) started first daily reporting on the emerging spot crude market in the now famous, 'Argus Telex'. It was followed by the London Oil Report (LOR) in 1980 and RIM Intelligence in Japan, in 1984.

Price reporting has played a major role in the price discovery process, making spot transactions transparent. What is more, it as made market-based pricing of hundreds of different kinds of oil possible. As discussed in the previous chapter, the Aramco partners agreed to use price formulae based on most frequently traded types of oil: Brent, WTI and Dubai. Such grades of oil are commonly referred to as benchmarks.

PRAs assess the value of benchmarks on daily basis and the value of all the other qualities of oil around the world are set as premiums or discounts to the benchmarks. When we refer to the 'price of oil', we normally have in mind the price of one of these three benchmarks. To smooth benchmark prices and avoid any short-term spikes that may cause volatility in the final, contractual price, traders normally use a number of daily PRA assessments, averaged out over a period of time. In Europe, five daily assessments around loading or delivery dates are common, while Asian markets generally use an average of the whole month of loading. For example, North Sea crude would normally price over a five-day period including two assessment days before loading, one on the loading ('bill of lading')[81] day and two days after the loading day.

The benchmarks, and the derivatives markets that emerged alongside them have enabled the participant to manage their price risk. Most importantly, the price-makers in those markets are the firms most active in trading those benchmarks, while the rest of the players are price-takers. A whole ecosystem of banks, traders, and brokers has grown around pricing of the benchmarks.

From the mid-1980s, the benchmarks became a pillar of the international oil pricing system. How benchmarks work, who and how they are traded is the subject of the rest of the book.

Oil Benchmarks

The most important characteristic of a benchmark is the trust by all the contracting parties that it reflects market value. To earn that trust, a benchmark needs to satisfy several criteria.[82] Firstly,[83] the oil needs to be produced in sufficient quantity to facilitate trading. Secondly, the production and consumption have to be diversified among a sufficient number of unrelated participants, so that no one buyer or seller can influence the price. Thirdly, the infrastructure should enable smooth delivery operations of the commodity. As we shall see later, operational bottlenecks, such as limitations of storage and loading facilities,[84] pipelines and even exposure to weather[85] can impact prices. Fourthly, the institutional framework has to allow for unrestricted trading. This is where the liberalisation of the 1980s played a key role, allowing for unregulated,[86] bilateral, and free-trading[87] of oil in the UK and US. Finally, an oil benchmark should reflect at least regional, if not global trade flows.

For all these reasons, Brent, WTI, and Dubai emerged as key regional benchmarks. Given the excellent infrastructure and the importance of the United States as both the biggest producer and consumer of oil at various points in time, WTI emerged as one of the most liquid oil contracts, in spite of the fact that it is land-locked and has often been de-coupled from the global oil flows. WTI contract is a showcase of the market dictum that liquidity of a contract is more important than the basis risk involved in using it.[88] Dubai emerged very early as a regional, Asian benchmark reflecting the fundamentals of the oil markets 'East of Suez'. As we shall explain soon, Dubai owes its liquidity and price level to Brent. In essence, it is closely linked to Brent, even though it has a vast derivative ecosystem associated with its own price. Finally, Brent has emerged as a premiere global oil benchmark, setting the price for most of oil traded outside the continental United States. Underpinned by English law, standardised contracts, no destination restrictions, and tax advantages in 'spinning' or 'churning' the cargoes, the North Sea Brent market developed as the premiere, transparent and liquid spot market. All these benchmarks will be discussed in detail in the subsequent chapters.

Notes

1. Between 1973 and 1979, Russian output increased from 8.4 to 11.4 mbd, Mexican output from 0.45 to 1.46 mbd and North Sea from virtually nothing

to 2 mbd. CIA (1980). Alaskan production picked up with the Prudhoe Bay coming online in 1977 and hitting the peak of 2 mbd in the late 1980s.

2. Shepherd (2015, p. 29). Much of the discussion about the early exploration is based on this source.

3. The company's oil assets were nationalised in Libya in 1971, in Kuwait in 1975, and in Nigeria in 1979.

4. Ibid., p. 37.

5. BP tried to charter it out but could not find any interest for it. Ibid., p. 39.

6. Standard Oil of New Jersey rebranded and changed name to Exxon Corporation in 1972. Its UK entity involved was Esso Exploration and Production UK.

7. McGrandle (1975, p. 25).

8. Ten fields in total: seven in the Brent and three in the Ninian system. Horsnell and Mabro (1993, p. 11).

9. BP produced 494 kbd, Shell 424 kbd, Esso 418 kbd and Statoil 206 kbd. Mabro et al. (1986, p. 33).Statoil was originally a Norwegian state oil company, partially privatised in 2001. It was renamed Equinor in 2018.

10. Shepherd (2015, p. 45).

11. The first four platforms were installed in the 1970s, while the Forties Echo platform was installed in the 1980.

12. https://www.offshore-technology.com/projects/forties-oilfield-a-timeline/.

13. BP Statistical Review (2020).

14. Mabro et al. (1986, p. 74).

15. The policies go back even further, back to the Great Depression of 1929, but become very apparent after the war.

16. Helm (2003, p. 1).

17. It mentioned privatisation only briefly: "sell back to private ownership the recently nationalised aerospace and shipbuilding concerns'. See: http://www.conservative-party.net/manifestos/1979/1979-conservative-manifesto.shtml.

18. Wassily Leontief received a Nobel in Economics in 1973. His input–output model is a matrix, representing the interdependencies between different sectors of the economy.

19. Bullard et al. (1978, p. 267).

20. In the twenty-first century, government monopolies would become great obstacles to energy transition.

21. Following Helm (2003, p. 39).

22. After 1972.

23. Monopsony is a monopoly in purchasing or employment.

24. BNOC was described as having three national objectives: To ensure that the government gets is 'fair share' of the oil wealth from the produced North Sea oil; to provide the government with information about the production and trade in oil there and to control development of oil E&P. See Krapels (1977, p. 20). However, security of supply was a very important objective as well, especially following 1979 oil price shock.The onshore oil pipeline network was

controlled within a subsidiary of BNOC, the Oil and Pipeline Agency, which operated behind a very strong Chinese wall with oversight by the MOD. It still exists.

25. In 1984, BNOC had 435 kbd of participation oil, 246 kbd of royalty in kind oil and 175 kbd of assigned purchases, mainly from smaller producers. Mabro et al. (1986, p. 103).

26. Ibid., p. 102.

27. BNOC employees were prohibited from calling them posted prices. They had to refer to them as quarterly negotiated prices. The sellers could challenge these prices with determination by an independent expert and buyers could terminate their contracts if they didn't like the price. Source: Interview with Liz Bossley.

28. Producers were obliged to sell their oil to BNOC, but in a force majeure situation, including domestic need, BNOC could suspend or cancel its resale contracts and divert oil to the refineries in the UK and its allies.

29. Mabro et al. (1986, p. 39).

30. Author's interview with Colin Bryce, December 2020. The quote refers to his time at the Pricing Unit of the BNOC roughly in the 1979–1981 period. Later, Colin was a head of oil trading at Morgan Stanley. Currently, he is with 'Energex Partners'.

31. Mabro et al. (1986, p. 106).

32. Author's interview with Liz Bossley, December 2020. At the time, Ms. Bossley worked at The Economic Intelligence Unit of BNOC. Ms. Bossley was later a trader at BNOC and then the head of oil trading at the privatised, Enterprise Oil. Currently, she is heading 'Consilience' consultancy.

33. Royalty was charged at 12.5%, PRT at 75% and Corporate tax at 53%, reduced to 35% in 1986. Effective rates were lower, see: Mabro et al. (1986, pp. 110–122).

34. In 1987, the Oil Taxation Office (OTO) refined their definition of non-arm's length deals and based them on market assessments.

35. Originally it was six months.

36. As the market volatility increased, the value of optionality increased as well. OTO had to find a way of reducing it.

37. Having sold a cargo, the company had until the end of the day, two working days following the sale, to declare if it was equity oil. So, a sale made on Monday (any time) had to be declared by end of working day on Wednesday.

38. Reported by Argus. Ibid., p. 163.

39. Ibid., pp. 164–165.

40. Mabro et al. (1986, p. 54).

41. The operator for Brent was Shell.

42. In the early 80s the deadline for nominating cargoes for month M was 5th M-1. The operator would confirm the programme before the 15th M-1- hence the choice of 15 days' notice in the forward market. As the nomination period expanded, a simple rule is that the loading programme is normally released just before that forward trading contract expires.

43. Over time, this range has gradually increased to 30 days (30-day Brent), in order to increase the volume of oil available for nominations and trading.
44. Referred to as contango.
45. For a 500,000 cargo (0.5 × 500,000).
46. There could be more than one cargo nominated on any particular day.
47. The average oil price, according to BP Statistical Review of 2020 was $31.61, or $111.31 in 2019 dollars.
48. Pearson and Watson (2012, p. 8).
49. E. Marshal was a managing director of the Office of Gas and Electricity Markets (OFGEM) and married to Prof. Robinson.
50. Colin Robinson was a free-market academic and the head of the economics department at Surrey University, where I completed my post-graduate studies in Energy Economics in the 1980s.
51. Helm (2003, p. 59).
52. BP was then fully privatised in 1987. British Gas was privatised a year earlier.
53. Deregulation and liberalisation are terms used interchangeably and with the same meaning—getting rid of various government controls, leaving more room and freedom for market forces to operate.
54. See https://www.bbc.co.uk/news/business-37751599.
55. House of Commons Research Papers (2014, p. 2).
56. https://www.legislation.gov.uk/ukpga/1982/23/section/1/enacted.
57. BNOC was forbidden by the Treasury to cut its quarterly negotiated prices, ostensibly to support OPEC. A more Machiavellian interpretation suggested by Liz Bossley is that BNOC was set up to fail so that it could be more easily privatised in keeping with the free market philosophy of Margaret Thatcher.
58. For which it was itself largely responsible.
59. BNOC continued for a while, even after Britoil (upstream) was privatised, citing the security of supply reasons: https://api.parliament.uk/historic-hansard/commons/1985/mar/13/british-national-oil-corporation.
60. Overall economic effects were not bad either. Some research points out that: '... *privatised NOCs over a period of seven years around the privatisation date improve their return on sales by 3.6 percentage points, increase total output by 40%, output per employee by 30% and capital expenditure by 47%, and decrease their employment intensity (relative to assets) by a total of 35%. In the run-up to the share sale the NOCs also manage to reduce unit operating costs by 11% and cut employment by 8%, but both trends are reversed immediately after the privatisation date as growth dominates further cost reductions in absolute terms.*' See Wolf and Pollitt (2008, p. 27).
61. Emerging US markets and WTI benchmark are discussed in Chapter 13.
62. 'Free on Board' means that oil was delivered to the ship at the loading port. Shipping and insurance are not included in the price.
63. It was a financially settled contract but a simple EFP transaction would ensure a physical delivery at S. Voe.

64. J. Aron was a small, family business, acquired by Goldman in 1981 precisely to take advantage of these liberalised and growing markets in the US and UK.
65. Horsnell and Mabro (1993, Table 7.4, p. 94).
66. Ibid., p. 80.
67. Arbitrage is a spread between two different markets. Cracks are spreads between crude oil and various petroleum products. Swaps convert 'floating' or indexed prices into a fixed price. We shall discuss most of these products later in the book.
68. Ibid., Table 7.5, p. 98.
69. This was a contractual feature of the 15-day Brent. It changed much later in 2002.
70. $22 − $21 = $1*5% = $0.05*500,000 = $25,000.
71. The opposite would happen if they had high purchases and low sales. If they kept the cargo as 'wet', they could minimise it and still make a profit (or minimise losses).
72. Author's interview with Colin Bryce, December 2020.
73. A product 'crack' is simply a differential between product and crude prices related to the same volume.
74. WTI reflected the fundamentals in the US continent, rather than Europe.
75. They were Colin Bryce and Marc Mourre.
76. Petróleos del Norte S.A. a Basque, Spanish oil and gas company.
77. London and Scottish Marine Oil (LASMO), It was acquired by ENI in 2001.
78. Johnson (2018, p. 43).
79. Discussed in earlier chapters. Freight element was added to the US Gulf price assessment.
80. They acquired the business from Platt in 1953: https://www.platts.com/IM. Platts.Content/AboutPlatts/Platts%20History-Full%20Summary_5-08-09F inal_pdf.pdf.
81. Bill of Lading is an essential document confirming the completion of loading of a cargo and includes quantity, date and time of loading.
82. International Organization of Securities Commissions (IOSCO) January 2013 definition of financial benchmarks is:

> *The Benchmarks in scope of this report are prices, rates, indices or figures that are:*
> (a) *Made available to users, whether free of charge or on payment;*
> (b) *Calculated periodically, entirely or partially by the application of a formula or another method of calculation to, or an assessment of the value of, one or more underlying assets, prices or certain other data, including estimated prices, rates or other values, or surveys; and*
> (c) *Used for reference for purposes that include one or more of the following: determining the interest payable, or other sums due, under loan agreements or under other financial contracts or instruments; determining the price at which a financial instrument may be bought or sold or traded or*

redeemed, or the value of a financial instrument; and/or measuring the performance of a financial instrument.' IOSCO (2013a, p. 48).

83. I am roughly following the points (while adding some of my own thoughts) by Horsnell and Mabro (1993, pp. 75–76).
84. Perceived shortage of storage at Cushing, Oklahoma, in April 2020 was a factor leading to negative prices of WTI crude.
85. For example, the Russian port of Novorossiysk in the Black Sea is usually affected by closures in the winter period, due to weather. This can cause significant price spikes.
86. Benchmarks were eventually regulated in REGULATION (EU) 2016/1011 OF THE EUROPEAN PARLIAMENT AND OF THE COUNCIL of 8 June 2016 on indices used as benchmarks in financial instruments and financial contracts or to measure the performance of investment funds and amending Directives 2008/48/EC and 2014/17/EU and Regulation (EU) No 596/2014. https://eur-lex.europa.eu/legal-content/EN/TXT/PDF/?uri=CELEX:32016R1011&from=EN.
87. Solid legal contractual basis is assumed. English law is a good example.
88. It will be discussed in more detail in the subsequent chapters.

References

BP Statistical Review (2020), https://www.bp.com/en/global/corporate/news-and-insights/press-releases/bp-statistical-review-of-world-energy-2020-published.html.

Bullard C.W., Penner P.S. and Pilati D.A. (1978): 'Net Energy Analysis: Handbook for Combining Process and Input Output Analysis', *Resources and Energy*, Vol. 1, No. 3, pp. 267–313.

CIA (1980): *International Energy Statistical Review*, National Foreign Assessment Centre, November 25, 1980.

Helm D. (2003): *Energy, the State and the Market, British Energy Policy Since 1979*, Oxford University Press.

Horsnell P. and Mabro R. (1993): *Oil Markets and Prices*, Oxford University Press.

House of Commons Research Papers (2014): *Privatisation*, Research Paper 14/61, November 20, 2014.

IOSCO (2013a): *Consultation Report*, The Board of the International Organisation Securities Commissions CR01/13, January.

Johnson O. (2018): *The Price Reporters, A Guide to PRAs and Commodity Benchmarks*, Routledge, London.

Krapels E. (1977): *Controlling Oil: British Oil Policy and the British National Oil Corporation*. US Government Printing Office, Washington, DC.

Mabro R., Bacon R., Chadwick M., Halliwell M. and Long D. (1986): *The Market for North Sea Crude Oil*, Oxford University Press for the Oxford Institute for Energy Studies.

McGrandle L. (1975): *The Story of North Sea Oil*, Wayland Publishers.

Pearson P. and Watson J. (2012): *UK Energy Policy 1980-2010, History and Lessons to be Learnt*, Parliamentary Group for Energy Studies.

Shepherd M. (2015): *Oil Strike, North Sea; A First-Hand History of North Sea Oil*, Luat Press Limited, Edinburgh.

Wolf & Michael G.P. (2008): *Privatising National Oil Companies: Assessing the Impact on Firm Performance*, Working Papers EPRG 0805, Energy Policy Research Group, Cambridge Judge Business School, University of Cambridge.

11

Benchmarks: Brent

The Brent Benchmark

Brent is the world's most important oil benchmark. It is a pricing reference for the Atlantic basin (North Sea, Mediterranean, and Africa) and for most 'sweet' (low sulphur) crude in Asia (Australia, Malaysia, Vietnam, and others).[1] It is generally accepted that Dubai, the main benchmark in Asia, or more generally, 'East of Suez', is essentially, a spread to Brent.[2] That would make Brent benchmarks responsible for setting the price for over 70% of world exported oil (by adding total shares of Brent and Oman/Dubai, see Fig. 11.1).

Brent 'paper' has evolved from being a 'forward'[4] market in physical cargoes in the 1980s, to become the most complex oil market in the world. It is a brand name of a benchmark that has reinvented itself many times since 1980s. Due to falling production, other sweet North Sea grades were gradually introduced into the Brent delivery mechanism forming what we now call a Brent or 'BFOET basket', comprising and named after: Brent, Forties, Oseberg, Ekofisk, and Troll grades of crude oil. Forties grade was introduced in 2002 (with the important Buzzard field entering production and feeding into the Forties stream in 2007), Oseberg in 2002, Ekofisk in 2007, and Troll in 2018. More additions are expected and will be discussed later in the chapter.[5] What is left of Brent blend crude oil, loading at Sullom Voe terminal,[6] is now just a brand name.

The physical volumes of oil in the 'Brent basket' have also been increased over time by widening the loading 'window' or the number of cargos which

© The Author(s), under exclusive license to Springer Nature Switzerland AG 2021
A. Imsirovic, *Trading and Price Discovery for Crude Oils*,
https://doi.org/10.1007/978-3-030-71718-6_11

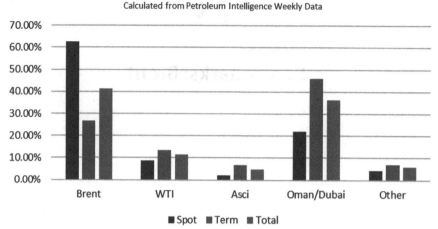

Fig. 11.1 Use of benchmarks in crude oil exports (%) (Calculated from the Petroleum Intelligence Weekly data[3])

qualify for the price assessment of Dated Brent. In the early days, from 1987 to 2002, this 'window' was from 7 to 15 days ahead of the date of assessment. In 2002, the window was expanded to 10–21 days ahead; in 2012 it was expanded to 10–25 days ahead. Finally, in 2015, it was extended yet again, this time to 10–30 days or one calendar month forward 'window'. Each of these changes added to the volume of oil included in the assessment. As we can see in the chart below, this has stabilised the volume of reported deals in the 'Brent basket'. The low volume of trades in 2020 should be attributed to the COVID-19 pandemic in this exceptional year (Fig. 11.2).[7]

Dated Brent

While Brent started trading as a 'forward' or 'cash' market, where oil was 'churned' for tax optimisation reasons,[8] Dated Brent is simply Brent with loading dates,[9] often referred to as 'wet' (as opposed to 'paper' Brent with no loading dates,[10] in the forward or futures markets). Being a price of actual prompt, physical oil, Dated Brent is generally used as a benchmark for physical trades of other types of crude oil. To understand what the actual Dated Brent benchmark price is, it is necessary to understand how its price is assessed. In a nutshell, it is based on four pillars or assessment values:

- Physical assessment of the value of the basket of Brent (BFOET)[11] grades.

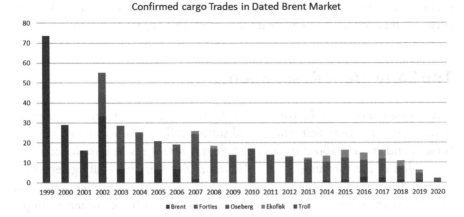

Fig. 11.2 Confirmed Dated Brent deals (Argus data)

- A forward curve based on the Dated swaps market.
- The fixed price of the forward or futures 'Brent' contract.
- Quality differentials or premiums (QP) of crudes other than Brent or Forties.[12]

Assessment of the Dated Brent forward curve allows for a wide range of crudes to be priced off this single benchmark. PRAs such as Platts and Argus report a wide variety of price differentials (for example, Urals, a variety of West African, Mediterranean, North Sea, and even Asia-Pacific, generally sweet crudes) vis-à-vis the Forward Dated Brent. This allows the refineries to compare the relative value of the different crudes and assess how different crudes are being valued in comparison to a common benchmark. This makes Dated Brent uniquely important in the global oil trade.

The most peculiar feature of the physical Brent market is that it is generally traded as a differential to itself (to Dated Brent). Therefore, the PRAs are challenged to assess the Dated Brent price based on physical trades which are themselves differentials to Dated Brent! Fortunately, the expected assessments for Dated Brent are traded in a liquid derivatives market as weekly swaps,[13] called Contracts for Difference or CFDs.[14] Historically, CFDs developed from a need to convert an outright Forward Brent price into a Dated Brent price plus a differential (and vice versa). In the 1980s and 1990s, most of the Forward Brent contracts were traded on an outright price basis.[15]

As different grades of oil used Dated Brent pricing around the Bill of Lading[16] as a reference or benchmark price, but often traded in very different time periods before loading,[17] there was a need to value them all, using a common denominator. Given that CFDs typically trade some 2–8 weeks forward, they are used to construct the Brent Dated forward curve.[18]

The Early Brent Assessments

Price assessments up to the turn of the century were not particularly rigorous. It was a job of a journalist who would simply call various oil companies and brokers and enquire about trades and values. Bids, offers, and trades could be concluded in the morning or late afternoon, but were normally given equal weight. Some trades went unreported, while others were recycled days after they were concluded. Some companies did not deal with each other or simply did not show bids and offers to others.

Making accurate and consistent assessments in such an environment was hard. At the same time, as demand grew and benchmarking would become increasingly important, there was a lot of pressure on the PRAs from the companies caught on the 'wrong' side of the price assessments. Streamlining the price assessments as we know today is generally credited to Jorge Montepeque, a Platts employee who arrived in Singapore in 1991 to head the office there. His motto was: *'Discipline, organisation, and transparency'*.[19] *'There were many languages spoken in the office and everything needed to be brought back to a common standard. I wanted numbers. We needed systems and technology. Everything needed to be collected and recorded, including dates, times, and prices. If anyone wanted to audit us, I wanted to be able to show what we did and why. The only way to do it was to store it electronically'*, said Jorge.

'We first used ICQ,[20] *but it did not have proper time-stamps, so we moved on to Yahoo Messenger. At first, companies did not want to use these systems, but we insisted and somehow, magically, they ended up using them'*, added Jorge. Companies would bid and offer and even agreed to trade—electronically. All the information had to be taken from Yahoo and entered into the Platts electronic system. *'But soon, it became clear that Yahoo was not good enough. We tried other systems, but they were never 'real time'. At the end, we moved to the Intercontinental Exchange (ICE) platform. As an exchange, they understood the importance of time. It took several years, but they delivered. There was a lot of internal fighting to get the right technology. At the end, I prevailed. Singapore was the first office to get linked'*.

In the meantime, Jorge moved to the London office to take care of pricing there. Brent was the most important energy commodity assessment there. *'It was 2001. I landed at London Heathrow on the expiry date of a contract and there was a Brent squeeze. I did a 'reset'. ICE did not like what I was doing.*

The industry was against it. The regulators prompted by traders, were against it. My guys in Platts were against it. Somehow, that year, our CEO, Mr. McGraw, picked me as one of the six employees featured in the annual report that year and I became 'bullet-proof, at least for a year. I went ahead and introduced the alternative delivery barrels into the Brent contract, Oseberg and Forties. Then it was BFO', Jorge concluded. Soon, the Platts 'eWindow' started on the ICE platform as well. It included only registered companies, authorised traders, and agreed credit terms between the parties. This was the assessment process we recognise today.

Assessing Brent Prices

The forward value of Brent is assessed at the same time as the Dated value, in the 'window', during 15.45–16.30 London time, with most of the trades done close to the end of the window. The forward Brents are usually traded in 100 kb partials (one-sixth of a cargo).[21] Figure 11.3 clearly shows that the trading in partials is concentrated with Shell Trading and Shipping Company (Stasco) being by far the biggest player. The top five traders make up almost 60% of all the trades. However, it does not necessarily mean they have a major influence on the outright prices. Brent is traded on the two exchanges[22] as well, and any major deviation from the exchange prices could be easily arbitraged by any other trader.

Major Brent Cash Partials Traders 2016-2019

Trader	%
Shell International Trading an...	16.47%
Vitol SA	11.62%
Gunvor SA	10.57%
Glencore Commodities Ltd.	10.01%
Hartree Partners, LP	9.80%
Mercuria Energy Trading SA	9.37%
SOCAR Trading UK Limited	8.94%
TOTSA Total Oil Trading SA	6.00%
BP Oil International	4.67%
ther	12.57%

Fig. 11.3 Major Traders in Cash Brent 2016–2019 (Using S&P Global Platts data)

The higher quality grades in the BFOET basket such as Ekofisk, Oseberg, and Troll have a quality premium (QP) applied[23] to 'normalize' the differentials for the assessment process. Brent's assessment is set by the grade with lowest value. From the refining point of view, it is usually Forties, due to its relatively high sulphur levels, and it commonly, but not exclusively, establishes the value of Dated Brent. The quality of Forties crude may sometimes vary depending on the contribution of the Buzzard field,[24] and a sulphur de-escalator is applied later, to compensate buyers when the level of sulphur is above 0.6 per cent.[25] This whole process happens in the London 'window' between 15.45 and 16.30 London time, with most trades being done during the last minute of the 'window'. This is a somewhat simplified rendition of the process.[26] Since the CFD curve is an integral part of the assessment process for the Dated Brent benchmark, it will be discussed in a little more detail.

Contracts for Difference (CFDs)

Like any contract for difference, the Brent CFD is a bet.[27] It is a bet that the spread between two Brent prices, the Dated Brent, and the Forward Brent,[28] will be higher or lower than some agreed amount over an agreed period.[29] Dated Brent (which reflects a Brent cargo to be delivered over the period 10 days to one month ahead) and Forward Brent (which reflects crude oil to be delivered further forward in time, usually up to four months ahead) are two key components of the Brent complex. This spread is highly volatile and reflects the prompt market fundamentals relative to the expected market in future. It can easily swing by more than a couple of dollars per barrel in a relatively short period of time.

CFDs have been trading since the early 1990s[30] and have become an essential component of the Brent complex.[31] CFD swaps provide a vital link between Forward Brent and Dated Brent. They play a key role in the price discovery process and the assessment of Dated Brent, a key reference price used in term contracts. CFDs are also an essential tool for hedging and speculation and are commonly used by market participants to manage risk. This risk normally comes from different pricing requirements between buyers and sellers. For example, a refinery would normally want their pricing exposure to be smooth, reflecting their production and sales of petroleum products. Dated Brent forward curve, represented by the CFD market, is an easy way to manage that exposure. Since the curve reveals the value of Dated Brent over time (relative to forward Brent), trading CFDs is a way to 'lock in' that value.

It is particularly useful in contracts where the buyer or seller have optionality in the agreed pricing period.[32] Originally, the swaps were traded primarily using Shell Trading and Supply Company (Stasco)[33] contract terms. Nowadays, virtually all CFD trades are traded or cleared on one of the two major oil exchanges (for an example of a Dated or CFD forward curve, see Fig. 11.4).

Similar to the Brent window forward or 'cash partials' trades, CFDs are concentrated in the hands of a few major players. As can be seen from Fig. 11.5 below, the top five players account for just over 50% of all CFD trades. Vitol and Gunvor were the most active CFD traders, possibly on the back of their large physical activity. CFDs are traded by a wider range of players compared to forward Brent, with the 'other' players accounting for over 30% of all the trades. This indicates that CFD market is utilised by a number of active hedgers or price-takers. While CFDs trade in large volume outside the pricing 'window', it is these 'window' trades that are used for assessing the value of Dated Brent. This peculiar feature of the Brent market sometimes leads to the criticisms that 'the (derivatives) tail is wagging the (physical crude oil value) dog'.[34]

Clearly, there was a small group of players (also Fig. 11.5), very active in trading both forward Brent and CFDs: Shell International Trading and Transport (Stasco), Vitol, Gunvor, BP and Mercuria. While the presence of liquid exchanges would make it hard to make a material difference to the Brent outright price, they are clearly price-makers, with potentially significant impact on the differential between Dated and forward Brent as well as EFP

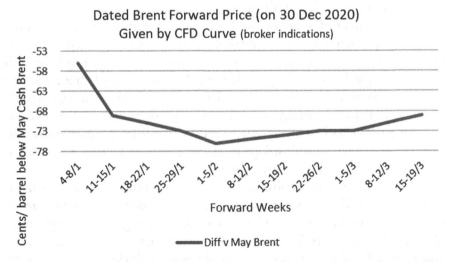

Fig. 11.4 CFD Curve or Forward Value of Dated Brent v May Cash Brent (From various broker indications)

Fig. 11.5 Major CFD Traders 2016–2019 (Platts data)

(Exchange for Physicals, or a spread between cash or forward, and futures Brent contracts).

Brent Derivatives and the Exchanges

Another important derivative linking Dated brent and futures Brent contracts is a 'Dated-to-Front Line' (DFL) swap. This product emerged in mid-1990s, following a retreat of some of the banks from the forward Brent market, which always carried a risk of physical delivery. Again, Morgan Stanley is usually credited for inventing this swap which prices over a calendar month as a differential between daily settlements for Platts Dated Brent and the first Brent forward month on the exchange.[35] The swap is a very flexible tool that can trade in pretty much any volume or period, and is used for hedging a whole variety of exposures such as petroleum product cracks and even whole refinery margins. Upstream companies producing oil which is sold on Dated-basis also frequently use it.

For this reason, DFL swaps, normally trade far into the future, as far as five years out.[36] This derivative instrument has provided further transparency in the dated Brent market which has helped, among other things, price discovery for some LNG long-term contracts based on oil-related pricing. Today, virtually all of these derivative products are both cleared and traded on the exchanges. But the path there was not a straight line and the exchanges had to move from open outcry to electronic transactions first.

As discussed previously, Brent has also been trading as a futures contract on the IPE, since 1988. The trading volumes were significantly lifted by the 1990–1991 Iraq war. As the IPE opened at AM 9.30 London time, well before NYMEX in New York, the Brent contract attracted a lot of trading liquidity, following the news from the Middle East. In just two months of the war, the volume of Brent trades on the exchange doubled.[37] The 1990s were the years of the 'dot.com' bubble and 'Enron Online'.[38] Any company with an 'e' in front or '.com' at the end of its name was appreciating in value. Enron was getting a lot of credit for their bilateral trading platform[39] even though most of the liquidity on the platform actually came from the market-makers such as Morgan Stanley, Goldman, BP, and Shell.

Eventually, these players, together with Elf (later bought by Total), Deutche Bank and Société Générale, bought into a separate platform, Continental Power Exchange, owned by Jeffrey Sprecher.[40] Sprecher renamed it to 'Intercontinental Exchange' (ICE), with a plan to bring in the NYMEX exchange[41] as a shareholder and partner and make it and OTC derivatives trading platform.[42] However, NYMEX board rejected the offer. ICE then approached the IPE, a smaller energy exchange with a well-functioning clearing house. In June 2001, IPE accepted a takeover offer from ICE, soon creating an electronic, energy-trading powerhouse.[43] Morgan and Goldman originally paid only about $8–9 million each and gave shares to the other participants, in return for commitments to trade certain volumes of contracts on ICE. Eventually, these shares were worth well over $1 billion to each bank.[44] Buying into ICE was one of their best trades, ever.

There is no franchise for the 'Brent' brand name and Brent contracts are listed on both ICE and CME exchanges now. Normally, they are financially settled[45] on the last day of trading based on an index[46] calculated by averaging the physical trades[47] on the last day of the contract. A trader with a futures position in Brent can easily turn it into a physical cargo using an 'EFP' contract, usually through a broker, in one simple transaction.[48] This establishes a pretty seamless link between futures, forwards, and actual physical oil, making Brent one of the most robust benchmarks in the world.

With development of liquid spot and futures markets, oil became commoditised, in many cases just another index in a wide portfolio of investments.

The Asian Link

In the 1980s and 1990s, a lot of the North Sea barrels moved to the largest consumer of oil in the world, the United States. However, with the rise of Asia and China in particular, as well as the growth of the United States shale production, the oil flows changed (see Fig. 11.6). With falling energy

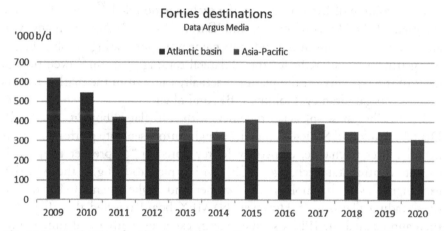

Fig. 11.6 Destination for the North Sea Forties crude over time (Argus Media data)

demand in Europe and growing Asian thirst for the commodity, since about 2010, selling the North Sea oil started to depend on Asian demand. The most common grade setting the Brent benchmark, Forties became popular in Asia.[49]

However, the dominant benchmark 'East of Suez' is Dubai. This is because the Middle East (ME) has historically been the key supplier of oil to this part of the world. While Brent represents the fundamentals in Europe, Dubai reflects the supply and demand realities 'East of Suez'. As a result, the interaction between the two benchmarks is a key indicator of the expected flows between the two key markets, the Atlantic basin and Asia. This interaction is discussed in the next chapter.

Notes

1. Brent is also used to price delivered crude into China. According to the Intercontinental Exchange (ICE) website (https://www.theice.com/brent-crude):' *Brent is the price barometer for 70% of global crude, with accessibility as a waterborne supply that is easily transported around the world.*' As we shall show, it is probably including Dubai benchmark as well.

2. Discussed in the next chapter on the Dubai benchmark.
3. PIW, Friday, 29 May 2020.
4. As explained in the previous chapter, forward Brent is simply a physical cargo sold 'forward' or in advance of the issue of the loading programme for that month, indicating loading dates.
5. Also, see Chapter 14.
6. In January and February 2021, there were only three cargoes of Brent per month.
7. According to Argus, other reasons for falling reporting are market participants' willingness is reduced due to changing company policies, given fear of regulatory consequences and different reporting structure—the market being forced into a narrow window where only what is explicitly to be used for setting Dated is declared.
8. Discussed in the previous chapter.
9. It means that the nomination procedure has been completed and a three-day laycan or loading window is known.
10. Except for the agreed month of delivery.
11. Brent and BFOET will be used interchangeably, both having the same meaning: the Brent benchmark basket.
12. Forties has a sulphur de-escalator (see endnote #70). This and quality premiums are discussed in the next section.
13. It is assessed on a weekly basis, because oil in Europe traditionally prices over a five-day range, usually around the 'bill of lading'.
14. CFD is a differential between physical or Dated Brent v forward (usually first) Brent. The swap is usually traded over one week period, mimicking a five-day pricing normally used for North Sea cargoes.
15. The seller of the physical cargo (say 15–17 January loading) would offer it at a price related to a forward Brent (say February Brent plus $0.10 a barrel). Once this differential was agreed by both parties, they would agree on the value of February Brent (say $25 a barrel). Finally, the seller would sell the physical cargo to the buyer at $25.10 a barrel and they would exchange February cargoes as hedges (the buyer of the physical Brent would sell a February forward Brent, and the seller of the physical would buy it).
16. Bill of Lading is the final document confirming all the loading details including volume, date and time of completion.
17. Urals would often trade shortly before or even after loading, while the West African cargoes would typically trade several weeks before loading.
18. CFD Brent swaps are differentials between Dated and forward Brent values. For example, 1–5 April CFD swaps may trade at June forward Brent, minus 50 cents per barrel (−$0.50). The following week (8–12 April), they may trade at −$0.30, and so on. PRAs need to establish these values (forward curve) as they are the key to resolving the circular problem where physical or Dated Brent, normally trades as a differential to Dated Brent! Let's take an example of a cargo of Forties crude (one of the grades in the 'Brent basket), loading 2–4 April,

traded at Dated + $0.50/bbl and another cargo of the same grade loading 9–11 April traded at Dated + $0.30/bbl. Given the above CFD values, they have both effectively traded at the same absolute price, equal to June forward Brent ($-$0.50 + $0.50 = 0$ and $-$0.30 + $0.30 = 0$). The actual value for June forward Brent is established at the end of a 'window' at 16.30 London time and the above differentials are added or subtracted from it.For more details on CFDs Fattouh B. and Imsirovic A. (2019).

19. From author's interview with Jorge Montepeque, November 2020.
20. ICQ ('I seek you') was one of the early, public, messaging platforms, originally developed by the Israeli company Mirabilis in 1996. It was bought by AOL in 1998.
21. Originally, Brent was trading in 600 kb cargoes. It switched to 500 kb and now the standard cargo size is 600 kb again.
22. CME and ICE.
23. It is applied at 60% of an established premium between Oseberg and Ekofisk and the cheapest grade. Troll QP was introduced in March 2019; see 'Platts Methodology and specifications guide Crude oil' available free online.
24. Introduction of Buzzard field into the Forties and therefore Brent basked caused a lot of controversy at the time, given its high sulphur content of 1.42% and lover API gravity. For example, with zero Buzzard added to it, Forties crude would be API 44 and 0.27% S. With 'normal', about 30% Buzzard in the blend, Forties crude is much lower API 39.6 and much higher S% of 0.68.
25. To compensate the buyers for sulphur levels over 0.6%. See: 'Methodology and specifications guide North Sea sulphur de-escalator', S&P Global Platts: 'https://www.spglobal.com/platts/plattscontent/_assets/_files/en/our-met hodology/methodology-specifications/northseadeescalator.pdf.
26. For now, we avoid discussing the issue of EFP in Platt's methodology. Traders hedging their physical oil with futures and CFDs take additional EFP risk as CFDs are based on the Dated and forward Brent differential and not on the Dated and futures Brent differential!
27. Modern betting systems are generally based on contracts for difference, offering markets for anything from the price of oil to a number of goals a football team may score in a particular time-period.
28. It can be any forward Brent, but the most liquid (the following month) is commonly used.
29. Brent CFDs can trade over any time period, but they are normally traded on weekly basis. For more details, see Fattouh and Imsirovic A. (2019).
30. The brokers embraced CFDs as they could charge commissions on both side of the trade! Early CFD brokers were United and First National.
31. Fattouh (2010), p. 4.
32. For details how to use CFDs in locking in this optionality, see Fattouh and Imsirovic A. (2020).
33. Original traders were brokered over-the-counter (OTC) using Stasco General Terms and Conditions (STASCO GT&CS).

34. The author does not necessarily share this view; see 'Do not blame PRAs for oil industry structural failures', *Financial Times*, 20 May 2013.
35. To avoid the last (contract settlement) day of the month, it normally uses the following month (M + 2) on the last day.
36. Obviously, players that far out are few and far in between and normally include specialised market-makers including banks.
37. Horsnell and Mabro (1993), p. 193.
38. Enron launched their trading platform 'Enron Online' in 1999.
39. The idea behind Enron Online was for Enron to be a market or price-maker for every trade. On the platform, one could not trade with any other company but Enron. This gave the company a trading advantage, being in the centre of the price, volume and trade information flow.
40. This is a short summary from my interview with Colin Bryce of Morgan Stanley, one of he key instigators of the deal, as well as from Morrison (2008), pp. 257–271.
41. WTI oil contract was trading there.
42. To avoid competing with NYMEX. ICE badly needed a clearing house, which both NYMEX and IPE had.
43. According to Colin Bryce: '*The present day ICE is a Sprecher creation. That man is one of the top five commodity heroes of our generation*'.
44. Ibid.
45. There is no physical delivery. Any outstanding long or short positions are settled against the Index, calculated at the end of a trading month.
46. The ICE Brent Index should represent the average price of trading in the BFOE (Brent-Forties-Oseberg-Ekofisk) 'cash' or forward ('BFOE Cash') market in the relevant delivery month as reported and confirmed by industry media. The ICE Brent Index is published by ICE Futures Europe on the day after expiry of the front month ICE Brent futures contract and used by the Exchange as the final cash settlement price. CME Brent Index is calculated in similar fashion.
47. In the absence of physical deals, various derivatives can be used (usually spreads and EFPs) to arrive at the final index.
48. For example, a long futures position is turned into a long forward or 'cash' position by purchasing an EFP (buyer gets a forward cargo in exchange for futures contract plus a premium).
49. Korea in particular. This has a lot to do with a tax treatment of European imports.

References

Fattouh B. (2010): *An Anatomy of the Crude Oil Pricing System*, OIES Paper WPM 40.

Fattouh B. and Imsirovic A. (2019): *Contracts for Difference and the Evolution of the Brent Complex*, Oxford Energy Comment, June.

Fattouh B. and Imsirovic A. (2020b): *Crude Oil Pricing Optionality and Contracts for Difference*, Oxford Energy Comment, June.

Horsnell P. and Mabro R. (1993): *Oil Markets and Prices*, Oxford University Press.

Morrison K. (2008): *Living in a Material World, A Commodity Connection*, Wiley, London, UK.

12

Dubai and Oman: Brent's Asian Relatives

A Grand Old Benchmark

Dubai crude oil has been the main Asian benchmark since the mid-1980s.[1] It's quality of just over 30 API and sulphur content of a bit over 2 per cent made it ubiquitous for most Asian refineries. It had no destination or resale restrictions and, as a result, it was freely traded on spot basis.

Just like Brent, Dubai production has diminished substantially. The government of Dubai does not release figures for its crude oil production but, from the loading data and sales, it can be deduced that production has fallen well below 70,000 b/d in 2021.[2] Additional grades of oil were added into the contract over time, bolstering volumes of oil available for assessment. Just like Brent, the Dubai benchmark has evolved into a 'brand name'.

For historical reasons, most grades of oil trading 'East of Suez' base their price formulae on the basis of monthly averages, the period normally being the month of loading. This has resulted in monthly Dubai swaps being the primary hedging instrument. These swaps are regularly traded as a differential to Brent futures, or EFS.[3] Dubai swaps can also be traded as a spread to Brent swaps (Brent/Dubai swap-swap spread). Dubai swap time-spreads (Dubai spreads) are especially liquid derivative instruments in their own right. Just like the Brent, a large derivatives market has grown around the Dubai 'brand name', feeding back into the price discovery of the benchmark itself.

Just like Brent, Dubai contract allows for the seller to deliver the most competitive grade[4] into the 'Dubai basket', traded during the so-called 'Platts Dubai window', between 15.45 and 16.30 Singapore time.[5] Trading in the

© The Author(s), under exclusive license to Springer Nature Switzerland AG 2021
A. Imsirovic, *Trading and Price Discovery for Crude Oils*,
https://doi.org/10.1007/978-3-030-71718-6_12

'window' is based on 25 kb cash 'partials'[6] in order to provide for more liquidity and continuous price discovery. Once two parties trade 20 partials for the same month of loading, the seller declares a grade to be delivered that month, and that is normally the cheapest of the five crudes in the Dubai basket.

Dubai production reached a peak of about 400,000 barrels in 1991. By the turn of the century, it fell significantly, making it small relative to the overall volume of oil pricing using the benchmark.[7] In January 2002, to avoid the benchmark being squeezed, Platts introduced Oman as alternative crude deliverable in the Dubai contract. This followed the same approach used in bolstering the Brent benchmark.[8] With over 800,000 barrels of production, and no destination and resale restrictions, Oman significantly boosted the overall volume of oil deliverable in the Dubai 'basket'.[9] In 2006, mimicking the widening of the Brent basket, Platts also added Abu Dhabi's Upper Zakum, grade[10] of oil. It was a controversial move as, prior to the introduction, Upper Zakum scarcely traded on spot basis. However, it proved to be the right decision, improving the overall liquidity of the Dubai 'brand'.[11]

The benchmark was relatively steady until 2014. Then, in August of that year, Chinaoil, a trading arm of Petro China, one of the Chinese majors, caused an upset in the market by buying 47 deliverable Dubai cargoes, or over 23 million barrels of 'Dubai basket'[12] grades of oil in a single month.[13] As a result, Platts started consultations with the industry players, and in 2016, introduced two additional grades of oil into the Dubai basket. They were Qatar's Al-Shaheen[14] and, more controversially,[15] Abu Dhabi's premiere, light, and medium-sulphur Murban.[16] All of the grades of oil in the Dubai basket are subject to a quality premium (QP), which is established along the same lines to that of the Brent basket.[17] While Al-Shaheen added only 200–250 kbd of deliverable oil into the Dubai contract, Murban potentially added over a million barrels a day.[18] The inclusion brought more liquidity and more importantly, stability[19] in the benchmark (See Fig. 12.1).

Changing Flows

The 1990s and early 2000s have witnessed two main themes in the world oil markets. The first is a shift in demand from the developed to the developing world, particularly towards Asia[20] and the Middle East (ME). The second is a large increase in light oil and gas production in the Americas.[21] The consequences for the crude oil flows to Asia, as well as main price benchmarks, have been profound.

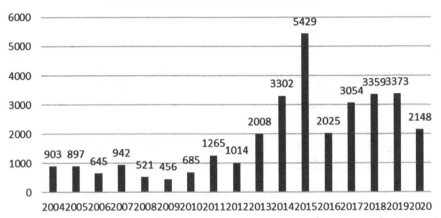

Fig. 12.1 Dubai Partials trades (numbers of 25 kbd partials) in Platts Window 2004–2020 (S&P Global Platts Data)

The United States East Coast (USEC) and Canadian refiners, traditional buyers of high gasoline yield crude oil from the North Sea, West Africa (WAF) and North Africa, essentially stopped importing these light grades, given the availability of locally produced, light sweet shale crude oil. Increased volume of sweet barrels from the Atlantic basin, which mainly trade on spot basis and have no destination restrictions (unlike most OPEC crude oil), became 'swing' barrels for the Asian refiners. They were ideal source of crude for new and expanding refineries looking for cheaper incremental feedstock.[22]

Given the weak domestic demand and persistently poor margins (see Fig. 12.2), the European refineries, especially the simple ones with limited upgrading capacity, have been closing down.[23] Most of the new and more sophisticated refinery capacity was being built in the Middle East and Asia at the expense of Europe. This was exacerbated by the Russian tax incentives to increase product exports at the expense of the traditional crude oil, in order to maximise revenue.[24] Despite the slowing Chinese economy, the main demand drivers in the oil markets continued to be China and the Middle East. As a result, the oil flows shifted towards Asia from almost all the producing areas.

Since the oil prices are set by the 'marginal' barrels, and the region is the main buyer of these barrels, Asia became the main driver of global oil prices. Delivered price of oil in Asia became a key signal for the world oil markets.[25] At the same time, the Middle East and other global producers became more dependent on Asian demand. This resulted in increased market

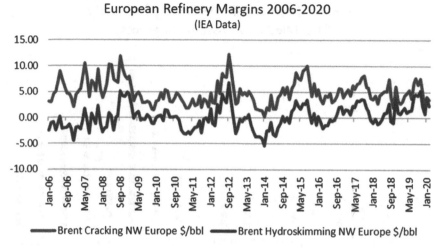

Fig. 12.2 European refinery margins (Author using IEA data)

power of the Asian consumers and ended the discussion about the so-called 'Asian premium'.[26]

The growing importance of Asia as a destination for oil from all over the world has profoundly impacted the Dubai market. 'Arbitrage' barrels from the Atlantic basin to Asia normally trade against Brent and WTI benchmarks. The end users in Asia are generally evaluating them on Dubai-related prices.[27] This means somewhere in the supply chain, prices may need to be converted from other benchmarks to Dubai prices. The process of arbitrage involves buying Brent, WTI[28] and selling Dubai swaps, in order to 'lock in' the differential at which oil is competitive in Asia.

The Brent-Dubai Link: The Heart of the Global Oil Flows

Dubai partials trade (on a fixed price basis, in dollars per barrel) only during the Singapore short pricing window. For the remainder of the trading day, all Dubai trades are still differentials to Brent futures (EFS), Brent swaps or spreads to other Dubai swap months (swap spreads, referred to as Dubai spreads). Even during the Singapore window, traders usually estimate their Dubai fixed price bids and offers based on the prevailing Brent futures prices, adjusted for the Brent/Dubai spread. As a result, Dubai does reflect the regional fundamentals, but its absolute price level is driven by the Brent benchmark.

Brent/Dubai spread also reflects two important global oil indicators, sweet-sour quality differential and arbitrage economics for Atlantic basin crudes to move to Asia. When there is a shortage of sour crude in Asia, as during OPEC production cuts for example, Brent/Dubai spread typically narrows.[29] The spread is an indicator as well as a liquid instrument, enabling signalling, hedging and speculation in the sweet-sour oil differential.

Given that Asia is short of crude oil, it pulls barrels from the Atlantic basin, which is long oil. A narrow Brent/Dubai spread (strong Dubai relative to Brent) would indicate healthy demand in Asia, abundant supply in the Atlantic, or both. If the spread (plus the cost of shipping oil from the Atlantic basin to Asia) is less than the Dubai-related bids in Asia, the 'arbitrage opens' and oil will likely flow between the two markets. In contrast, a wide Brent/Dubai spread is normally an indicator of relatively poor demand in Asia, tight supply in the Atlantic, or both.

Brent/Dubai EFS tends to be the dominant trading link between the two benchmarks.[30] For example, importing Brent-related barrels, such as North Sea or African oil, loading in the month of January to Asia and converting its price into a Dubai-related one, would normally involve a purchase of January EFS (buying January Brent futures and selling January Dubai swaps can be done as one trade by buying the January EFS). Then, as the cargo has 'priced in', during the loading period of January,[31] Brent futures are sold rateably.

The arbitrage closes when a sufficient volume of oil has been hedged and the Brent/Dubai spread has been driving higher until enough barrels have moved and the arbitrage is closed. The spread is bid to a level where the arbitrage economics (difference in prices minus transportation, financing, and insurance costs) do not work any longer. Eventually, a closed arbitrage would put pressure on the Atlantic basin and Brent would fall until it is cheap enough relative to Dubai for the arbitrage to open again.[32] The arbitrage is also driven by the costs of moving the barrels between regions. Therefore, freight costs tend to be essential in making the arbitrage work. The higher the freight element is in the cost of moving the barrels between the two markets, the less likely it is to happen. If this is the case, the bids for imported oil in Asia, Dubai being a common pricing denominator for most of them, may have to increase further to facilitate the needed imports. This would tend to narrow the Brent/Dubai spread.[33]

The spread works like a pump, sending a price signal and then sucking in the barrels. When the demand has been met, the spread resets until another cycle begins. Brent/Dubai spread is the heart of the global oil flows.

Price Discovery for Dubai Is a Little Different

Unlike Brent and WTI, Dubai has no liquid, functioning futures markets.[34] However, the Dubai derivatives such as Dubai swaps, EFS, Brent-Dubai swap spreads and Dubai (swap) spreads frequently trade both in the OTC markets and the exchanges. The way to establish a value of a Dubai swap is to use Brent and apply the prevailing EFS value to it. This is best illustrated by an example. Physical Dubai cargoes traditionally trade as a differential to Dubai swaps (equal to swap value during the month of loading). For example, physical Dubai loading in the month of October will trade as a premium or a discount to October Dubai swaps,[35] and would normally trade about two months earlier, during August. Also, in August, the most liquid EFS market will be October (which is a spread between October Brent futures and October Dubai swaps). By applying October EFS to October Brent futures, a trader can obtain the October Dubai swap value. During August, when October Dubai normally trades, its value is equal to the calculated October swap, plus some differential (positive or negative), depending on the fundamentals of the market.[36] To obtain a value of any forward month of Dubai, say twelve months forward, a very liquid Dubai (swap) spread market is used.

Just like Dated Brent, the Singapore window is dominated by a small elite of self-selected 'price makers'[37] and there is even more concentration among the top players. Shell and the trading arms of the two Chinese majors, Unipec and China Oil, accounted for almost 60% of all the trades (between 2018 and 2020, see Fig. 12.3). Half a dozen players accounted for almost all the deals. No national oil companies (NOCs) were involved.[38] The rest of the market were price-takers.

It is a shame as PRAs generally encourage as wide participation in the price-setting process as possible. The reasons for relative low participation are likely to be risk aversion, lack of trading know-how, and potentially high transaction costs. Normally, there are many cash partials trades during the course of the window at prices different from the final assessment. Any company involved in the process may end up with one or more physical cargoes long or short. This introduces risk and most refiners and upstream companies simply lack the authority to take on such risk. Equally, they may not accept additional cost, given uncertain outcomes, and may not have the necessary know-how to manage the resulting risk exposures appropriately. This is gradually changing as some refiners such as Reliance, SK Energy and upstream companies such as ADNOC and ARAMCO are setting up their own trading arms,[39] along the lines of the majors BP, and Shell.

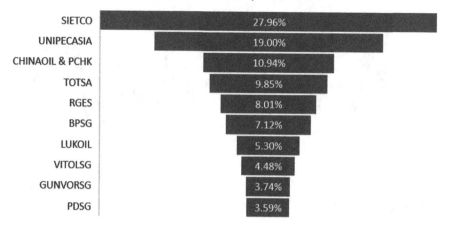

Fig. 12.3 Dubai Platts Window Trades (both buy and sell partials) from Jan 2018 to Jun 2020 (Platts data)

The oil pricing system 'East of Suez' also includes the Oman benchmark, which had been largely neglected before the launching of the Oman futures contract in 2007.

Oman: Dubai's Neglected Sibling

A number of OPEC producers such as Saudi Arabia, Kuwait, Iran, and Iraq base their pricing formula on both Dubai and Oman.[40] Omani government sets the price of its crude based on the average of the monthly settlements of the Oman futures contract on the Dubai Mercantile Exchange (DME).[41] More interestingly, the official price of the Dubai crude oil itself, is based on the DME Oman settlements. Given that the physical Oman crude often trades on Dubai Platts quotations,[42] most newcomers to the Asian oil market will find it mind-bending.[43]

Oman is lighter, with lower sulphur content, making it a higher value grade of oil and it normally trades at a premium to Dubai.[44] It is well accepted by most Asian refiners, has no destination restrictions, and is frequently transacted in the spot market. With at least fifty physical cargoes produced every month[45] and loading outside the Strait of Hormuz,[46] it has many characteristics of a good benchmark. It is a part of the 'Dubai basket' and deliverable into the Platts Dubai contract.

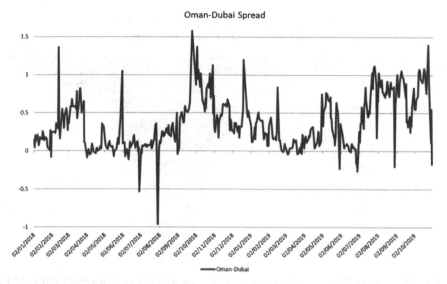

Fig. 12.4 Oman v Dubai differential ($/bbl) (S&P Platts data for Dubai and DME for Oman)

It can be seen (Fig. 12.4) that Oman and Dubai prices, or a spread, can diverge by a dollar per barrel, and often more. While this difference can be significant, historically Asian refiners done little to hedge it.[47] The evidence for this is a relatively low volume of Oman trading on the DME exchange outside the 'pricing window' and the trading on the exchange seems to be primarily for the reasons of physical delivery.[48]

Similarly, to most oil futures contracts, DME Oman futures settle daily, based on a weighted average of trades between 16.25 and 16.30 Singapore time (Exactly the same time as the closing minutes of the 'Singapore Dubai window'). In line with the usual timing of Asian oil purchases, the contract trades two months before the actual month of loading. For example, during January, the front-month contract is March. The Oman official selling price (OSP) is simply a monthly average of the DME Oman daily settlements. Physical Oman also trades as a differential to this OSP.[49]

Just a Minor Benchmark?

Even though Oman is used as a pricing basis by some of the most important producers in the world and is widely traded, it has remained a minor benchmark overshadowed by Dubai. This is partly to do with a difference in philosophy between some Middle East producers and the reporting agency

S&P Global Platts, mainly used for Dubai pricing purposes. For Platts, there is only one Middle East benchmark, and that is Dubai. Platts Dubai benchmark already includes Oman as an alternative delivery grade of oil. But given the mentioned producers' preference for the 'Oman/Dubai' formula, Platts has no choice but to continue publishing the 'Oman' assessment as well.[50] Indeed, the Oman assessment is not even included in the 'Key Benchmarks' section of their flagship publication, Crude Oil Marketwire.

In October 2018, Saudi Aramco changed their oil price formulae to the DME Oman settlement (instead of Platts Oman assessment), in its pricing formula for Asian customers. Saudi Aramco's move from Platt's Oman to the DME Oman assessment was driven in part by the higher volume of daily trades of Oman crude on the DME compared to alternative Oman assessments. For example, the November 2018 DME Oman contract traded on average 1860 lots (1.8 million barrels per day), while on many days it traded well over 4000 lots.[51] During the same period, Platts Oman bids and offers were scarce.[52]

However, the Saudi decision made little if any impact on the volumes of Oman traded. This seems to confirm the 'rule' about benchmarks in general[53] traders prefer liquidity over basis risk. In other words, they are prepared to take some risk (pay some risk premium) and use an imperfect, but liquid instrument rather than eliminate this risk by trading an illiquid contract (which carries its own risks and possibly costs). So, most Asian refiners stick to the liquid Dubai contract, often ignoring their Oman/Dubai spread risk.

Another problem with an Oman benchmark is the fact that most of the grade ends up in China. In 2020, up to 80% of all the cargoes went there.[54] It does not necessarily follow that the Chinese majors control the Oman contract, but they could certainly have a leverage over it if they wished to do so. Finally, DME Oman has had some issues with the expiry of the contract when the liquidity dried up and caused elevated levels volatility. This was probably caused by traders 'squaring up' their positions early, before delivery volumes are decided, making any late adjustments difficult in thin market. Some adjustments to the contract including introduction of an alternative delivery mechanisms (additional deliverable grades) would certainly make Oman a more robust Middle East regional benchmark.[55]

As we shall see in the next chapter, it is the oil flows which determine the importance and use of particular benchmarks. WTI is a good example of how a regional benchmark with ample liquidity can play an important role in the oil markets. Equally, changing flows and poor policy can make it, at least temporarily, irrelevant.

Notes

1. See Fattouh, Bassam. (2012), '*The Dubai Benchmark and Its Role in the International Oil Pricing System*', Oxford Energy Comment.
2. At the time of writing, there are about 3 cargoes of Dubai available for loading each month.
3. EFS stands for Exchange of Futures for Swaps, where (Brent) futures contracts are exchanged for a (Dubai) swap contract. Brent/Dubai swaps (swap v swap) are also traded frequently as a spread.
4. Subject to the quality premium or QP applicable to Oman, Upper Zakum, Al Shahen and Murban. It is set in a similar fashion to the QP for the Brent basket. See the previous chapter.
5. Platts uses the Market on Close (MOC) to assess prices for crude oil, petroleum products and related swaps. The MOC is a structured process in which bids, offers and transactions are submitted by participants to Platts' editors. Following the close, Platts' editors examine the data gathered through the day and develop price assessments that reflect an end-of-day value. The Platts 'window' is the term market participants use to refer to the 30 to 45-minute period before the close of the market, when Platts no longer accepts new bids or offers in the price assessment process. More on this at: http://www.platts.com/IM.Platts.Content/MethodologyReferences/Method ologySpecs/Crude-oil-methodology.pdf.
6. They are cash partials because, when added up to a full cargo (20 partials of 25 kb each), they become a full physical cargo of 500 kb.
7. In November 2000, Dubai production was only 160 kbd. See Rushforth and Blei (2020), p. 4.
8. Discussed in the previous chapter.
9. Platts Oman assessments reflect the value of Middle East sour crude oil, where the buyer is willing to accept delivery of Oman itself, or alternative delivery of Murban, at the seller's option. In all cases, cargoes must be free of any restrictions or limitations placed on the buyer, such as resale or destination clauses. The operational tolerance for these cargoes is ±1000 barrels at the buyers' option. Source: S&P Global Platts.
10. API 33.9 and 1.84% sulphur.
11. At the time of the introduction, this author was questioning the relevance of UZ to the Dubai liquidity because the spot trades were scarce. But with the first deliveries of the grade in the Dubai trade, the author proved to be wrong. The UZ production is about 630 kbd at the time of writing.
12. Dubai, Oman and Upper Zakums.
13. It was trading during the month of August. See 'China Imports Record Crude as Price Collapse Spurs Buying Spree', Bloomberg News, 13 January 2015.
14. API 28.10 and 2.37% sulphur.

15. The introduction of Murban was and still is controversial as it does not quite reflect the fundamentals of the traditional, Middle East medium heavy, sour crude such as Dubai.

16. API 40.20 and 0.79, % sulphur. It was and remains controversial as all the other grades in the Dubai basket are medium and high sulphur crude oils.

17. For detailed methodology, see: https://www.spglobal.com/platts/plattscontent/_assets/_files/en/our-methodology/methodology-specifications/apag-crude-methodology.pdf.

18. Only cargoes with no destination restrictions are deliverable. Proportion of such cargoes is hard to estimate, but they are a fraction of the total of about 1.2 mbd at the time of introduction.

19. Making it harder for any one large player to influence price outcomes.

20. See Imsirovic (2014), p. 3.

21. For a more detailed discussion see: Imsirovic, Adi. 'Asian Oil Market in Transition' Journal of Energy Security, April 2014 (http://www.ensec.org/index.php?option=com_content&view=article&id=520:asian-oil-markets-in-transition&catid=143:issue-content&Itemid=435).

22. See Fattouh, Bassam and Sen, Amrita. (August 2014), '*New Swings for West African Crudes*', Oxford Energy Comment.

23. Europe lost a nominal refinery capacity of about 2 million b/d between 2009 and 2021. Another couple of million b/d of capacity may need to be shut before 2022. At the same time, the Chinese new greenfield refinery projects between 2014 and 2022 amount to an additional capacity of about four million b/d. Planned Middle East refinery projects excluding Iraq, between 2014 and 2020, amount to about 3 million b/d. (Calculated from various announcements).

24. In spite of this, Russians have been able to increase their crude oil sales to Asia through the ESPO pipeline.

25. See Imsirovic (2014), p. 2.

26. See Doshi, T. K, and Imsirovic, A. (2013).

27. There are clearly exceptions to this. Most Angolan barrels sold to China are often priced on Dated Brent basis. India buys WAF oil on the same basis. Chinese independents buy delivered oil on Brent exchange prices. It is impossible to know internal benchmarking for each refiner, but it is generally accepted that Dubai is the prevalent benchmark in Asia. This large Brent/Dubai exposure may be too large for the Asian paper markets to bear, resulting in refiners either internalising the exposure within their trading arms (such as Unipec being a trading arm of China Petroleum & Chemical Corporation, or Sinopec) or demanding Bent exposure which is easier to manage.

28. Often it is both in sequence: WTI/Brent, then Brent/Dubai.

29. All other things being equal. Many other factors influence the spread. For details see Imsirovic and Pryor (2018), pp. 3–4.

30. As the Atlantic basin crude oil is normally purchased on pricing period a few days around or after the bill of lading, Brent futures are the common way to

hedge such price. On the other hand, there is no liquid futures market for Dubai. Given that the ME producers and Asian refiners have traditionally been using the whole month of loading for the pricing period, making Dubai swaps a more convenient method of hedging Dubai price.

31. As the oil is normally purchased well over a couple of months before delivery, January EFS may well be the most liquid month. As the delivery approaches, January Brent futures will have to be 'rolled' to March, the first or most prompt contract in the month of January. Therefore, the trader would likely be 'rolling' her futures hedges from January to March Brent.

32. The existence of large buyers and sellers as well as greater liquidity in the Brent contract can make the spread a bit 'sticky'. See Imsirovic, A. (2014), p. 3.

33. Depending on the shipping market. If the market is weak, ship owners may have to absorb the additional cost. However, in a balanced market, they are likely to pass the cost on to the charterer.

34. Dubai swaps, swap spreads and Brent—Dubai swap spread and EFS do trade on ICE and CME. These are normally based on Platts assessments (for Dubai). But there is no futures contract for the actual Dubai crude oil contract.

35. I am using trading jargon here. October swap value is an average of all daily Platts assessments for Dubai first month (the most prompt month) cargoes.

36. The conclusion that Dubai is a benchmark derived from Brent and not a centre of absolute price discovery remains valid: Horsnell, P. (1997).

37. See Fattouh, Bassam. (2012), 'The Dubai Benchmark'. Of course, participation of one or more large producers could also produce a biased benchmark. It should be said that the Brent market also involves a small 'self-appointed elite' of participants. However, unlike Dubai, Brent has a hugely liquid futures market working in tandem with the PRA assessment process in providing the price discovery.

38. It is becoming increasingly hard to distinguish 'oil traders' from the other market participants. For many years now, most majors have had trading arms (Stasco, a trading arm of Shell, is possibly the biggest trading company in the world). However, more and more refiners (Unipec, China Oil, Reliance, and others) have their own trading companies. NOCs such as Oman, Abu Dhabi and Saudis now have active trading arms, to be discussed in the final chapter. Finally, trading houses such as Glencore, Vitol and others have had both upstream and downstream assets for quite some time.

39. This will be discussed in the last chapter of the book.

40. They use 50% Dubai and 50% Oman based on Platts quotations. In 2018, Saudis changed from Platts Oman to DME futures Oman.

41. DME is a joint venture between Dubai Holding, Oman Investment Authority and CME (exchange) Group plus some energy trading firms such as Goldman Sachs, J.P. Morgan, Morgan Stanley, Shell, Vitol, and Concord Energy. DME exchange was launched in June 2007.

42. As it is common 'East of Suez', average month quotations during the month of loading.

43. Dubai OSP is essentially a small differential (usually about plus/minus 10–30 cents a barrel) to the Oman OSP. Because the Asian refiners tend to benchmark their crude oil purchases relative to Dubai, most spot Oman and Dubai crude is traded on Dubai quotations during the month of loading plus a premium or discount.

44. Oman API of 30.5 is almost identical to Dubai API of 30.4. However, Dubai sulphur content of 2.13% is far higher than Oman's 1.38%. They also have very different yields.

45. At the time of writing, the production of Oman was about 950 kbd.

46. The Straight is close to the Iranian maritime border, making it a major potential choke-point in the international oil trade.

47. Until Oman moved to the DME settlement as a basis for their OSP, there was some trading in the MOG (Ministry of Oil and Gas, Oman)/Dubai swap.

48. DME contract is a physical delivery futures contract.

49. If the contract has already 'priced in' most of the OSP (say in the middle of December for February loaded cargoes), Oman will trade on Dubai swap basis—calendar January Dubai swap plus a differential or discount. This is one of those curiosities of the Asian benchmarks—Dubai OSP is actually set base on the DME Oman settlements!

50. Historically, physical Oman used to be traded extensively. Platts introduced a weekly Oman assessment in 1983 and a daily one two years later. Hence the origins of the Platts Oman assessment and its inclusion into the Saudi pricing formula.

51. Data from DME and Platts.

52. Since then, liquidity in the Platts Oman has improved, but the Saudi decision to stick to DME Oman has remained.

53. This particularly applies to WTI benchmark and will be discussed in the next chapter.

54. In July 2020, 77.6% of all the Oman went to China. Clipper data.

55. For detailed discussion about the contract and possible solutions, see Imsirovic A. (2018).

References

Doshi T.K. and Imsirovic A. (2013): 'The 'Asian Premium' in Crude Oil Markets: Fact or Fiction?' in: Daoijong Z. (Ed), *Managing Regional Energy Vulnerabilities in East Asia*, Routledge. ISBN:978-0-415-53538-0, January, https://doi.org/10.13140/2.1.4053.6009.

Horsnell P. (1997): *Oil in Asia*, Oxford University Press.

Imsirovic A. (2014): *Changes to the 'Dated Brent' Benchmark: More to Come*, Oxford Energy Comment, March 2019.

Imsirovic A. (2018): *What Next for Asian Benchmarks? – A Footnote*, Oxford Energy Comment, November.

Imsirovic A. and Pryor B. (2018): *IMO 2020 and the Brent Dubai Spread*, Oxford Energy Comment, September.

Rushforth J. and Blei V. (2020): *Yields vs. Sulphur: What Is Driving Crude Benchmarks in 2020?* Oxford Energy Comment, July.

13

US Oil and the WTI Benchmark

The Cushing Hub

Throughout the modern history, the United States has been the world single largest regional oil market.[1] Cushing, Oklahoma is at the crossroads of the vast US pipeline system linking the oil producers in Oklahoma, West Texas (Midland), and Canada to the refining centres of the Midwest, Midcontinent and US Gulf Coast (USG). Pipelines deliver crude oil from Canada and the United States shale oil regions such as Bakken, Permian, and Niobrara. From Cushing,[2] the crude oil is fed to the two key refining centres in the Administration for Defence Districts[3] (PADDs): PADD 2 (Midwest) and PADD 3 (USG). The USG is of course, the main export outlet as well.

Given the extent of these connections, West Texas Intermediate crude oil (WTI) is traded at a number of points such as Cushing, Midland, Magellan East Houston (MEH), and the Enterprise Houston Echo hub. The benchmark WTI assessment is based on one of the world's most liquid contracts that is physically delivered in approved storage in Cushing. Massive storage capacity there[4] and a large number of participants provide ample liquidity for trading this light sweet crude oil.[5]

Like all benchmarks, WTI is shaped by oil flows. The key to this benchmark is the Cushing hub. The interaction between the oil gathering centres, two dozen pipelines of almost 4 million barrels per day of pipeline capacity,[6] over 90 million barrels of storage capacity, refining, and import/export facilities are the key to understanding the history, development, and dynamics of the WTI benchmark. Being land-locked, oil balances at the Cushing storage

© The Author(s), under exclusive license to Springer Nature Switzerland AG 2021
A. Imsirovic, *Trading and Price Discovery for Crude Oils*,
https://doi.org/10.1007/978-3-030-71718-6_13

hub are subject to changes in the infrastructure in and around the hub. As domestic production and refining changed, so did the infrastructure linked to Cushing. The pipeline links to the US Gulf Coast are essential in keeping the benchmark linked to the international oil markets.

Rebirth of a Market

Spot, forward, and options oil contracts were flourishing at a number of exchanges throughout the United States in 1880.[7] Then, in January 1895, Rockefeller finally stamped his authority as a monopolist[8] by ending his purchases of oil at the exchange prices (as was the norm at the time[9]). Instead, his buying agent simply decided or 'posted' prices at which it would buy oil for his refineries. Once proud US oil market entered the Dark Ages of monopoly power, governed by large corporations and governments.

Perhaps the darkest episodes for the oil markets occurred during the period when President Nixon's advisor, Henry Kissinger[10] directed a policy of United States support for dictators such as the Shah of Iran,[11] which encouraged higher international oil prices and Nixon's price controls in 1971 (through the Economic Stabilization Program, followed by Ford's Energy Policy and Conservation Act[12]), discouraging domestic oil exploration and production, feeding ever higher petroleum prices. This sad period of energy and foreign policy-making culminated in the 1977 ban on the US oil exports.[13]

At the end of the decade, sick of shortages and ever-increasing prices, voters in Britain and the United States, gave a chance to pro-market ideas of Thatcher and Regan.[14] After a landslide victory, President Regan took only two months to lift the last price controls on US-produced oil.[15] Following the 'decontrol'[16] of prices in 1981, spot physical oil trade grew quickly, and PRAs started surveying and publishing prices for WTI as well as the Louisiana Light Sweet (LLS) and West Texas Sour (WTS).[17]

Soon, the first successful oil futures contract was launched at the New York Mercantile Exchange (NYMEX). The exchange, which was originally operating as the Butter, Cheese and Egg Exchange[18] (staple diet of the times) was in crisis, due to the war restrictions on trading butter and eggs. It launched potato futures, with spuds from Maine providing most of the liquidity. Unfortunately, the potato contract proved popular with a few large and unscrupulous speculators, employing dubious trading strategies. In 1976, the May potato contract collapsed after a large speculator, short a staggering 50 million pounds of potatoes, defaulted.[19] Looking for something else to trade, the exchange launched a heating oil contract[20] in 1978, the first modern energy futures contract. The contract gradually picked up and the market-friendly policies of the Regan administration encouraged the launch of a gasoline futures contract three years later. The gasoline futures contract eventually proved a big success.

The launch of the NYMEX WTI futures contract in March 1983 heralded a return of the oil exchanges in the United States and the world. Timing of the launch was perfect, as OPEC was struggling to control the market and price volatility was growing. With a well-established base in the physical trades around the Cushing area, the physically delivered WTI futures oil contract gradually took off. It was the 1986 and the OPEC subsequent abdication of price-setting role that really spurred the crude oil contract. The first users of the NYMEX oil futures were local fuel distributers, storage operators, refiners, and oil companies.[21] They were soon to be joined by oil traders such as Phibro[22] and banks such as J. Aron[23] and Morgan Stanley.[24] With a steady growth in volumes and open interest (see Fig. 13.1), the exchange and the contract took off.

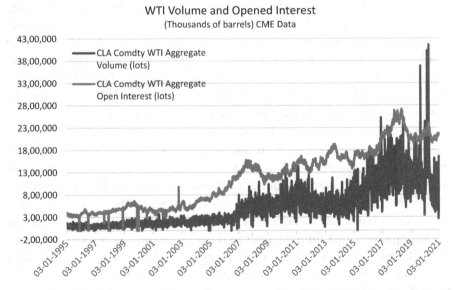

Fig. 13.1 WTI Volume and Open Interest on the CME Exchange (Number of contracts, each 1000 barrels) indicating a relentless growth in oil trading over time (Data CME)

Challenges

Being land-locked, WTI has had a fair share of problems over the years.

One of the first crises was caused by the oil price crash of 1986. It had a dramatic effect on the domestic production, which fell by over 1.5 mbd,[25] causing over 25,000 wells to be shut, many of the permanently.[26] In that year, total open interest in the WTI contract fell to less than 100,000 contracts.[27] Starved of the local crude oil supply, the inland refineries had to import oil from the US Gulf (USG), using reversed pipeline flows.[28] Foreign oil imports became competitive and the NYMEX soon introduced an 'alternative delivery procedure', which allowed for the foreign sweet crudes to be delivered into the contract. The procedure allowed for delivery of a number of light, sweet types of crude oil including Brent,[29] Oseberg, Bonny Light, Qua Iboe, and others. This increased the 'depth' of the market as there was more oil to be delivered into the contract and more new players were able to do it. Open interest in the contract took off and grew steadily to about half a million contracts in 1990s (Fig. 13.1).

Quite the opposite challenge for the WTI benchmark followed the subsequent increases in the Canadian and then domestic shale oil production. This trend started in the mid-1990s, with increasing Canadian oil sands production, mainly exported to the United States where the Midwest and Midcontinent refineries. They invested in upgrading their facilities to take advantage of these cheap, but harder to process grades of oil.[30] Spurred by the rocketing oil prices in 2007 and 2008, Canadian production continued a relentless growth towards the four million barrels a day mark.[31]

Around the same time,[32] United States shale oil production picked up substantially, resulting in domestic oversupply, especially in Cushing. Flooded with crude oil, which was banned from being exported, WTI Benchmark started trading at deep discounts to Brent (see Fig. 13.2). In September 2011, this differential exceeded $32 a barrel. Against the LLS, it traded at a discount of over $29 a barrel. The WTI benchmark became meaningless in signalling the market fundamentals to the international, waterborne markets. USG Coast refineries and exporters of sweet crude from Europe and West Africa started to rely on LLS,[33] as an indicator of market fundamentals at the USG Coast refining hub.

In 2009, unhappy with the discounts of WTI against other international oil prices,[34] Saudi Aramco switched their pricing formula for sales into Americas from Platts WTI assessment to The Argus Sour Crude Index[35] ('ASCI'). They were soon followed by Kuwait and Iraq. The future of the benchmark

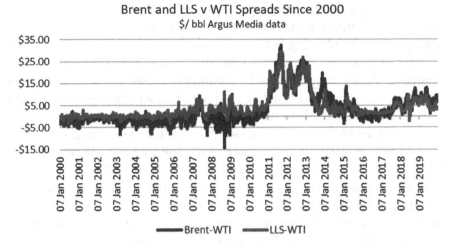

Fig. 13.2 Brent and LLS c WTI Spreads in $/bbl (2000–2020) (Argus Media data)

was seriously in question. Eventually, in May 2012, the underutilised, 669-mile Seaway pipeline system, originally feeding the imported oil from the Gulf Coast to Cushing was reversed.[36] Quickly, the WTI discount to Brent and other international, sweet grades of oil started to narrow.[37]

The WTI price disconnect with the rest of the world was finally resolved when common sense prevailed among the US legislators, and the US oil export ban[38] was lifted in December 2015. Immediately, this relieved the glut at Cushing, lifting the domestic oil prices. WTI price reconnected with the international oil markets (see Fig. 13.2), increasing, and eventually achieving record volumes of open interest[39] (Fig. 13.1).

NYMEX, the original home of the WTI futures contract, also faced fundamental changes. In 2006, the ICE introduced a WTI contract on its electronic platform.[40] After a string of failures in acquiring the IPE, merging with ICE, and delays in setting up electronic trading, NYMEX was bought by the Chicago Mercantile Exchange (CME) in 2008.[41] Originally a hog and cattle futures exchange, CME embraced electronic trading and turned itself to a for-profit organisation early. Its Globex electronic platform turned out to be a better place for the WTI contract, quickly killing the 'open outcry' trading in the pit.[42]

The growing shale oil production and Canadian imports[43] challenged the quality or WTI contract as well. The 'original' WTI quality comes from the Permian producing region in Midland, Texas. The CME Cushing WTI contract is referred to as 'NYMEX WTI Light Sweet Crude Oil' (ticker symbol CL), a blend of oil which simply has to meet certain quality parameters[44] such as gravity between 37 and 42 API and no more than 0.42%

sulphur content. Given that Cushing is a very large blending hub for oil coming from different parts of the Americas, it is very tempting to meet these quality criteria by blending heavy, sour Canadian or West Texas Sour (WTS) oil with light, sweet condensates from the various shale plays. While more profitable, these blends may not be consistent or yield the same quality and volume of products as 'Midland WTI'. For this reason, they generally trade at a discount to the 'pure' Permian WTI oil.[45] The growing availability of other types of oil for blending was a serious problem for the exchanges[46] making it impossible to determine the source of oil delivered in Cushing,[47] forcing CME to tighten its delivery specifications from January 2019.[48]

It is important to emphasise that, even during the self-imposed imposed export ban, the sheer size of the US market provided the trading liquidity in the contract, maintaining the position of WTI as one of the two most important global oil benchmarks. This proves one very important point regarding benchmarks in general: liquidity of the contract and the confidence that traders get from it is often far more important than the basis risk[49] involved.

The market liquidity and the price transparency were further enhanced by the shale revolution and growing US exports. Trading of WTI picked up in the European and Asian time zones by importers of US oil, making a profound change in the way the contract was used. WTI was going international again. However, it brought about challenges as well. Before we discuss them, it is important to talk about the rise of shale oil production helped by high oil prices which were accompanied with the usual 'peak oil' narrative.

Peak Oil (Again, Again)

While the 1980s markets were turbulent, the following decade and a half saw some price stability around $20 a barrel.[50] The Iraq war in 1991 was followed by a large release of oil from the US Strategic Petroleum Reserve (SPR) and the prices eventually stabilised. Another market event in this period was the 1997–1999 Asian Financial Crisis when the prices fell from the peak of about $25 to $10, but eventually recovered and picked up in 2000s. However, it was the geopolitical events of '9/11' terrorist attack and the subsequent invasion of Iraq in March 2003 that rattled the market and increased volatility. Driven by low investments in new production in the previous decade and booming Chinese (and other Asian) economies, WTI crossed the $50 mark at the end of 2004.

The tight market remained, and prices accelerated and peaked close to $150 a barrel, until the Great Recession,[51] starting another wave of 'peak oil' debates.[52] In 2004 and 2005, books titled 'The Long Emergency', 'The End of Oil', 'Beyond Oil', 'Out of Gas', 'Party's Over' started to appear. But none of them matched the impact of the 'Twilight in the Desert: The Coming Saudi Oil Shock and the World Economy' by Matthew Simmons.[53] Using the recycled arguments of the Club of Rome,[54] Simmons focused on the Saudi oil reserves. He argued that oil production in the major producing countries such as Saudi Arabia was unlikely to increase enough to meet the growing demand. In other words, he argued that the world was running out of oil.

Of course, the proved reserves of any resource were a function of price and technology, both of which were to change substantially for oil and prove him wrong.[55] It was a collection of technologies that would take advantage of high oil prices and create a revolution in the industry, increasing the global oil resources by 11% and gas resources by a staggering 47%.[56]

Shale Oil

The advent of shale was not just a game-changer for the US oil production. It was a set of technologies that would change the structure and workings of the global oil industry itself.

Shale is a type of sedimentary rock composed of flaked layers of minerals that may contain organic matter, resulting in deposits of gas and oil.[57] The technique of extracting hydrocarbons from this rock is hydraulic fracturing or 'fracking'. Oil produced from shale is often referred to as 'tight' oil.[58] Fracking is a collection of technologies, developed over time and adopted to particular rock formations, involving horizontal drilling. First experiments with rock fracturing go back to nineteenth century.[59] In the mid-1970s, the US Department of Energy (DOE), the Gas Research Institute (GRI), and some private partners, worked to develop a technology for the commercial production of natural gas from the Devonian (Huron) shale in the eastern United States.[60] Large-scale shale gas production is associated with Mitchell Energy and the Barnett Shale in Texas, in 1980s.[61]

Amid collapsing oil prices, it was the worst possible time to experiment with a new and relatively expensive methods of extracting hydrocarbons. Like many larger than life figures in the oil industry, George Mitchell, the company founder, persisted and eventually succeeded. The full potential of the technology for both gas and oil production was recognised at the turn of the century, resulting in a massive investment from the Wall Street[62] and a production boom. For a change, timing was fortunate. The Asian (mainly

Chinese) demand was booming and conventional oil production (due to low prices and lack of investment in the previous decade) was slow to pick up. Early in 2008, oil prices rallied over $100 a barrel,[63] giving investors a massive incentive to put their money to work in the shale plays. Between 2008 and 2012, $133.7 billion of foreign capital was also invested in shale plays in the United States.[64]

The US oil production almost doubled between 2007 and 2014.[65] In spite of the price collapse at the end of 2014, the US production exceeded that of Saudi Arabia by 2017 and a year later (see Fig. 13.3), the country became the largest oil producer in the world.[66] Fracking boosted the oil reserves as well. At 47.1 billion barrels, US proved reserves of oil in 2019 remain at the record level set in 2018.[67] The magnitude and speed of this growth was such that the IEA commented: *'The US shale revolution has reshaped the energy landscape at home and abroad'.*[68]

The advent of shale oil[69] production is important for a number of reasons. The shale basins are enormous and widely spread across the globe.[70] While it takes a significant effort to produce shale hydrocarbons, there is far less uncertainty in the shale exploration and production. The investments can be distributed over a number of small plays and require short-cycle financing, making the price risk easy to hedge. For example, an exploration rig for drilling in the US Gulf could cost almost $300,000 a day, making the cost of just one test well easily reach $100 million in expenses.[71] And it was often dry.[72] By the time production started, project costs could run in billions of dollars.

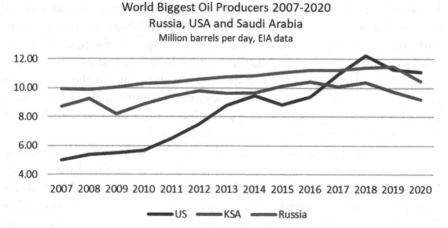

Fig. 13.3 Oil Production by Russia, USA, and Saudi Arabia 2007–2020 (EIA data)

A good conventional well could produce for several decades (large North Sea fields have been producing oil for over four decades now), but it was very hard to hedge the price risk of such a large volume of oil so far out into the future.[73] On the other hand, a typical shale well produced just over a thousand barrels a day[74] with overall exploration and production costs in 'only' millions of dollars.[75]

Such production is predictable for periods of 1–2 years, before new investment is needed to maintain or increase output. Therefore, it is possible to calculate the economics of such operations and hedge the anticipated revenue, 'locking in' the return on borrowed funds. The shale production is more manageable and fundamentally less risky. In the process of hedging (selling forward), the shale oil producers tend exert downward pressure on the forward oil price curve, dampening the price outlook.[76]

For this reason, shale oil production is highly price-sensitive. As soon as the market price exceeds the cost[77] of production, shale oil output normally starts to bounce back. This, coupled with continuing cost reductions and improvements in productivity, make the shale oil production very resilient. After the price collapse at the end of 2014, the production growth stalled (see Fig. 13.3), but bounced back and rapidly continued to grow after 2015. Even after the demand shock and price collapse of 2020, there were signs of shale gradually picking up.[78] In spite of the price and output collapse that year, shale oil accounted for about 70% of the US oil production.[79]

Such production makes shale oil a nightmare competitor for the short-term revenue maximising cartel such as OPEC.[80] What is more, the new shale production technologies are likely to be exported and applied globally, boosting the international oil reserves and productivity.[81] As technology becomes ubiquitous, the unconventional production methods eventually become conventional.

The US oil export ban was lifted in December 2015 relieving the pressure at Cushing and WTI connected again with the international markets, increasing, and eventually achieving record volumes of volume of open interest.[82] What followed was a relatively calm period for the benchmark, until the 2020 Covid-19 pandemic. The massive demand shock following the measures to contain the pandemic, rattled the oil market, prices, and benchmarks. But WTI contract was rattled more than most. On 20 April 2020, the contract settled for the day at −$37.63 a barrel!

WTI Goes Negative

That day, May delivery WTI contract price fell from $17.73 into a negative territory, settling at a shocking level of −$37.63 a barrel (see Fig. 13.5).

Any storable commodity can, reach a point where its price becomes negative. Natural gas prices in Waha hub in the Permian were frequently trading at negative prices.[83] This point is reached when the cost of storage[84] becomes greater than the value of the commodity itself. If a commodity is abundant and cheap, demand for storage normally increases and as the tanks fill up, the cost of storing it can increase exponentially. If there is no storage available at all at a contractual delivery point, the cost of moving and storing the commodity at an alternative location sets the price.

CME Group's WTI crude oil futures contract is physically deliverable in Cushing, Oklahoma. Traders who expire a long position in the contract are responsible for arranging storage space in order to accommodate the delivery of oil there. Due to a massive price shock resulting from the COVID-19 pandemic, Cushing stocks started a rapid rise in April that year (see Fig. 13.4). As they approached the maximum working storage levels,[85] a possibility of negative WTI prices at Cushing became a distinct possibility. As the Figure shows, similar inventory levels were reached before, in 2016–2018 period. In spite of the lifting of the export ban in December 2015, the stock builds were the result of the continuing shale oil boom[86] and a lack of sufficient pipeline capacity[87] from the new production areas and Cushing to the export terminals in the US Gulf.[88]

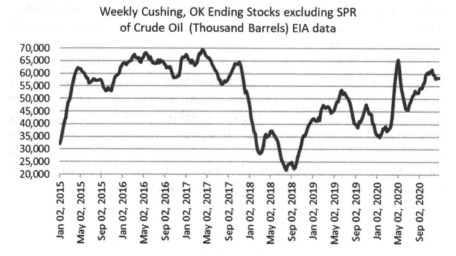

Fig. 13.4 Weekly Oil Stocks in Cushing, OK (EIA data)

Given the magnitude of the demand shock in 2020 (the fall in demand was estimated globally to be about 8.7 mbd), and the speed of the inventory build, there was a perception that 'tank tops' were soon to be reached.[89] Indeed, the CME exchange itself anticipated this possibility, and about a week before the event, it switched on the facility allowing for negative prices.[90]

While it was not surprising for a land-locked contract with limited options for alternative delivery locations and storage to go negative,[91] the extent of the price fall was certainly very odd. On the same day, the next delivery month of June settled $58.06 a barrel higher.[92] At that price differential (spread), alternative outlets could and should have been found in other locations, such as Houston. The additional cost of transporting and storing the oil and then delivering it back into the subsequent contract in Cushing was unlikely to be more than $5 a barrel.[93] Any trader buying oil at that settlement price, taking physical delivery, storing oil in an alternative location,[94] and delivering it back into the June contract could have made over $50 a barrel.[95]

So, what happened? Sadly, it is impossible to know without detailed exchange data regarding players and positions held on that day. This information is not publicly available. However, it can be made available to the Commodities and Trading Commission (CFTC), which is responsible for policing of the commodity markets in the United States. On 23 November 2020, after seven months of deliberations, the Commission issued a preliminary report[96] examining the events. It was very disappointing. The report pointed to the obvious factors contributing to the price fall such as: '*an already oversupplied global crude oil market at the beginning of 2020; an unprecedented reduction in demand caused by COVID-19; and Concerns about availability of global crude oil storage*', but no explanations regarding the extent of the price fall.[97]

Some anecdotal evidence[98] points to the role played by the Exchange Traded Funds (ETFs) as a possible cause (and the victims) of the event. Oil ETFs are funds marketed to the retail investors keen on having some oil exposure in their portfolios.[99] These funds can have very large positions and the way they are managed is often publicly available.[100] In other words, the professional traders, or price-makers, are generally aware when these funds open and close their positions in particular contracts. The funds generally rely on derivative instruments such as 'Trade at Settlement' (TAS)[101] to do so. If a relatively small player 'rolls' positions from one delivery month to the next one, on a pre-announced date, it is not a problem. However, as ETFs have grown in size, that information became increasingly important as the 'roll' can move the market.

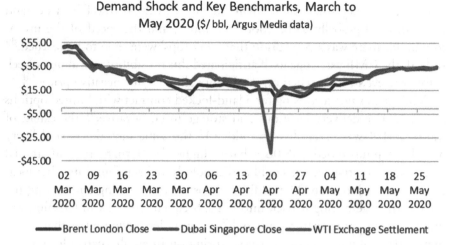

Fig. 13.5 WTI, Brent, and Dubai Prices, March to May 2020 (Argus Media data)

There is a distinct possibility that, on April 20, one or more of such ETFs were victims of a long squeeze.[102] On that day, the price-makers (smart money) in WTI tures contract probably knew that funds were closing a large, long position in the May contract and bought a large volume of TAS futures from them. Indeed, the CFTC report points out that, at 31.1 per cent, TAS futures were the largest constituent of '*All Traded Sides of May 2020 NYMEX WTI Contract*'.[103]

As the market settlement approached, the price-makers might have added to their positions by selling additional values of May futures, forcing the market to settle at a very low, negative price. In other words, the price-takers (ETFs) were already committed to sell TAS contracts at whatever price the price-makers (professional traders) decided it to be (Fig. 13.5). While by no means a proof, there is anecdotal evidence that the professional traders did very well out of the event.[104]

If this were the case, it would certainly amount to a foul play and indicate possible dangers involving the use of derivatives contracts.[105] So far, the CFTC interim report implied that the cause of the crash was the incompetence of some of the retail investors entering complex contract without understanding them. While this was very likely a contributing factor, it is unlikely to be the whole story.[106]

The Pandemic of 2020 was certainly a test for all the oil markets and benchmarks. The WTI was briefly shaken more than most other benchmarks. How benchmarks may change and hopefully improve is the subject of the next chapter.

Notes

1. At the time of writing, US oil demand is close to 20 mbd and production almost 12 mbd.
2. 'The Cushing location not only represented a gathering hub for the local crudes for refiners in Oklahoma, Kansas and Missouri, but it also was the central gathering point for terminus of pipelines originating in Texas and Oklahoma with onward distribution to the main refining centres in the central and eastern Midwest markets in Indiana, Illinois and Ohio.' Purvin and Gertz (2010), p. 24.
3. The US is divided into five Petroleum Administration for Defence Districts, or PADDs: Pad1 (East Coast), PADD2 (Midwest), PADD3 (USG), PADD4 (Rocky Mountains and PADD 5 (West Coast). See EIA. These were created during World War II under the Petroleum Administration for War to help organise the allocation of fuels derived from petroleum products, including gasoline and diesel (or "distillate") fuel. Today, these regions are still used for data collection purposes. For more details, see: https://atlas-eia.opendata.arc gis.com/datasets/petroleum-administration-for-defense-districts-padd.
4. At the time of writing in 2019, about 77 million barrels of working storage capacity (91 million barrels of total shell capacity) in 20 terminals was available in Cushing.
5. To be delivered as WTI, oil has to meet the following specifications: Sulphur: 0.42% or less; Gravity: Not less than 37° API, nor more than 42 API Viscosity: Maximum 60 Saybolt Universal Seconds at 100°F; Reid vapour pressure: Less than 9.5 lb per square inch at 100°F; Basic Sediment, water, and other impurities: Less than 1%; Pour Point: Not to exceed 50°F. Source: NYMEX/CME.
6. Inflow is about 3.7 mbd and outflow 3.1 mbd. See Brusstar and Karas (2020), p. 1.
7. Discussed in Chapter 3.
8. Strictly speaking, as a monopsony buyer of oil.
9. Directly or indirectly, it is a norm now.
10. He served as National Security Advisor and Secretary of State under President Richard Nixon and continued as Secretary of State under Nixon's successor Gerald Ford. It is widely believed that he had a free hand and was responsible for the policies.
11. See Chapter 7.
12. See Chapter 8, 'Oil Production and Price Regulation in the US'.
13. Although the role of President Trump in brokering an agreement between OPEC and Russia in orchestrating a major production cut in 2020 is a pretty good candidate for the saddest policy episode. For a good commentary on the US export ban, see https://www.wsj.com/articles/the-oil-export-ban-a-relic-of-the-1970s-1429913717.

14. Discussed in Chapter 11.
15. See New York Times: PRESIDENT ABOLISHES LAST PRICE CONTROLS ON U.S.-PRODUCED OIL, 29 Jan. 1981.
16. Liberalisation and decontrol will be used interchangeably, presuming the same meaning.
17. For a historical overview see: Purvin and Gertz (2010).
18. It started in 1872 as Butter and Cheese Exchange. It was renamed NYMEX in 1882. See Morrison (2008), p. 251.
19. The speculator was J.R. "Jack" Simplot, a self-made billionaire. See: https://www.newenglandhistoricalsociety.com/the-great-maine-potato-war-the-year-the-spuds-didnt-show-up/.
20. The refined product contracts built on the earlier launches of Rotterdam crude oil and US propane futures by the NY Cotton Exchange, which shared a trading floor with NYMEX.
21. It was important enough for BP to send their start trader, Andy Hall to New York in 1980. Bower (2010), p. 47.
22. In 1981, Phibro bought Salomon Brothers, a profitable Wall Street investment bank. In 1988 Phibro became the largest independent oil refiner in the US. So, it may not be strictly labelled as trading house. http://www.phibro.com/history.
23. Goldman Sachs commodity trading arm.
24. Morrison (2008), p. 254.
25. The fall was much greater for the inland refineries because the 1.5 fall was cushioned by the 1978 discovery and then production from Alaska.
26. 'WTI dropped to near $10/Bbl at the lows in 1986... 25,000 producing wells were lost in 1986 and by 1990, that drop had approached 45,000 wells versus the peak number in 1985.' Purvin and Gertz (2010), p. 6.
27. Ibid., p. 5.
28. Seaway pipeline was converted (again) from gas to oil and started importing USG oil in 1996.
29. In 2020 Platts and Argus are considering inclusion of WTI into the 'Brent' contract. How times have changed.
30. Many Canadian grades are heavier with a higher sulphur content and require deeper conversion de-sulphurisation (hydrotreating) facilities. This is because most of the oil comes from oil sands which contain bitumen. Bitumen is then extracted and then 'upgraded'—mixed with dilutants such as condensates for the refineries to be able to transport and process it. For more details, see: https://www.nrcan.gc.ca/science-data/data-analysis/energy-data-analysis/energy-facts/crude-oil-facts/20064.
31. 4 mbd was reached and exceeded in 2013. See https://www.eia.gov/opendata/qb.php?sdid=INTL.55-1-CAN-TBPD.A.
32. The shale clearly became a significant factor in the US oil production after 2011 when it grew aby about 1 mbd in a single year (from 5.67 to 6.52 EIA annualised data).

33. Light Louisiana Sweet is a crude with 36.6 API gravity and sulphur content of 0.37%.

34. There might have been other reasons for the change, including the timing of the settlement of the contract.

35. The ASCI is a volume-weighted average of all trades for Mars, Poseidon, and Southern Green Canyon (SGC), crudes that are produced in the US Gulf coast.

36. 'The Seaway pipeline, which goes to Freeport and Houston, opened in 1995 with a south-to-north flow. A surge in Canadian oil sands output and U.S. shale oil production, however, has rendered the south-to-north flow unnecessary. Interest in reversing Seaway to flow north-to-south intensified in the past 18 months as Cushing inventories surged and NYMEX WTI fell to unprecedented discounts'. https://www.reuters.com/article/us-oil-seaway-startup-idUSBRE84 I0EC20120519.

37. 'The spread between U.S. benchmark West Texas Intermediate and global benchmark Brent, similar crudes historically priced at near parity, narrowed to $15 from almost $19 Wednesday. It was as much as $28 late last year, costing U.S. and Canadian oil producers billions but boosting profits for Midwestern U.S. refiners.' Ibid.

38. See Chapter six about the government involvement and the imposition of the export ban.

39. 'According to exchange data, the total volume of NYMEX WTI Futures traded for year-to-date (through December 31 2016) was 1.1 million contracts per day compared to 785,000 lots per day in ICE Brent Futures. Over the full-year 2015, WTI average daily volume was 800,000 lots per day, and Brent average daily volume was 685,000 lots per day. Year on year growth in WTI Futures is around 36%.' Source: https://www.cmegroup.com/education/articles-and-reports/wti-and-the-changing-dynamics-of-global-crude-oil.html.

40. https://s2.q4cdn.com/154085107/files/doc_news/archive/ab0adf49-ed97-4932-b815-ead557c8f334.pdf.

41. https://www.reuters.com/article/us-cme-nymex/cme-eyes-nymex-for-11-billion-idUSWNAS802220080129.

42. Morrison (2008), p. 267.

43. Up to 1 million b/d of Canadian crude arrives at Cushing via the Keystone, Spearhead, Flanagan South andPony Express lines. See S&P Platts Insight: 'WTI: what's in a name?'https://www.plattsinsight.com/insight/commodity/oil/wti-whats-in-a-name/, p. 49.

44. Sulphur: 0.42% or less by weight specific Gravity: 37–42° API, BSW (sediment, water and other impurities): Less than 1% Pour Point: No greater than 50°F. https://www.cmegroup.com/trading/energy/nymexs-physically-delivered-light-sweet-crude-oil-futures-faq.html.

45. See S&P Platts Insight: 'WTI: what's in a name?'https://www.plattsinsight.com/insight/commodity/oil/wti-whats-in-a-name/.

46. Blending also affects the quality (and prices) of WTI, NYMEX-suitable WTI, and Domestic Sweet (DSW). This has led to the use of the terms 'Midland' and 'Permian' to differentiate oil (WTI) that moves directly to the USGC as opposed to the blended WTI delivered to Cushing.

47. From 2000 to 2011, total asphaltenes were 0.2%–0.5%. Since 2013, they have been in the range of 0.7%–1%. A high range is 0.2%–0.4%. Ibid., p. 48.

48. Additional specifications were: MCR (Micro Carbon Residue): Less than 2.40% by weight, TAN (Total Acid Number): Less than 0.28 mg KOH/g, Nickel: Less than 8 ppm by weight, Vanadium: Less than 15 ppm by weight.

49. Basis risk is a degree of correlation between the contract and underlying commodity being hedged. The higher the coefficient, the less basis risk there is in using the contract.

50. Between 1990 and 2004 (annualised Brent prices, inclusive) averaged $21.89 (PB Statistical Review).

51. 2007–2008. WTI was hitting peaks of over $145 a barrel in July 2008.

52. On the early 'peak oil' myths, see Chapters 6 and 8. For further reading, I recommend: Mills (2008) and Lynch (2016).

53. Simmons (2005).

54. See Chapter 8.

55. He famously made a sizeable bet with a NY Times reporter John Tierney that the average price of oil in 2010 would exceed $200 and lost. For details, see https://www.nytimes.com/2010/12/28/science/28tierney.html.

56. See EIA Report, Table 1 at https://www.eia.gov/todayinenergy/detail.php?id=14431.

57. *'The organic matter content of carbonaceous and bituminous shales are generally above 10%. The organic matter induces black or grey colour to the shales.'* https://geologyscience.com/rocks/sedimentary-rocks/shale/.

58. "Tight" oil refers to the crude oil produced from shale, sandstone and limestone formations, as typically found in the Permian Basin, Bakken, and Eagle Ford areas.

59. See Chapter 3, 'The First Killer App: Lighting'.

60. See: https://www.eia.gov/analysis/studies/usshalegas/.

61. See Zuckerman (2014), p. 17.

62. *'As of 2012, some of the biggest shale players in the lower 48 included Bakken, Eagle Ford, Permian, Marcellus, Anadarko-Woodford, Granite Wash, and Niobrara. During 2012 alone, these top US shale companies spent a total of $54.3 billion on oil shale production.'* https://kirkcoburn.com/2020/08/27/the-us-shale-industry-from-boom-to-bust/.

63. In Jul 2008, Brent, WTI, and LLS averaged $133.98, $133.81, and $137.80, respectively. Argus Media prices.

64. Investment in shale plays in the United States totalled $133.7 billion between 2008 and 2012. https://www.eia.gov/todayinenergy/detail.php?id=10711#:~:text=Investment%20in%20shale%20plays%20in%20the%20United%20Stat

es,foreign%20companies%20accounted%20for%2020%%20of%20these%20investments.

65. It rose from 5 mbd to 9.45 mbd. EIA data.

66. On 12 September 2018, the EIA published their Short-Term Energy Outlook with a headline: '*The United States is now the largest global crude oil producer*'. https://www.eia.gov/todayinenergy/detail.php?id=37053#.

67. Source: https://www.eia.gov/naturalgas/crudeoilreserves/.

68. IEA Policy Review, September 2019:https://www.iea.org/news/the-us-shale-revolution-has-reshaped-the-energy-landscape-at-home-and-abroad-according-to-latest-iea-policy-review.

69. Shale gas is at least as important, but we are focused on oil here.

70. See: https://www.eia.gov/todayinenergy/detail.php?id=14431.

71. See Bower (2010), pp. 28–29.

72. In 1980's, Shell spent $300 million drilling dry holes in Alaska. Ibid., p. 21.

73. It is possible, but very costly. Normally, price is hedged as far forward as liquidity would allow, say 2–5 years, and then hedges would be regularly 'rolled' (as the prompt month approaches, the contract is bought back and the following liquid month is sold).

74. See: https://www.rystadenergy.com/newsevents/news/newsletters/UsArchive/shale-newsletter-oct-2019/.

75. According to EIA, onshore wells typically cost between $4.9 million and $8.3 million, including land acquisition, drilling, completion, facilities, operating expenses, and gathering processing and transport costs.

76. 'U.S. shale producers lock in future sales as oil prices rise to one-year high'— Reuters News, 16-Jan-2021.

77. In 2019, average anticipated cost of new wells was roughly in the $45 to $52 range for WTI. See Kilian (2020), p. 4.

78. At the time of writing, there was a continuous increase in the number of drilling rigs for several months. The oil rig count rose from the low of 172 in August to 214 on 25/11/20.

79. Ibid., p. 2.

80. Long-term implications will be discussed in the final chapter of the book. Shale is a nightmare for the analyst too. Normally, balances are estimated first and price forecasts follow. With shale oil, price feeds back to the balances, creating a system of non-linear simultaneous equations which is hard to solve.

81. This very much depends on the prevailing legal and political frameworks. In Europe and the UK legal systems (Napoleonic and Customary laws), the subsoil belongs to the state, making exploration and production rather unattractive to the owners of the land. The 'rule of capture' in the US makes leasing of the land a profitable enterprise for the owners. As a result, fracking is nowhere near as unpopular in the US as it is across the Atlantic.

82. This was not a smooth process. With shale output increasing by over 1 mbd on annual basis, the offtake pipeline capacity was lagging behind until almost 2020.

83. Due to lack of pipelines. Associated gas was produced with crude oil which was more profitable. Given limitations for flaring, it still made sense to produce and sell crude and sell gas at negative prices (i.e. pay for it to be taken away. See: https://www.reuters.com/article/us-usa-natgas-texas-waha-natgas-prices-drop-to-negative-now-but-soar-post-coronavirus-idUSKCN2231TD.

84. Including insurance and any other transaction costs.

85. See endnote 3.

86. Overall US oil production increased between 2015 and 2017 by over 2 mbd (from 8.85 to 10.96 mbd). EIA data.

87. '2016 U.S. Oil Pipeline Report: Downturn Leads to Delay', https://napipelines.com/2016-u-s-oil-pipeline-report/ also https://www.reuters.com/article/uk-usa-pipeline-oil-factbox-idUKKBN0MX1CD20150406?edition-redirect=uk.

88. Up until the lifting of the export ban, the top destination for the US oil was Canada (over 300 kbd in 2016), which was not subject to the restrictions.

89. Traders of WTI reserve storage in Cushing. Hence tanks do not have to be full not to be available.

90. 'Testing opportunities in CME's "New Release" environment for negative prices and strikes for certain NYMEX energy contracts.' CME Advisory Notice, CME Group, 15 April 2020: '*Recent market events have raised the possibility that certain NYMEX energy futures contracts could trade at negative or zero trade prices or be settled at negative or zero values, and that options on these futures contracts could be listed with negative or zero strike prices.*'

91. Low commodity price minus the high cost of alternative delivery and storage can easily be a negative number.

92. Commodity Futures Trading Commission (2020), p. 9.

93. Pipeline cost is normally no more than $2 a barrel each way.

94. '*According to EIA, the 75.8 million barrels of storage capacity in Cushing represents about 44% of all crude oil working storage capacity in the Midwest (as defined by Petroleum Administration for Defense District 2), and about 11% of all commercial crude oil storage in the U.S. as a whole*'. Ibid., p. 13.

95. As May delivery settled $58.06 below June delivery, buying May and selling June (buying May/June spread) would 'lock in' the profit equal to that spread minus the cost of additional transportation plus one month of storage.

96. Commodity Futures Trading Commission (2020).

97. The report simply stated the fact that: '*The speed and magnitude of the price moves observed on April 20 in the May Contract, particularly between 1:00 p.m. and the end-of-day settlement at 2:30 p.m. Eastern Time, were exceptional despite the triggering of exchange-based control mechanisms designed to impose pauses in the event of rapid or large price moves.*' Ibid., p. 3.

98. For example, see: https://asia.nikkei.com/Opinion/Negative-oil-price-teaches-mom-and-pop-investors-a-costly-lesson.

99. For example, the OTC contract, known as Yuányóu Bǎo, sold by the Bank of China. See: https://www.reuters.com/article/china-bank-of-china-oil/upd ate-1-bank-of-china-deeply-disturbed-about-investors-loss-on-oil-products-idUKL3N2CC3JV?edition-redirect=uk andhttps://www.reuters.com/article/china-bank-of-china-oil-regulator/regulator-fines-bank-of-china-over-loss-mak ing-product-linked-to-crude-oil-idINKBN28F0EA.
100. Rolling long ETF positions is usually done on pre-announced dates, before the expiry of the contract.
101. This is simply an agreement to buy or sell a volume of commodity at whatever price the exchange settles.
102. A market 'squeeze' happens when a player buys all the commodity available in the contract, making the short players pay an extortionate price to close their position. 'Long squeeze' is the opposite. Any long player h is forced to settle (sell their long position) at a very low price. See: https://www.forbes.com/sites/michaellynch/2020/04/21/negative-oil-prices-are-a-long-squeeze-not-a-crisis/?sh=4a00481713ec
103. Commodity Futures Trading Commission (2020), p. 15. Table 1. 31.1% includes TAS spreads.
104. See: https://www.bloomberg.com/news/articles/2020-08-04/oil-s-plunge-below-zero-was-500-million-jackpot-for-a-few-london-traders.
105. So called 'leveraged play' will be discussed in the final chapter.
106. CFTC publishes weekly open interest data in its Commitment of Traders (COT) report which shows the positions held by different categories of traders. The commercials, hedgers, and speculators were holding larger than normal positions prior to expiry, possibly due to the uncertainty about delivery alternatives in an over-supplied market during the pandemic. One explanation was that, due to the extraordinary market events resulting from the pandemic, there was a large market imbalance between longs and shorts that had to be cleared at the expiration of the WTI futures contract, and this led to higher volatility and negative pricing. Again, this explanation was not sufficient to explain the extent of the negative price.

References

Bower T. (2010): *The Squeeze*, Harper Press.
Brusstar and Karas (2020): *Why Cushing Matters: A Look at the WTI Benchmark*, OIES, May 13, 2020,
Commodity Futures Trading Commission (2020): 'Trading in NYMEX WTI Crude Oil Futures Contract Leading up to, on, and around April 20, 2020' Interim Staff Report, November 23, 2020, https://cftc.gov/PressRoom/PressReleases/8315-20.

Killian Lutz (2020): 'Would Shale Impede or Accelerate the Global Energy Transition?', Presentation to the KAPSARC Virtual Workshop Agenda, December 9.

Lynch C.M. (2016): *The "Peak Oil" Scare and the Coming of Oil Flood*, Praeger Publishers.

Mills M.R. (2008): *The Myth of the Oil Crisis*, Praeger Publishers.

Morrison K. (2008): *Living in a Material World, A Commodity Connection*, Wiley, London, UK.

Purvin and Gertz (2010): *The Role of WTI as a Crude Oil Benchmark*, January.

Simmons M. (2005): *Twilight in the Desert: The Coming Saudi Oil Shock and the World Economy*, Wiley.

Zuckerman, G. (2014): *The Frackers*, Portfolio Penguin.

14

Global Oil Markets: Lessons from the 2020 COVID-19 Pandemic

The 2020 Demand Shock

The demand collapse following the 2020 COVID-19 pandemic was massive and historic[1]. The measures to contain the pandemic around the world hit mobility particularly hard with global road transport falling by 50% and air travel in parts of Europe falling by more than 90%.[2] In March that year, the world oil demand plummeted by a record 10.8 mb/d (see Fig. 14.1) below the previous year.[3] The collapse was swift, leading to some of the highest levels of volatility in oil prices ever recorded.[4] As we saw in the previous chapter, WTI May futures contract went into deep, negative territory. The impact on the oil market was profound, exposing all the weaknesses in the pricing structure as well as the industry as a whole. It was a glimpse of what the future oil market might look like when we transition away from oil, and demand for the commodity begins to fall.

The sharp demand fall exposed the land-locked Cushing delivery point for the WTI benchmark as a possible weakness.[5] Other, seaborne delivery points had the whole world to ship and store oil and were highly unlikely to get choked to the point where prices turn negative. As the United States became a major oil exporter again, following the lifting of the export ban in 2015, the focus of price discovery in the United States started to shift to the loading ports on the US Gulf Coast. The events of April 2020 and the issues with the Cushing delivery benchmark are only likely to accelerate that shift. With the US crude becoming a base slate of many European and Asian refineries, its

© The Author(s), under exclusive license to Springer Nature Switzerland AG 2021
A. Imsirovic, *Trading and Price Discovery for Crude Oils*,
https://doi.org/10.1007/978-3-030-71718-6_14

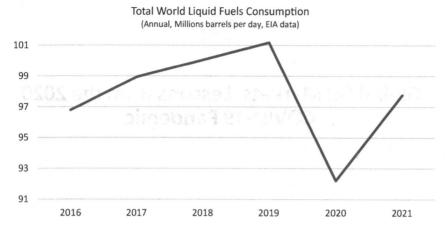

Fig. 14.1 World Liquid Fuels Consumption (Million barrels per day, EIA data)

price at the loading port has become an important indicator for global oil markets.

The two biggest PRAs and the two major oil exchanges all developed waterborne price assessments: Argus and CME Group focused on the WTI Houston (Permian), while S&P Global Platts and ICE focused on WTI delivered in the Magellan East Houston (MEH) terminal.[6] Also, in 2020, both Argus and Platts started publishing the American Gulf Coast Select (AGS) assessments of the waterbourne light, sweet crude oil, loading 15–45 days forward from the USG Coast region. These prices originally started a differential to WTI Cushing, but their introduction improved a price discovery for all the buyers of American oil in Europe and Asia.

The growing United States exports intensified the competition between Brent and WTI for pricing of these FOB[7] barrels. Once loaded on a ship at the US Gulf Coast, the oil essentially 'became Brent', in the sense that it was of similar quality and Brent was the main pricing reference point for exports both to Europe and Asia. WTI competes directly with lighter grades in the BFOET or 'Brent' basket, particularly Ekofisk and Oseberg. In the Mediterranean, it directly competes with Saharan blend.[8]

Brent Survived

Following the WTI dip in the negative territory, all eyes were on the June Brent contract expiring at the end of April.[9] However, the Brent complex performed relatively well. The brunt of the impact of the demand shock was absorbed first by the physical, Dated Brent which collapsed into a deep discount relative to forward (and futures) Brent contracts. Quality differentials relative to Dated Brent also collapsed (See Fig. 14.2). While there were arguments that the absolute price level was defying gravity,[10] the price of physical crude such as naphtha-rich CPC Blend from Kazakhstan fell below $5 a barrel.[11] The fall in Dated values was followed by a large fall in Brent spreads, sending a strong price signal and incentive for excess barrels to be stored.

While the Brent complex performed relatively well, the falling volume of the physical crude underpinning the benchmark was becoming a concern. BFOET or 'Brent' grades made up only about 800,000 barrels a day[12] at the time of writing.[13] As a 'rule of thumb', this was a volume where additional barrels were needed to maintain a heathy liquidity, enough oil to prevent a squeeze. The only problem was that, from the quality point of view, few other grades fitted into the Brent basket. From 1 November 2019, Platts included offers of Brent cargoes on a CIF Rotterdam basis in their BFOET assesment, adjusted by prevailing freight for a typical Aframax[14] cargo. Using a well-established procedure—making the delivered oil price quotation using the freight cost assessments—was a steppingstone to the inclusion of other delivered grades into the 'Brent' basket. From the quality point of view, the obvious candidates were the delivered US grades such as WTI Midland.

In February 2019, Argus introduced a 'New North Sea Dated' assessment which included delivered Rotterdam prices for a number of other grades delivered to this port. The idea was to make this methodology the basis of

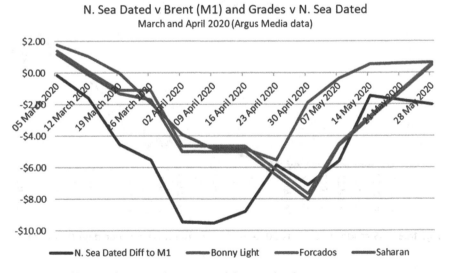

Fig. 14.2 Differentials to North Sea Dated (Argus data)

its main 'North Sea Dated' index. WTI proved very competitive and became one of the main grades setting the price of the 'New North Sea Dated', reflecting its competitiveness in the European market. Judging from the Argus experience with 'New North Sea Dated', the inclusion delivered WTI (see Fig. 14.3) could increase liquidity, prevent spikes in 'Dated Brent', and hence provide an effective 'cap' on its price and allow the negotiated differentials to Dated Brent for other grades to remain more stable.

In September 2018, Platts started publishing assessments for WTI Midland and Eagle Ford 45 delivered in Rotterdam and Augusta. The obvious next step was the inclusion of WTI Midland[15] into its flagship Dated Brent basket, announced at the end of 2020.[16] The grade had a typical average monthly export volume of just over one million barrels a day,[17] roughly half of which was exported to Europe. The new assessment was to start from March 2022.[18]

However, engineering the inclusion of WTI Midland into the FOB Brent basket will be far from easy. Sue to the lack of published loading programmes for the US grade and the complexity of the Brent benchmark (based on forward, Dated and futures contracts as well as a plethora of derivatives instruments), both forward and Dated Brent will have to be assessed on the same delivery basis. Any difference between them would result in a lack of convergence at the expiry of the forward contract, affecting all the key derivative contracts such as CFDs, DFLs and EFPs.

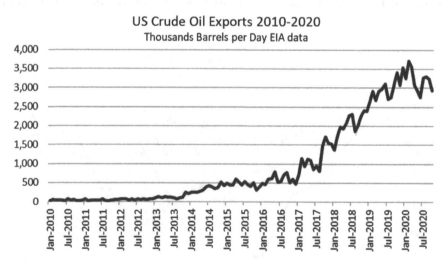

Fig. 14.3 US crude oil exports 2010–2020, (thousand barrels per day) (EIA data)

While the Brent and WTI benchmarks may continue to compete for global supremacy, the announced changes were likely to strengthen both, creating more liquidity, transparency, and arbitrage opportunities.

Asian Disconnect

The demand shock of 2020 created some disconnect in the Asian benchmarks. As discussed in Chapter 12, both Dubai and Oman Platts benchmarks allow for the delivery of Murban crude, a high-quality light sour grade, normally trading at a couple of dollars premium above Dubai.[19] When Murban was first introduced into the Dubai basket in 2016, it was seen as a safety valve, used only in case of a severe squeeze on the benchmark. As gasoline and jet became the main casualties of the demand collapse, naphtha was so weak as to make Murban even less valuable than the Qatari heavy and high sulphur Al-Shaheen,[20] thus setting the price of the Dubai benchmark.

This resulted in heavy discounts for Murban crude (see Fig. 14.4), making it the cheapest grade in the Dubai and Oman baskets, setting the price for both Platts Asian benchmarks. On the other hand, DME Oman, exchange contract with a single delivery grade, continued to reflect the value of a single grade, Oman. As a result, the two Oman assessments (DME Oman and Platts Oman) were reflecting values of very different crudes. This was creating a historically large price divergence between the two benchmarks. On 22 April

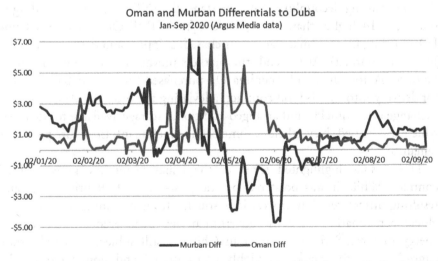

Fig. 14.4 Oman and Murban differentials to Dubai in 2020 (Argus Media data)

2020, the price differential between the two Oman assessments reached $6.56 per barrel.[21]

While this divergence proved to be only a temporary phenomenon, it exposed the structural differences between the two benchmarks, methodologies, and the crudes they represent.[22]

Problems with the Shanghai Exchange Oil Contract

With encouragement from the top of the Chinese leadership, the Shanghai International Energy Exchange (INE) launched its own crude oil futures on 26 March 2018. The contract is for delivered (into designated bonded shore tanks so that the price is net of tax) medium-sulphur grades of crude oil (32 API and 1.5 per cent sulphur), priced in Chinese yuan (RMB). The deliverable grades of oil include domestic Shengli and seven other Middle Eastern grades: Basrah Light, Oman, Dubai, Upper Zakum, Murban, Qatar Marine, and Masila. The contract was almost an instant success, with volume of trades quickly exceeding those on the DME exchange, making INE the third-largest oil exchange in the world.

Amplified by the shock from the COVID-19 pandemic, the INE crude oil contract increased both in liquidity and volatility (see Fig. 14.5). However, the July delivery contract decoupled from the international markets.[23] Just like in the case of the WTI price collapse, it was the buying by retail investors that was causing decoupling.[24] At one stage, the INE contract was trading as much as $14 higher than the equivalent June DME Oman contract (June FOB loading DME Oman can be purchased, shipped, and delivered into the July INE contract). At the end, the markets prevailed. The state companies Sinopec, PetroChina, and Zhenhua Oil purchased Oman and Basrah Light for delivery into the INE oil contract, alleviating the problem. Also, the INE exchange acted quickly and arranged additional storage available for delivery, which also helped. Nevertheless, some of the pipeline infrastructure problems remained.[25]

The episode highlighted some of the issues facing the growing INE contract. While it was bolstered by the post-COVID-19 price crash and resulting attractively low prices, it is still far from becoming a regional or global benchmark. While the government has been gradually liberalising energy markets,[26] the oil market in China is still subject to a tight state control. Also, the market is highly concentrated and dominated by the

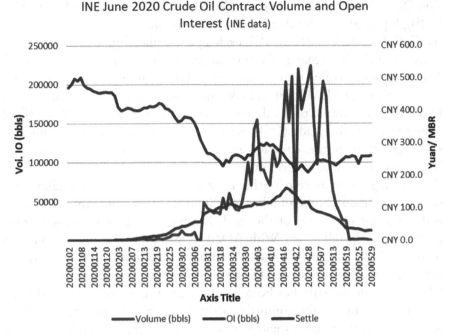

Fig. 14.5 Shanghai Exchange (INE) June Oil Contract Volume and OI (INE data)

three biggest national oil companies: PetroChina Company Limited, Sinopec Group, and China National Offshore Oil Corporation.

The lesson from history[27] is that a liberalised market is a precondition for a well-functioning futures market. This would involve the privatisation of state oil companies; abolition of all price controls, including those in the currency and capital markets; encouragement of transparency; and access to key infrastructure for all market participants. Given it is a top-down measure, it should not be an impossible task for the Chinese leadership.

The events of 2020 generated a healthy debate on the usefulness and limitations of the benchmarks 'East of Suez', whether PRAs needed to adjust their underlying assessment methodologies, whether the producers needed to revisit their pricing formulae, or whether some new benchmarks should be introduced.

Murban: Another Middle East Benchmark?

While the demand shock of 2020 might have shifted the focus and pricing power from sellers to buyers, the Middle East producers were not sitting idle.

Abu Dhabi National Oil Company (ADNOC) was working hard on placing its flagship crude oil, Murban, at the centre of the price-making process in the Gulf. In March 2021, the ICE exchange was planning to launch the ICE Futres Abu Dhabi exchange (IFAD) featuring a Murban futures contract.[28] Not all details regarding the contract[29] were known at the time of writing, but it was likely to be a DME Oman look-alike, based on convergence of a settled futures position into a physical delivery of Murban crude oil.[30] The official selling price for the grade (OSP) would be set on the basis of the monthly settlement of the futures contracts and the remaining ADNOC grades would be set as a differential to this settlement price.

Murban grade of oil certainly has the required ubiquity and liquidity. UAE can produce about 3 mbd of oil or 50 million barrels per month and Murban makes up just over 50% of the total. Murban is one of the largest crude grades in the Middle East. With ADNOC plans to raise production to 5 mbd by 2030, it potentially makes it a viable, long-term stream of crude for setting prices. Virtually all of Murban production is exported to Asia-Pacific. Globally, crude oil slate has been getting lighter and sweeter and Murban quality is not unlike the competing delivered barrels in the region: North Sea Forties, Russian ESPO and US WTI.[31] As such, it is highly accepted by the refineries throughout Asia, particularly South East Asia and Japan. Historically, setting OSPs as a differential to the Dubai benchmark had mixed reception, particularly in the case of Murban. Spot prices have frequently traded below the OSP, causing the term lifters problems (Fig. 14.6). Using the exchange settlement price would certainly take a subjective element out of the equation.

But the key point regarding the new Murban futures contract is often missed. For the first time since the creation of OPEC, a Gulf member of the

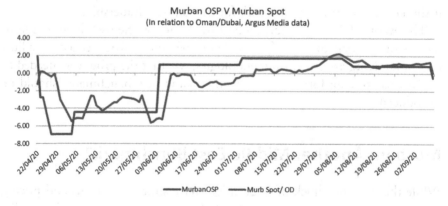

Fig. 14.6 Murban Official Selling Prices v Spot Prices in 2020 (Argus Media data)

organisation is giving up a pricing link to a benchmark, making its crude a benchmark itself. In the process, Abu Dhabi is giving up resale and destination restrictions, conceding even more control to the market. What is more, the UAE participation in a major OPEC production cut, such as the one in October 2020[32] could severely disrupt the orderly functioning of an exchange contract. The very role of UAE within OPEC itself may have to be questioned. This question prompted Bloomberg to speculate: *'Could the UAE Prompt Opec's House of Cards to Collapse?'*[33] While the rumours of a discord within OPEC were quickly denied, questions remained, given the UAE's ambitious plans to expand its future production capacity.[34] Lastly, if the Murban exchange contract was successful, what would be the response of Saudi Arabia? Would they follow?

Lessons for OPEC

Oil producers were particularly hard hit by the slump in demand and scared by negative oil prices.[35] The shock of the events in April 2020 helped Saudi Arabia rally the OPEC members and expand the scope of its wider OPEC+[36] alliance to arrange 'orderly' production cuts[37] and support prices. The result was the largest ever output cut of 9.7 mbd, agreed by the alliance in April that year.[38]

The very creation[39] of a wider alliance betrays the inability of the cartel to control the market. OPEC's members only supply about a third of the global oil (see Fig. 14.7) and have about 80 percent of proven global oil reserves. By expanding the alliance to twenty-four member countries, Russia being the most important one, their share of production exceeds well over a half of the global supply and the proven reserves increase to about 90%. On the other hand, the alliance has became large, containing diverse economies, policies, and views on the oil market. Outside the core OPEC members, cheating is endemic.[40] The alliance is only kept together by fear of another price collapse and the leadership, including voluntary cuts by Saudi Arabia.[41] For this reason, OPEC+ name may stay with us for a while, but the alliance is unlikely to be effective in the long run.

More importantly, the events linked to the pandemic have made it clearer that all the oil producers will have to face two simple facts. One is the abundance of oil, especially following the new production technologies associated with the shale revolution. The other is the urgent need to stop climate change. Global proved reserves of oil have been increasing from 1277 trillion barrels in 1999 to 1532 trillion in 2009 and 1734 trillion barrels in 2019.[42]

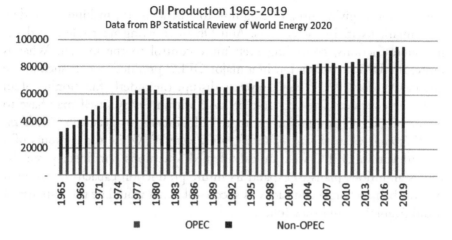

Fig. 14.7 OPEC and non-OPEC Oil Production Since 1965 (Data from BP Statistical Review of World Energy 2020)

Even at pre-pandemic levels of consumption, we have enough oil for at least another fifty years,[43] even without finding another single new barrel. The definition of proved reserves[44] is based on prevailing technology and price. As the oil price increases, reserves increase too.[45] There is plenty of oil. And thanks to shale revolution, it may come from many places outside the Middle East,[46] reducing the geopolitical risks usually associated with the region and oil prices.

At the same time, oil demand is unlikely to grow forever, especially given the limitations of the planet's remaining carbon budget.[47] The events of 2020 have shown us what the low-demand world may look like. Oil consumption simply has to be in line with the goals of the Paris agreement[48] and limiting global warming below two degrees Centigrade.[49] In their 2020 World Energy Outlook (WEO 2020), The International Energy Agency (IEA) created a Sustainable Development Scenario (SDS) which relied on efficiency to reduce the demand for oil after the early 2020s. In this scenario,[50] oil demand would fall by a third by 2040s.

Similarly, BP's 'Energy Outlook 2020'[51] presented two global oil demand scenarios consistent with the Paris goals.[52] In both of these scenarios, oil consumption fell immediately after 2020. These projections were not unrealistic. The OECD oil demand peaked back in 2005.[53] The remaining carbon budget should simply be seen as a boundary condition,[54] and if we do not rise to the challenge and meet it, oil prices will be the least of our worries.[55]

From the OPEC perspective, the conclusion is simple. On one hand, there are large and growing reserves of oil. On the other, most of them must be left in the ground. In the long run, the only oil producers left standing should be the low-cost products. This includes most Gulf, OPEC countries.[56] However, they are likely to face shrinking demand, coupled with higher costs of carbon.[57] In WEO 2020, the IEA sees the price of carbon, consistent with SDS, reach $140 per tonne by 2040.[58] While the energy transition from oil is likely to be associated with high oil prices, these are more likely to come from various forms of carbon tax.[59]

In 2020, the three key players in achieving climate goals aligned. Europe was launching its Green Deal which included tightening the Emissions Trading System (ETS)[60] and proposals for EU carbon border adjustment mechanism for selected sectors. At the same time, China announced the launch of the world's biggest ETS scheme.[61] Lastly, the new US administration was spending some $2 trillion for 'a clean energy revolution and environmental justice'.[62]

All these developments are likely to leave cash from higher oil prices in the pockets of consuming, rather than producing countries.[63] None of this bodes well for the future of OPEC, unless it aligns itself with the realities of the climate emergency.[64]

2020 Oil Balances in Real Time

The pandemic of 2020 and the general market selloff resulted in substantial losses incurred by quantitative traders.[65] As a result, the existing approaches to applying AI in trading came under serious scrutiny.

Attempts to implement machine learning and artificial intelligence (AI) trading have a long history.[66] In essence, most of such price forecasting are based on some form of time series models,[67] just like stochastic and 'ordinary' regression models.[68] Most of the original models were based on high-frequency data and some algorithm such as neural networks, genetic algorithm, or a hybrid combination of two or more algorithms.[69] The attraction of these 'black box' models was their ability to accommodate most functional forms, including non-linear ones. Their serious drawback was the inability to understand the drivers of their forecasts, hence the term 'black box'. Their forecasts were based on back-testing the data, picking the best fitting model, without much insight into the drivers of such outcomes.

The failure to predict the 'Black Swan' event of 2020 has led to a revival of fundamental principles in forecasting. The traditional 'fundamental' analysis in trading always had an Achille's heel in the quality and timing of data. Even the best data was backward looking, usually delayed by weeks, if not months.[70] However, the availability and quality of real-time data such as satellite imaging,[71] automatic identification system (AIS), and others had been around for some time and caused a proliferation of companies specialising in providing such information.[72]

Suddenly there was too much data, much of it of dubious quality. For example, ships loading at the Saudi port of Ras Tanura may end up in exports as well as floating storage. They may load different grades of oil, for different destinations. The satellite images of such vessels need to be cross-checked with shipping fixtures, loading or discharge documentation and other available sources of information.[73] Oil tanks usually have roof-tops and inventories can be estimated by their height. Given a large number of tank farms around the globe, machine learning algorithms and AI are ideally placed to use satelite images to use a vast amount of information and estimate storage levels.

Not only can a machine cross check the real-time information, but it can also do it against the past information: Has this vessel loaded at this port before? Was the charterer the same company and was it a regular occurrence? This automated process of validating the real-time data is often referred to as 'Nowcasting'. The back-testing of the data is used for validation of concepts, relationships, and theories and not for forecasting. '*It used to take me on average one hour to reconcile around 10 shipping broker reports. Now, with the use of AI, we can process thousands of reports of documents in two seconds*' said Florian Thaler, the CEO of OilX. His goal is to empower the forecasters and decision makers, rather than replace them. Since 2020, the goals of AI suddenly became more modest but more useful.

The tragedy of the 2020 COVID-19 pandemic aside, the shocks it caused was a real life experiment in the behaviour of the international oil markets under a large demand shock. Overall, the international oil market worked well and fulfilled its function. The key international oil Benchmark, Brent worked well with Dated Brent and physical quality differentials taking the brunt of the short-term adjustments.

There were temporary issues with some Asian benchmarks such as Dubai, INE crude contract, and DME Oman which need some fixing. WTI had major problems and although they were very temporary, they will need further examination by all the stakeholders in the contract. In the long run, a waterborne WTI contract, set around the Houston area may be a solution.

OPEC managed to reinvent itself in a form of OPEC+ alliance, due to the sheer shock of negative prices but also through a determined leadership of Saudi Arabia. The kingdom used its spare production capacity and economic muscle to stamp its role as the undisputed leader, not only among OPEC members, but also among the oil producers at large. In spite of the Saudi efforts, only growing demand can ensure the survival of OPEC+ alliance. However, given the limits imposed on the industry by the carbon budget, such a diverse alliance of oil producing countries is highly unlikely to survive in the long run.

Notes

1. https://www.reuters.com/article/us-global-oil-yearend-graphic-idUSKBN29 30FJ.
2. Even as late as October 2020: '*International passenger demand in October was down 87.8% compared to October 2019, virtually unchanged from the 88.0% year-to-year decline recorded in September. Capacity was 76.9% below previous year levels.*' See: https://www.iata.org/en/pressroom/pr/2020-12-08-01/.
3. IEA figures. https://www.iea.org/reports/global-energy-review-2020/oil#abs tract.
4. On April 21st, CBOE Crude Oil Volatility Index (^OVX) closed at 325.15, the highest level ever recorded and roughly a tenfold increase compared to usual levels.
5. For a detailed discussion, see the previous chapter.
6. The CME WTI contract is delivered at Houston terminals owned by Enterprise Products Partners, with API within 40–44 degrees, and sulphur content of max 0.275% plus maximum metal content of four parts per million of nickel and vanadium. ICE's contract is delivered at Houston terminals owned by Magellan Midstream Partners, with API within 36–44 degrees and a sulphur limit of 0.45%.
7. FOB stands for Free on Board. These are good traded at the loading port where the title is also transferred. The buyer is responsible for the sipping.
8. For a detailed discussion, see Imsirovic (2019), p. 6.
9. See: https://www.reuters.com/article/idUSL5N2CG86S.
10. See Fattouh and Imsirovic (2020a), p. 2.
11. On April 21, Argus assessed CPC Blend at $3.670.
12. '*Platts also considers offers for, and any resulting transactions of, recently loaded physical BFOE crude oil* via *ship-to-ship (STS) transfers at Scapa Flow in Scotland, provided the seller agrees to cover all additional costs incurred by the buyer lifting oil on an STS basis.*' STS barrels are not included here. https://www.spglobal.com/platts/PlattsContent/_assets/_files/en/our-met hodology/methodology-specifications/emea-crude-methodology.pdf.
13. March 2021 programme had about 42 cargoes or about 25 million barrels: 3 Brents (one cargo often gets cancelled), 14 Forties, 4 Oseberg, 13 Ekofisk, and 8 Troll cargoes.
14. About 80,000–120,000 MT or 500,000–800,000 barrels sized ship.

15. For different qualities of WTI, see the previous chapter.
16. https://www.spglobal.com/platts/en/market-insights/latest-news/oil/120320-sampp-global-platts-proposes-inclusion-of-wti-crude-in-dated-brent-benchmark.
17. In 2020.
18. Platts said was inviting feedback on its proposal by 5 Feb. 2021 (at the time of writing) with a potential implementation for March 2022.
19. Mainly because of its high naphtha content.
20. Al-Shaheen is deliverable into the Dubai basket. Being heavier with a higher sulphur content, it is generally cheaper than other grades, thus setting the basket (benchmark) price. See Chapter 12.
21. Fattouh B. and Imsirovic A. (2020b), p. 6.
22. For detailed discussion and possible solutions, see: Fattouh and Imsirovic (2020c), p. 10.
23. For more detail, see: Imsirovic A. (2020b), p. 33.
24. Most of the volume of the oil contract on INE is traded by retail and financial participants with limited access to international oil exchanges.
25. See: 'Shandong pipelines face overload', 29 May 2020, Argus Media.
26. Import licenses have regularly been granted to at least 60 'independent' companies.
27. See Chapters 10 and 13.
28. At the time of writing. See: https://ir.theice.com/press/news-details/2021/ICE-Provides-Update-on-ICE-Murban-Futures-Ahead-of-Launch-of-ICE-Futures-Abu-Dhabi-on-March-29-2021/default.aspx.
29. https://www.theice.com/murban.
30. See Mehdi et al. (2019).
31. Forties is 37.3 API, 0.54 s%; Murban 40.2 API, 0.79%S; WTI 40.8 API, 0.42%S, ESPO 34.7 API and 0.55%S.
32. 'UAE'S ADNOC cuts October crude oil term supplies by 30% in surprise move'—Reuters News 31-Aug-2020.
33. https://www.bloomberg.com/opinion/articles/2020-11-22/could-the-uae-prompt-opec-s-house-of-cards-to-collapse.
34. https://www.bloomberg.com/news/articles/2020-12-06/opec-wrangle-puts-uae-s-ambitions-on-display.
35. The negative pricing of the May WTI contract impacted on crude import prices into the US, even for those crude exporters that don't use WTI as their main benchmark. In 2009, Saudi Arabia, Kuwait, and Iraq shifted from WTI to the Argus Sour Crude Index (ASCI) for pricing their crude exports into the US. The ASCI is a volume-weighted average of all trades for Mars, Poseidon, and Southern Green Canyon (SGC), crudes that are produced in the US Gulf coast. However, given that CME's settlement of WTI futures constitutes the underlying fixed price for the ASCI, the protection was limited. For example, while Mars went from +$1.75 on April 17 to +$11.00 on April 20, Mars ended the day with a negative $26.63, as the physical differential is applied

to the WTI futures settlement. On Monday April 20, Middle East exporters who use ASCI as a benchmark and whose crudes are not landlocked, had to settle for deeply negative prices for that day. This is a failure of the benchmark which did not accurately reflect the value of the delivered crude on the day. No producer would willingly sell a waterborne crude with storage options (including underground) at a negative number. See Fattouh B. and Imsirovic A. (2020b), p. 4.

36. OPEC + is a loose association of oil producers which, aside from the 14 OPEC members includes Russia, Azerbaijan, Bahrain, Brunei, Kazakhstan, Malaysia, Mexico, Oman, South Sudan, and Sudan.

37. Details and nuances of the OPEC + deal are well explained in the OIES podcast: https://www.oxfordenergy.org/publications/the-impact-of-the-opec-meeting-and-the-covid-19-pandemic-on-global-oil-markets/For.

38. https://www.reuters.com/article/us-global-oil-opec-deal/opec-agrees-largest-ever-oil-output-cut-of-9-7-million-bpd-sources-idUSKCN21U0QO?edition-redirect=uk.

39. The cooperation goes back to 2016 following a joint pledge to cut production by 1.8 million b/d (600,000 b/d non-OPEC and 1.2 million b/d by OPEC).

40. See: https://www.bloombergquint.com/markets/opec-gets-cheats-in-line-as-angola-makes-new-oil-cut-pledge.

41. See: 'Saudis pledge to cut oil output despite Russian increases', *The Financial Times*, 5 January 2021.

42. BP Statistical Review of World Energy (2020), p. 15.

43. Oil reserves to production ratios have been either constant or increasing. Ibid.

44. *'Proved reserves are those quantities of petroleum which, by analysis of geological and engineering data, can be estimated with reasonable certainty to be commercially recoverable, from a given date forward, from known reservoirs and under current economic conditions, operating methods, and government regulations.'* See: https://www.spe.org/en/industry/petroleum-reserves-definitions/.

45. It has to be repeated that this simple point is at the heart of the arguments against 'peak oil' theories. Only a fraction of oil can be extracted from the ground economically and with the existing technology. As technology, prices and costs change, so do the reserves because more of the oil will be extracted.

46. See the previous chapter, discussion on shale.

47. Carbon budget is the amount of carbon dioxide emissions permitted over a period of time to keep within a certain temperature threshold. See: https://carbontracker.org/carbon-budgets-where-are-we-now/.

48. Conference of the Parties or COP21 agreement on climate change of December 2015. For details see: https://unfccc.int/process-and-meetings/the-paris-agreement/the-paris-agreement.

49. *'Its goal is to limit global warming to well below 2, preferably to 1.5 degrees Celsius, compared to pre-industrial levels. To achieve this long-term temperature goal, countries aim to reach global peaking of greenhouse gas emissions as soon as possible to achieve a climate neutral world by mid-century.'* Ibid.

50. IEA (2020), p. 171.
51. See: https://www.bp.com/en/global/corporate/energy-economics/energy-out look/demand-by-fuel/oil.html.
52. '*The demand for liquid fuels in Rapid and Net Zero never fully recovers from the fall caused by COVID-19, implying that oil demand peaked in 2019 in both scenarios. The consumption of liquid fuels falls significantly over the Outlook in both scenarios, declining to less than 55 Mb/d and around 30 Mb/d in Rapid and Net Zero respectively by 2050. The falling demand is concentrated in the developed world and China, with consumption in India, Other Asia and Africa broadly flat over the Outlook as a whole in Rapid, but falling below 2018 levels from the mid-2030 s onwards in Net Zero.*' Ibid.
53. In 2005, OECD oil consumption was 49.76 mbd. In 2019 it was 45.82 mbd. See the BP Statistical Review of World Energy (data).
54. In a mathematical sense. A boundary condition is a constraint necessary for the solution of a mathematical problem.
55. For a wonderful summary of the effects of climate change, see: https://www.nat ionalgeographic.com/environment/global-warming/global-warming-effects/.
56. https://knoema.com/infographics/vyronoe/cost-of-oil-production-by-country
57. In the sense that they are likely to bear the cost of emitting carbon.
58. IEA (2020), p. 81.
59. It may be called 'pollution tax' or some other, more appealing name, ideally not referring to tax at all.
60. See https://ec.europa.eu/clima/policies/ets_en. At the time of writing, ETS prices were over $35/mt.
61. https://www.climatechangenews.com/2021/01/07/china-launches-worlds-lar gest-carbon-market-power-sector/.
62. https://joebiden.com/climate-plan/.
63. Through higher raxes.
64. For some policy options, see Fattouh (2021), pp. 11–15.
65. De Prado M. and Lipton A. (2020), p. 2.
66. See the 2012 FT article: https://www.ft.com/content/da5d033c-8e1c-11e1-bf8f-00144feab49a.
67. Cross sectional data were also used in asset pricing models.
68. Sehgal N. and Pandey K. (2015), Fig. 1.
69. Ibid., p. 1.
70. For example, consumption and inventory data by IEA, DOE, etc.
71. Synthetic Aperture Radar (SAR) satellite data is normally used for measuring storage levels in tanks, as it is not weather dependent.
72. ClipperData, OilX, Vortexa, Tanker Trackers and others.
73. Such data often comes in very different formats such as spreadsheets, PDF documents, emails and so on.

References

BP Statistical Review (2020), https://www.bp.com/en/global/corporate/news-and-insights/press-releases/bp-statistical-review-of-world-energy-2020-published.html.

De Prado M. and Lipton A. (2020): 'Three Quant Lessons from COVID-19 (Presentation Slides)', SSRN, May 2020. https://papers.ssrn.com/sol3/papers.cfm?abstract_id=3562025.

Fattouh B. (2001): Saudi Oil Policy: Continuity and Change in the Era of the Energy Transition, Oxford Energy Comment, January 2021.

Fattouh B. and Imsirovic A. (2020a): Shocks and Differentials: How Are Oil Markets Coping? Oxford Energy Comment, April.

Fattouh B. and Imsirovic A. (2020b): Oil Benchmarks Under Stress, Oxford Energy Comment, April.

Fattouh B. and Imsirovic A. (2020c): Middle East Benchmarks and the Demand Shock, Oxford Energy Comment, July.

Imsirovic A. (2020): 'Chine and Asian Oil Benchmarks: Where Next?', OIES Forum, No. 125 (September), p. 33.

International Energy Agency (2020): World Energy Outlook 2020, www.iea.org/weo.

Mehdi M. et. al. (2019): Murban: A Benchmark for the Middle East? Oxford Energy Comment, October.

Sehgal N. and Pandey K. (2015), Artificial Intelligence Methods for Oil Price Forecasting: A Review and Evaluation, Energy Systems, November.

15

Epilogue

The Oil Market Survived the Pandemic

The events following the COVID-19 pandemic and the resulting demand shock have been quite revealing about the state of the international oil market and its likely development in future. While the overall market functioned well throughout the crisis, some oil benchmarks showed weaknesses which needed to be fixed.[1]

It is not clear[2] why the May WTI futures contract went negative to the extent that it did on 20 April 2020. If the main reason was the perceived lack of storage at the WTI hub in Cushing, Oklahoma, and resulting panic and poor management of the ETFs, more should be done by the exchanges to issue early warnings and advise on alternative delivery locations.

On the other hand, if the contract collapsed because of large, highly leveraged derivatives positions,[3] the regulator[4] would have to do a lot more work explaining the crash and making sure it does not happen again.

Derivative or 'paper' oil markets trade in multiples of the actual physical commodity. That leaves a possibility that traders with large paper positions can use few barrels of the underlying physical commodity to influence price assessments and make money on their large derivative positions. In the modern oil markets, these 'leveraged plays' are a distinct possibility, could lead to disconnects in prices, and hedge losses for price-takers.

Even the best functioning benchmarks depend on a relatively small number of price-makers. In the London Brent 'window',[5] which sets forward

© The Author(s), under exclusive license to Springer Nature
Switzerland AG 2021
A. Imsirovic, *Trading and Price Discovery for Crude Oils*,
https://doi.org/10.1007/978-3-030-71718-6_15

Bent, top five traders make up almost 60% of all the trades.[6] This concentration of trading firepower is even more obvious in the Dubai market, where top three players account for almost 60% of the trades.[7] Two of those three are trading arms of the Chinese major oil companies.[8] In August 2014, one of them bought over 23 million barrels of oil deliverable into the 'Dubai' benchmark in a single month, prompting Platts PRA to initiate industry-wide consultations, leading to addition of two more grades of crude deliverable into the benchmark.

While oil benchmarks are the backbone of the global oil price system, not all market participants are involved in setting those prices. The market can be divided into those actively involved in trading the benchmarks during the assessment process and those who simply use those assessments for pricing of physical crude and hedging.[9] In an ideal world, benchmarks should be set by all the market players participating in the price-setting process[10]; but this is not the case. This is a problem as it is sometimes suggested the benchmark price is 'too high' or 'too low'; but if the 'too high' prices are not sold into, and 'too low' prices are not bought by the market, there is no mechanism to 'correct' the benchmark price.[11] What is more, markets are not 'perfect' in the economic-theory sense: As already mentioned, oil is dominated by a handful of very large players and setting benchmark prices is often left to large traders or trading arms of large oil companies. As a result, there is no perfect oil price benchmark.

But PRAs and the exchanges can only do so much. Markets work on a principle of 'one dollar, one vote'. Large players are likely to have more influence on prices than smaller ones. It is the role of governments and their regulators have to make sure there is a level playing field for all the participants and the rules of fair play are observed.

Lessons from History

The international oil markets have barely ever been 'free'[12] While the industry has some characteristics, which make large firms more likely,[13] significant market power has largely been the result of a lack of proper regulation and in many cases, direct government action. Up until 1980s, the conventional wisdom was that markets were inadequate in providing energy supplies. In most European countries, competition in the energy sector was essentially illegal.[14] The resulting inflexibility and inefficiency of our energy systems and oil in particular was unable to respond to challenges and oil shocks of the 1970s.

History of the oil market has a number of important lessons for us. Free markets are fragile and need constant support in terms of legal and regulatory framework within which they can operate. It is too tempting for legislators to get involved in the workings of the market even when they function well, because it gives them political power. President Nixon's advisor, Henry Kissinger directed a policy of US support for dictators such as the Shah of Iran, encouraging higher international oil price, paid by Europe, Japan, and the US taxpayers. In return, the administration could circumvent a democratic process without asking the Congress for funding of such policies. President Nixon's price controls of 1971, discouraged the domestic exploration and production, feeding oil dependency and exacerbating the oil shocks of the 1970s. President Ford's Energy Policy and Conservation Act of 1975, separating the US production into 'old' oil and 'new' oil discouraged production of any oil, and production seriously declined after 1973, at the time when it was needed most.[15]

This sad period of policy-making included the European and Japanese protectionism of their monopolised domestic energy industries[16] and the 1977 ban on the US oil exports. They all exacerbated oil crises, increased oil dependence, and helped oil cartels increase their power and prominence.

It is often hard and tedious for politicians to ensure smooth working of markets, perhaps because they get little personal benefit out of it. One early example is failed regulation of a new transportation technology in the United States at the end of the nineteenth century—the railways. The resulting chaos of differential rates, discounts, and drawbacks[17] enabled Henry Flagler and John D. Rockefeller to create one of the greatest monopolies in history, the Standard Oil Company. The lessons have not been learned and today we still struggle to regulate the new technology giants such as Amazon, Alphabet, Twitter, and Facebook.

Thankfully, some leaders had courage and vision to withdraw the government intervention from markets where it was doing harm and set solid framework for their functioning. Such were policies in the UK and the United States in the early 1980s. Price controls and other obstacles to trade were removed, ingenuity was unlocked, and free markets flourished. Prices gave appropriate signals and new oil resources were found and prospered. It is not a coincidence that the back of the OPEC cartel was broken in the mid-1980s.[18]

But markets are fragile, and people have short memories. In 2020, another US president, decided it was a good idea to broker a deal between the OPEC and other oil producers led by Russia, to create an even bigger oil cartel, OPEC+.[19] In order for the President to score some short-term political points and support a small constituency at home, the world economy was 'rewarded' with higher oil prices at the time when it could least afford it. Fortunately, markets do work, and higher prices eventually incentivise new supply.[20] But the volatility of these booms and busts remains.

Markets and Energy Transition

The lessons from the oil markets need to be remembered especially now, at the age of energy transition. Countries struggling to move on to new, cleaner forms of energy are precisely the ones with sclerotic energy monopolies with little reason to change status quo. Shambolic regulation of nuclear plants and slow pace of liberalisation of the energy sector in Japan are good examples. In the winter of 2021, Prices on the Japan Electric Power Exchange (JEPX) hit a record high of about $2390 per megawatt hour of electricity, the highest price on record anywhere in the world, and the country narrowly avoided black-outs.[21] New, smaller players in the Japanese market were starved of access to data on supply, demand, reserve capacity, and fuel inventories, finding it hard to plan their purchases of power on the exchange. In the same part of the world, some prices of liquefied natural gas (LNG) continued to be based on oil indices. As prices of oil and gas diverge, disconnects become obvious, causing stress among both producers and consumers. Such arrangaments are fossilised remains of a bygone era of monopolies which simply passed the cost onto the consumer.

Throughout the world, even the most liberalised electricity systems have little or no markets at the retail level. As a result, consumers have no incentive to save power when power is scarce and wholesale prices are high (in the power sector, price spikes can easily be 1000% or more[22]) and use more when they are low. As a result, peak demand is usually met by switching on the plants powered by fossil fuels.[23] This lack of market response and flexibility which it provides seriously curtails our efforts to stop climate change.

Of course, markets fail as well and the provision of public goods such clean environment are a good example of this. But we know-how to deal with market failure. Commons do not work[24] and making polluters paying for the damage they cause does work. The Acid Rain Program initiated in the United States, back in 1995 was based on a sulphur dioxide (SO_2) emissions trading scheme. It targeted coal-burning power generating plants, forcing them to buy and sell SO_2 emission permits ('allowances'). It was so successful that acid rain is rarely talked about these days.[25] Putting a price on carbon and implementation of some form of carbon market is absolutely necessary before we even begin to limit our greenhouse gas emissions. The proof is in the fact that our non-renewable resources such as oil and gas, which operate in functioning markets, are plentiful while our renewable resources such as drinking water, forests and fisheries, which are generally outside assigned property rights and markets, tend to be struggling. Yet some 'environmentalists' continue to oppose the market-based solutions, seriously hampering our efforts to fight against climate change. In doing so, they go hand-in-hand with the fossil industry lobbyists and politicians who were, for years, happy to give away free permits in the European Trading Scheme (ETS), making it largely ineffective.[26]

But there are plenty of good examples too. In 2018, India established an online capacity trading platform, providing transparency in these markets. In 2020 China, the government promoted creation of China Oil & Gas Piping Network Corporation (PipeChina),[27] an independent operator of gas pipelines, liquified natural gas import terminals, and storage facilities.[28] These developments are in line with the liberalisation of markets in the United States and UK in the early 1980s. Only the policies of keeping the infrastructure operators independent from supply incumbents, ensuring that the markets are transparent, market rules clear and competitive, can be a framework for flexible, responsive, yet stable, and reliable energy system. Only such policies can attract the new private investment needed to meet growing energy demand for clean energy and prevent the new technologies become new monopolies.

The other exciting market development is the use of the artificial intelligence (AI) which has moved on from the 'black box' modelling to 'back to basics' forecasting of oil balances, but this time in real time.[29] Using the AI to cross-reference a huge amount of data, this approach validates and supplies far more accurate and reliable, real time (as opposed to 'rear mirror view') data and puts the traders and decision makers back in the driving seat. Most importantly, it provides additional market transparency, so much needed for its proper functioning.

The energy industry is at an important crossroad. Facing a limited carbon budget, we must stop burning carbon by the middle of this century or find economical ways of removing the greenhouse gasses emitted in the process. As a result, oil demand is likely to fall significantly.[30] But oil is unlikely to disappear. Most of the growth in oil demand is likely to come from the petrochemical industry which is likely to face challenges of its own.[31] In such an environment, the low-cost oil producers in the Middle East are likely to be the 'last men standing' in the oil industry. In spite of low cost, the transition away from oil is likely to be associated with high prices of petroleum products. Only this time, the high price will come from carbon tax and other measures to reduce environmental pollution. To achieve this transition, we shall need smart policies and well-functioning international energy markets. The lessons learned from the history of the oil markets will help.

Notes

1. For discussion, see Chapter 14.
2. At the time of writing, and about 10 months after the event, there are opened questions about the event. See Chapters 13 and 14 for details.
3. Trading at Settlement or 'TAS' derivatives as discussed in Chapter 14.
4. Commodity Futures Trading Commission (CFTC) in this case. Ibid.
5. This is the Platts window for Brent cash partials. See Chapter 11.
6. The concentration in the CFD market is somewhat lower, about 50% for the top five players (again, see Chapter 11).
7. See Chapter 12.
8. They are Unipec, a trading arm of Sinopec and Chinaoil, a trading arm of Petro China. See Chapter 12.
9. For great arguments on how the Saudis could bridge the gap from a price taker to a price maker, see J. Luciani: 'From Price taker to Price maker: Saudi Arabia and the World Oil markets' in 'Saudi Arabia in Transition' ed. B. Haykel et al. Cambridge University Press 2015.
10. In theory, if all the global trades were done and recorded through blockchain or some similar technology, it would be possible to create and index or a series of indices that would reflect all the deals done. Perhaps, one day we shall have perfect benchmarks?
11. See A. Imsirovic: 'Don't blame PRAs for oil industry's structural failures', the FT, 21 May 2013.
12. Very roughly, from the first Drake's well in 1959 to Standard Oil's 1995 order to buy at 'posted' prices and somewhat free after 1986 OPEC abdication of the price-making role in favour of markets, even though the cartel had influence on the market.
13. See Chapter 2 for details.
14. See Chapter 10.
15. These policies were discussed in Chapter 8.
16. Also discussed in Chapter 8.
17. Discussed in Chapter 4. Regulation of companies involving different states was a major issue as well.
18. See Chapters 9 and 10.
19. Discussed in Chapter 14.
20. Ibid.

21. See: 'Out in the cold: how Japan's electricity grid came close to blackouts'—Reuters News, 05-Feb-2021.
22. They are so high precisely because of the lack of demand response.
23. So called 'spinning capacity' is generally met by gas-powered plants.
24. See G. Hardin's seminal paper: 'The Tragedy of the Commons'. https://www.bing.com/search?q=tragedy+of+the+commons&cvid=053a253c7d3047b9bb 54f809f977417e&FORM=ANAB01&PC=DCTS.
25. https://blog.epa.gov/2010/04/08/whatever-happened-to-acid-rain/.
26. Up to about 2018, ETS prices were in single digits, mainly due to a large number of permits given. Economist believe that a carbon price of at least $70 per tone is needed to make a significant impact on greenhouse gas emissions. For historical ETS prices, see: https://ember-climate.org/data/carbon-price-vie wer/.
27. For a good analysis, see: https://www.energypolicy.columbia.edu/research/ commentary/reform-pipelines-pipechina-and-restructuring-china-s-natural-gas- market.
28. Also see an excellent article on the subject: https://www.iea.org/commentaries/ asia-s-record-gas-prices-underline-the-need-to-make-its-markets-more-resilient.
29. It is discussed in Chapter 14 under '2020 Oil Balances in Real Time'.
30. See Chapter 14 about details.
31. The problem of plastic pollution. Ibid.

Correction to: Trading and Price Discovery for Crude Oils

Correction to:
A. Imsirovic, *Trading and Price Discovery for Crude Oils,*
https://doi.org/10.1007/978-3-030-71718-6

The original version of this book was inadvertently published with an incorrect affiliation in the copyright page, which has now been corrected. The corrections to the book have been updated with the changes.

The updated version of the book can be found at
https://doi.org/10.1007/978-3-030-71718-6

© The Author(s), under exclusive license to Springer Nature
Switzerland AG 2021
A. Imsirovic, *Trading and Price Discovery for Crude Oils,*
https://doi.org/10.1007/978-3-030-71718-6_16

Bibliography

Adelman M.A. (1955): 'Concept and Statistical Measurement of Vertical Integration', in *Business Concentration and Public Policy*, Princeton University Press for National Bureau of Economic Research, Princeton.

Adelman M.A. (1965): 'An Economist Looks at The Sherman Act', *Section of Antitrust Law*, Vol. 27, Proceedings at the Spring Meeting, Washington, DC., April 8–9, pp. 32–46.

Adelman M.A. (1972): *The World Petroleum Market*, The Johns Hopkins University Press.

Adelman M.A. (1973): 'Is the Oil Shortage Real? Oil Companies as OPEC Tax-Collectors', *Foreign Policy*, No. 9 (Winter, 1972–1973), pp. 69–107.

Adelman, M.A. and Lynch, M.C. (1995): 'Fixed View of Resource Limits', *Oil & Gas Journal*, April 7 1997.

Adelman M.A. (1995): *The Genie Out of the Bottle, World Oil Since 1970*, The MIT Press.

Adelman M.A. (2001): 'The Clumsy Cartel: OPEC's Uncertain Future', *Harvard International Review*, Vol. 23, No. 1 (Spring), pp. 20–23.

Adelman L. (1995): *Fixed View of Resource Limits, Oil & Gas Journal*, July 4, 1997.

Aguilera R.F. and Radetzki, M. (2016): *The Price of Oil*, Cambridge University Press.

Akin E.N. (1988): *Flagler: Rockefeller Partner and Florida Baron*, University Press of Florida.

Al-Naimi A. (2016): *Out of the Desert: My Journey From Nomadic Bedouin to the Heart of Global Oil*, Penguin.

Allsopp C. and Fattouh B. (2008): *Oil Prices: Fundamentals or Speculation?* Bank of England, June 13, 2008 OIES.

American Petroleum Institute (1959): *Petroleum Facts and Figures*, 9th Edition.

© The Editor(s) (if applicable) and The Author(s), under exclusive license to Springer Nature Switzerland AG 2021
A. Imsirovic, *Trading and Price Discovery for Crude Oils*,
https://doi.org/10.1007/978-3-030-71718-6

Annual Report to the Secretary of the Navy, 1867. US Government Records.

Ansari AM (2001): 'The Myth of the White Revolution: Mohammad Reza Shah, 'Modernization' and the Consolidation of Power', *Middle Eastern Studies Journal*, Vol. 37, No. 3 (July), pp. 1–24.

Argus (2020): *Opec at 60: 'Road to Stability Long and Bumpy*, September 14, 2020.

Babaev E. (2009): *Dmitriy Mendeleev: A Short CV, and A Story of Life*, http://www.chem.msu.ru/eng/misc/babaev/papers/139e.pdf.

Begg D, Gianluigi V., Stanley F. and Rudiger D. (2014): *Economics*, 11th Edition.

Bhattacharyya S.C. (2011): *Energy Economics: Concepts, Issues, Markets and Governance*, Springer.

Blair J.M. (1976): *The Control of Oil*, Pantheon Books, New York.

Bower T. (2010): *The Squeeze*, Harper Press.

BP Statistical Review (1951), https://www.bp.com/en/global/corporate/energy-economics/statistical-review-of-world-energy/downloads.html.

BP Statistical Review (2020), https://www.bp.com/en/global/corporate/news-and-insights/press-releases/bp-statistical-review-of-world-energy-2020-published.html.

Brown JH and Partridge M (1998): 'The Death of a Market: Standard Oil and the Demise of 19th Century Crude Oil Exchanges', *Review of Industrial Organization*, Springer, Vol. 13, No. 5 (October), pp. 569–587.

Brusstar and Karas (2020): *Why Cushing Matters: A Look at the WTI Benchmark*, OIES, May 13, 2020,

Bullard C.W., Penner P.S. and Pilati D.A. (1978): 'Net Energy Analysis: Handbook for Combining Process and Input Output Analysis', *Resources and Energy*, Vol. 1, No. 3, pp. 267–313.

Commodity Futures Trading Commission (2020): 'Trading in NYMEX WTI Crude Oil Futures Contract Leading up to, on, and around April 20, 2020' Interim Staff Report, November 23, 2020, https://cftc.gov/PressRoom/PressReleases/8315-20.

Chatham House (1959): 'The First Arab Petroleum Congress', *The World Today*, Vol. 15, No. 6 (June), pp. 246–253, Royal Institute of International Affairs.

Chalabi F.J. (2010): *Oil Policies, Oil Myths*, I.B. Tauris & Co. Ltd. London.

Christakis F. (2011): *Connected*, Harper Press.

CIA Intelligence Memorandum (1970): *Algeria: The Importance of the Oil Industry*, Directorate of Intelligence, October 1970.

CIA Intelligence Assessment (1986): *The Libyan Oil Industry: Dependence on Foreign Companies*, Directorate of Intelligence, January 1986.

CIA (1980): *International Energy Statistical Review*, National Foreign Assessment Centre, November 25, 1980.

CIA (1987): *International Energy Statistical Review*, Directorate of Intelligence, November 27, 1987.

Comptroller General of the United States (1980): *Report to the Congress of the United States: The United States Exerts Limited Influence On The International Crude Oil Spot Market*, August 21, 1980.

Coase R. (1937): 'The Nature of the Firm', *Economica*, pp. 386–405.

Craig J., Gerali F., Macaulay F. and Sorkhabi R. Eds. (2018): *The History of the European Oil and Gas Industry (1600s–2000s)*, Geological Society, London, Special Publications, 465, pp. 1–24.

Copetas A.C. (1985): *Metal Men*, Futura Publications.

De Prado M. and Lipton A. (2020): 'Three Quant Lessons from COVID-19 (Presentation Slides)', SSRN, May 2020. https://papers.ssrn.com/sol3/papers.cfm?abstract_id=3562025.

Derrick's (1884): *Hand-Book of Petroleum*, Derrick Publishing Company.

DOE/EIA (1980): *Price Controls - and International Petroleum Product Prices*, February.

Doshi T.K. and Imsirovic A. (2013): 'The 'Asian Premium' in Crude Oil Markets: Fact or Fiction?' in: Daoijong Z. (Ed), *Managing Regional Energy Vulnerabilities in East Asia*, Routledge. ISBN:978-0-415-53538-0, January, https://doi.org/10.13140/2.1.4053.6009.

Erickson E.W. (1970): 'Crude Oil Prices, Drilling Incentives and the Supply of New Discoveries', *Natural Resource Journal*, Vol. 10, No. 1 (Winter).

Ezzati A. (1976): 'Future OPEC Price and Production Strategies as Affected by Its Capacity to Absorb Oil Revenues'. *European Economic Review*, Vol. 8, pp. 107–138.

Fattouh B. (2010): *An Anatomy of the Crude Oil Pricing System*, OIES Paper WPM 40.

Fattouh B. and Economou A. (2020): *OPEC at 60: The World with and Without OPEC*, Technical Workshop on OPEC at 60: Contributions to the Global Economy and Energy Markets, OIES, June 23, 2020.

Fattouh B. and Mahadeva L. (2013). 'OPEC: What Difference Has It Made?' *Annual Review of Resource Economics*, Vol. 5, pp. 427–443.

Fattouh B., Poudineh R. and Sen A. (2016): 'The Dynamics of the Revenue Maximization–Market Share Trade-Off: Saudi Arabia's Oil Policy in the 2014–15 Price Fall', *Oxford Review of Economic Policy*, Vol. 32, No. 2, pp. 223–240.

Fattouh B. and Imsirovic A. (2019): *Contracts for Difference and the Evolution of the Brent Complex*, Oxford Energy Comment, June.

Fattouh B. and Imsirovic A. (2020a): *Shocks and Differentials: How Are Oil Markets Coping?* Oxford Energy Comment, April.

Fattouh B. and Imsirovic A. (2020b): *Crude Oil Pricing Optionality and Contracts for Difference*, Oxford Energy Comment, June.

Fattouh B. and Imsirovic A. (2020c): *Oil Benchmarks Under Stress*, Oxford Energy Comment, April.

Fattouh B. and Imsirovic A. (2020d): *Nigerian Barrels and the Demand Shock: Differentials and Changing Oil Trade Flows*, Oxford Energy Comment, June.

Fattouh B. and Imsirovic A. (2020e): *Middle East Benchmarks and the Demand Shock*, Oxford Energy Comment, July.

Fattouh B. (2001): *Saudi Oil Policy: Continuity and Change in the Era of the Energy Transition*, Oxford Energy Comment, January 2021.

Federal Oil Conservation Board (1926): *Public Hearing*, May 27, 1926, Office of Board, Washington, DC.

Feis, H. (1944): *Petroleum and American Foreign Policy*, Food Research Institute, Stanford University.

Final Communiqué of the Asian-African Conference, Bandung from the 18th to the 24th April 1955. https://www.cvce.eu/en/obj/final_communique_of_the_asian_african_conference_of_bandung_24_april_1955-en-676237bd-72f7-471f-949a-88b6ae513585.html.

Frankel P.H. (1969): *Essentials of Petroleum, A Key to Oil Economics*, Chapel River Press, Andover, Hants.

Garavini G. (2019): *The Rise and Fall of OPEC in the Twentieth Century*, Oxford University Press.

Grossman, S.J. and Hart O.D. (1986): 'The Costs and Benefits of Ownership: A Theory of Vertical and Lateral Integration', *Journal of Political Economy*, Vol. 94, No. 4, pp. 691–719.

Granitz A. and Klein B. (1991): 'Monopolization by "Raising Rivals' Costs": The Standard Oil Case', *The Journal of Law & Economics*, Vol. 39, No. 1.

Gibson, M.W. (2012): *British Strategy and Oil, 1914-1923*, PhD thesis, http://theses.gla.ac.uk/3160/1/2012gibsonphd.pdf.

Golombek R., Irarrazabal A.A. and Ma L. (2018): OPEC's Market Power: An Empirical Dominant Firm Model for the Oil Market, *Energy Economics*, Vol. 70, pp. 98–115.

Haight, G.W. (1972): 'Libyan Nationalization of British Petroleum Company Assets', *The International Lawyer*, Vol. 6, No. 3 (July), pp. 541–547.

Hearing Before the Committee on Energy and Natural Resources (1983): 'World Petroleum Outlook – 1983', US Government Printing Office, Washington, DC.

Helm D. (2003): *Energy, the State and the Market, British Energy Policy Since 1979*, Oxford University Press.

Henry J.T. (1873): *The Early and Later History of Petroleum*, Jas. B. Rodgers Co. Printers, Philadelphia.

Hidy R. and Hidy M. (1957): *Pioneering in Business: History of the Standard Oil Company* (of New Jersey), Harper and Brothers, New York.

Horsnell P. and Mabro R. (1993): *Oil Markets and Prices*, Oxford University Press.

Horsnell P. (1997): *Oil in Asia*, Oxford University Press.

House of Commons Research Papers (2014): *Privatisation*, Research Paper 14/61, November 20, 2014.

Howarth S. (1997): *A Century in Oil, The Shell Transport and Trading Company 1897-1997*, Weindenfeld & Nicholson, London.

Hussin, N. (2007): *Trade and Society in the Straits of Melaka*, NUS Press, Singapore.

Imsirovic A. (2014): *Oil Markets in Transition and the Dubai Crude Oil Benchmark*, Oxford Energy Comment, October.

Imsirovic A. (2018): *What Next for Asian Benchmarks? – A Footnote*, Oxford Energy Comment, November.

Imsirovic A. and Pryor B. (2018): *IMO 2020 and the Brent Dubai Spread,* Oxford Energy Comment, September.

Imsirovic A. (2014): *Changes to the 'Dated Brent' Benchmark: More to Come,* Oxford Energy Comment, March 2019.

Imsirovic A. (2020a): *The US Should Avoid Repeating Past Mistakes,* Petroleum Economist, April 2.

Imsirovic A. (2020b): 'Chine and Asian Oil Benchmarks: Where Next?', *OIES Forum,* No. 125 (September), p. 33.

Imsirovic A. (2021): 'The Trading and Price Discovery for Crude Oils', in: Hafner M. and Luciani G. (Eds), *Handbook of International Energy Economics,* Palgrave Macmillan.

International Energy Agency (2020): *World Energy Outlook 2020,* www.iea.org/weo.

IOSCO (2013a): *Consultation Report,* The Board of the International Organisation Securities Commissions CR01/13, January.

IOSCO (2013b): *Consultation Report,* The Board of the International Organisation Securities Commissions CR01/13, April.

Johnson O. (2018): *The Price Reporters, A Guide to PRAs and Commodity Benchmarks,* Routledge, London.

Kent M. (1993): *Moguls and Mandarins, Oil, Imperialism and the Middle East in the British Foreign Policy, 1900-1940,* Franc Cass & Co. Ltd.

Killian Lutz (2020): 'Would Shale Impede or Accelerate the Global Energy Transition?', Presentation to the KAPSARC Virtual Workshop Agenda, December 9.

Kinzer S. (2003): *All the Shah's Men,* Wiley, Hoboken, NJ.

Krapels E. (1977): *Controlling Oil: British Oil Policy and the British National Oil Corporation.* US Government Printing Office, Washington, DC.

Lilian L. (2020): 'The Future of the U.S. Shale Oil Industry', Presentation to KAPSARC virtual Workshop, December 9.

Langstroth C. and Stilz W. (1899): *Railway Co-operation,* University of Pennsylvania series in Political Economy and Public Law, No. 15.

LeClair, M.S. (2000): *International Commodity Markets and the Role of Cartels,* 2015 Edition, Routledge, New York, NY.

Leeman, W.A. (1962): *The Price of Middle East Oil: An Essay in Political Economy,* Cornell University Press.

Liebeler J. (1976): *Integration and Competition,* in: Mitchell E.J. (Ed), 'Vertical Integration in the Oil Industry'.

Lloyd H.D. (1881): *The Story of a Great Monopoly,* The Atlantic, March.

Longhurst H. (1959): *Adventure in Oil, Story of British Petroleum,* Sidgwick and Jackson Ltd.

Lynch C.M. (2016): *The "Peak Oil" Scare and the Coming of Oil Flood,* Praeger Publishers.

Mabro R. (1975) 'OPEC After the Oil Revolution', *Millennium,* Vol. 4, No. 3, pp. 191–199.

Mabro R. (1991). 'OPEC and the Price of Oil', *The Energy Journal*, Vol. 13, No. 2, pp. 1–17.

Mabro R., Bacon R., Chadwick M., Halliwell M. and Long D. (1986): *The Market for North Sea Crude Oil*, Oxford University Press for the Oxford Institute for Energy Studies.

Magueri L. (2006): *The Age of Oil, The Mythology, History and Future of the World's Most Controversial Resource*, Praeger, Westport, Connecticut.

Marvin C. (1891): '*The Region of Eternal Fire*, W.H. Allen & Co. Ltd.

McGrandle L. (1975): *The Story of North Sea Oil*, Wayland Publishers.

McKie J.W. and McDonald S.L. (1962): 'Petroleum Conservation in Theory and Practice', *The Quarterly Journal of Economics*, Vol. 76, No. 1 (February), pp. 98–121.

McLaurin J.J. (1896): *Sketches in Crude Oil*, Harrisburg, PA.

McNally R. (2017): *Crude Volatility*, Columbia University Press.

Meadows D.H., et. al. (1972): *The Limits to Growth, A Report for the Club of Rome Project on the Predicament of Mankind*, A Potomac Associates Book.

Megginson W.L. (2005): *The Financial Economics of Privatisation*, Oxford University Press.

Miller E.C. Ed. (1968): *This Was Early Oil, Contemporary Accounts of the Growing Petroleum Industry, 1848–1885*, Commonwealth of Pennsylvania, The Pennsylvania Historical and Museum Commission, Harrisburg, 1968.

Miller N.Y. (2018): *The United States, Britain and the Marshall Plan: Oil and Finance in the Early Post-War Era*, Economia e Sociedade, Campinas, Unicamp. IE, https://doi.org/10.1590/1982-3533.2017v27n1art12.

Mills M.R. (2008): *The Myth of the Oil Crisis*, Praeger Publishers.

Mitchell E.J. (1976): 'Vertical Integration in the Oil Industry', *National Energy Study*, No. 11 (June).

Morrison K. (2008): *Living in a Material World, A Commodity Connection*, Wiley, London, UK.

Murphy R. (2018): *The Crazy Crude Oil Price Controls of the 1970s*, Institute for Energy Research Commentary, April 18.

National Petroleum Council Report (1964): *Impact of Oil Exports from the Soviet Block, Supplement to the 1962 Report*, MPC, March 19, Washington.

Nevins A. (1859): *John D. Rockefeller: Study in Power*, one volume abridgement by William Greenleaf, Charles Scribner's Sons, New York.

Newbery D.M. (1982): *Manipulation of the Futures Market by a Dominant Producer*, The World bank, Development Research Department. Discussion Papers No. 39.

Odell R.P. (1986): *Oil and World Power*, Penguin Books.

OPEC Secretariat (2012): *General Information*, Organization of the Petroleum Exporting Countries, https://www.opec.org/opec_web/static_files_project/media/downloads/publications/GenInfo.pdf.

OPEC (1968): 'Guidelines for Petroleum Policy in Member Countries', *International Legal Materials*, Vol. 7, No. 5 (September), pp. 1183–1186, Cambridge University Press.

Para F. (2004): *Oil Politics, A Modern History of Petroleum*, I.B. Taurus Co. Ltd.

Pearson P. and Watson J. (2012): *UK Energy Policy 1980-2010, History and Lessons to be Learnt*, Parliamentary Group for Energy Studies.

Purvin and Gertz (2010): *The Role of WTI as a Crude Oil Benchmark*, January.

Posner A. (1979): 'The Chicago School of Antitrust Analysis', *University of Pennsylvania Law Review*, Vol. 127, No. 4 (April), pp. 925–948.

Preliminary Report on Trusts and Industrial Combinations, Together with Testimony, Review of Evidence, Charts Showing Effects on Prices, and Topical Digest (1899) Govt. Print. Off., Washington, DC, USA.

Priest G.L. (2014): 'Bork's Strategy and the Influence of the Chicago School on Modern Antitrust Law', *The Journal of Law & Economics*, Vol. 57, No. S3, The Contributions of Robert Bork to Antitrust Economics (August), pp. S1–S17.

Proceedings of the Special Committee on Railroads (1879): Appointed under a Resolution of the Assembly to Investigate *Alleged Abuses in the Management of Railroads Chartered by the State of New York*, The State of New York.

Puntigliano A.R. and Appelqvist O. (2011): Prebisch and Myrdal: Development Economics in the Core and on the Periphery, *Journal of Global History*, Vol. 6, pp. 29–52, London School of Economics and Political Science.

Report to the Committee of Foreign Relations, United States Senate by the Subcommittee on Multinational Corporations (1975): *Multinational Oil Corporations and the US Foreign Policy*, January 2, US Government Printing Office, Washington.

Rhodes R. (2018): *Energy, A Human History*, Simon and Schuster.

Rockefeller J.D. (1933): *Reminiscences of Men and Events*, Doubleday, Doran & Company, Inc., Garden City NY.

Rubino A. (2008): *Queen of the Oil Club*, Beacon Press, Boston.

Rushforth J. and Blei V. (2020): *Yields vs. Sulphur: What Is Driving Crude Benchmarks in 2020?* Oxford Energy Comment, July.

Salop S.C. (2114): 'What Consensus? Why Ideology and Elections Still Matter to Antitrust', *Antitrust Law Journal*, Vol. 79, No. 2, pp. 601–648.

Sampson A. (1988 ed.): *The Seven Sisters*, Cornet Books.

Schumpeter J.A. (1943): *Capitalism, Socialism and Democracy*, 1976 Edition, George Allen & Unwin Ltd.

Sehgal N. and Pandey K. (2015), *Artificial Intelligence Methods for Oil Price Forecasting: A Review and Evaluation*, Energy Systems, November.

Select Committee on Small Business, US Senate (1952): *The International Petroleum Cartel*, Staff Report to the Federal Trade Commission submitted to the Subcommittee on Monopoly of the Select Committee on Small Business, US Senate, Government Printing Office, Washington, August 22.

Sharkey W.W. (1982): *The Theory of Natural Monopoly*, Cambridge University Press, Reprinted version 2008.

Shepherd M. (2015): *Oil Strike, North Sea; A First-Hand History of North Sea Oil*, Luat Press Limited, Edinburgh.

Shiller R. (2019): *Narrative Economics*, Princeton University Press.

Simmons M. (2005): *Twilight in the Desert: The Coming Saudi Oil Shock and the World Economy*, Wiley.

Smil V. (2017): *Energy and Civilization, A History*, The MIT Press.

Smith E.V. (1887): *Plain Truths About Stock Speculation, How to Avoid Losses in Wall St.*, Brooklyn, NY.

Soglio R. and Jaffe A.M. (2000): *A Note on Saudi Arabian Price Discrimination*, The *Energy Journal*, Vol. 21, pp. 121–134.

Steffen W., Broadgate, W., Deutsch L., Gaffney O. and Ludwig C. (2015): 'The Trajectory of the Anthropocene: The Great Acceleration', *The Anthropocene Review*, January 16.

Wendy Broadgate, Lisa Deutsch, Owen Gaffney, Cornelia Ludwig.

Stoff M.B. (1981): 'The Anglo-American Oil Agreement and the Wartime Search for Foreign Oil Policy', *The Business History Review*, Vol. 55, No. 1 (Spring), pp. 59–74.

Talman C.F. (1919): *The Story of Oil*, The Mentor (The Scientific American), Department of Science, Serial Number 189, October 15.

Tarbell I.M. (1904): *The History of Standard Oil Company*, Brief Version, Chalmers D.M. (Ed), Dover Publications. Reprint 2015.

Telser (1960): 'Why Should Manufacturers Want Fair Trade?', *The Journal of Law & Economics*, Vol. 3 (October), pp. 86–105.

Telser (1985): 'Cooperation, Competition, and Efficiency', *The Journal of Law & Economics*, Vol. 28, No. 2 (May), pp. 271–295, Antitrust and Economic Efficiency: A Conference Sponsored by the Hoover Institution.

The New York Times (2000): *Secrets of History: The C.I.A. in Iran -- A Special Report*, April 16, https://www.nytimes.com/2000/04/16/world/secrets-history-cia-iran-special-report-plot-convulsed-iran-53-79.html.

Trebat, N.M. (2018): 'The United States, Britain and the Marshall Plan: Oil and Finance in the Early Post-War Era', *Economia e Sociedade, Campinas*, Vol. 27, No. 1 (62), pp. 355–373, abr. 2018.

United Nations Human Rights, Office of the High Commissioner, General Assembly resolution 1803 (XVII) of "Permanent Sovereignty Over Natural Resources", December 14, 1962, https://www.ohchr.org/EN/ProfessionalInterest/pages/NaturalResources.aspx.

United Nations Secretariat (1962): *Agreement Concerning the Creation of the Organization of Petroleum Exporting Countries (OPEC)*. Done at Baghdad, on September 14, 1960, United Nations Treaty Series UN Resolution No. 6363, https://treaties.un.org/doc/Publication/UNTS/Volume%20443/volume-443-I-6363-English.pdf.

United States Senate (1945): *American Petroleum Interests in Foreign Countries*, Hearings Before a Special Committee Investigating Petroleum Resources, 79th Congress, June 27 and 28, 1945.

United States Tariff Commission (1973): *World Oil Developments and the US Oil Import Policies*, A Report Prepared for the Committee on Finance, US Senate, TC Publication 632, Washington, DC.

White J.H. (1979): *A History of the American Locomotive: Its Development, 1830-1880*, Dover Publications New York.

Williamson H.F. and Daum A.R. (1959): *The American Petroleum Industry, 1859-1899 The Age of Illumination* (Vol. 1), Northwestern University Press.

Williamson H.F., Andreano R.L., Daum A.R. and Klose G.C. (1963): *The American Petroleum Industry* (Vol. 2), Northwestern University Press.

Winthrop, G.H. (1972). Libyan Nationalization of British Petroleum Company Assets', *The International Lawyer*, Vol. 6, No. 3 (July 1972), pp. 541–547, American Bar Association.

Williamson O.E. (1971): 'The Vertical Integration of Production: Market Failure Considerations', *The American Economic Review*, Vol. 61, No. 2.

Wolf & Michael G.P. (2008): *Privatising National Oil Companies: Assessing the Impact on Firm Performance*, Working Papers EPRG 0805, Energy Policy Research Group, Cambridge Judge Business School, University of Cambridge.

Wright J.D. (2012): 'Abandoning Antitrust's Chicago Obsession: The Case for Evidence-Based Antitrust', *Antitrust Law Journal*, Vol. 78, No. 1 (2012), pp. 241–272, an Economic Association, pp. 112–123.

Wright, T. (1854): *The Travels of Marco Polo, the Venetian*,http://public-library.uk/ebooks/60/81.pdf.

Zuckerman, G. (2014): *The Frackers*, Portfolio Penguin.

Zweifel P., Praktiknjo A., and Erdmann G. (2017): *Energy Economics, Theory and Applications*, Springer.

Index

© The Editor(s) (if applicable) and The Author(s), under exclusive
license to Springer Nature Switzerland AG 2021
A. Imsirovic, *Trading and Price Discovery for Crude Oils*,
https://doi.org/10.1007/978-3-030-71718-6